THE ART OF
MAKING MONEY

THE ART OF MAKING MONEY

THE STORY OF A
MASTER COUNTERFEITER

JASON KERSTEN

GOTHAM
BOOKS

GOTHAM BOOKS
Published by Penguin Group (USA) Inc.
375 Hudson Street, New York, New York 10014, U.S.A.
Penguin Group (Canada), 90 Eglinton Avenue East, Suite 700, Toronto, Ontario M4P 2Y3, Canada
(a division of Pearson Penguin Canada Inc.); Penguin Books Ltd, 80 Strand, London WC2R 0RL, England;
Penguin Ireland, 25 St Stephen's Green, Dublin 2, Ireland (a division of Penguin Books Ltd); Penguin
Group (Australia), 250 Camberwell Road, Camberwell, Victoria 3124, Australia (a division of Pearson
Australia Group Pty Ltd); Penguin Books India Pvt Ltd, 11 Community Centre, Panchsheel Park, New
Delhi—110 017, India; Penguin Group (NZ), 67 Apollo Drive, Rosedale, North Shore 0632, New Zealand
(a division of Pearson New Zealand Ltd); Penguin Books (South Africa) (Pty) Ltd, 24 Sturdee Avenue,
Rosebank, Johannesburg 2196, South Africa

Penguin Books Ltd, Registered Offices: 80 Strand, London WC2R 0RL, England

Published by Gotham Books, a member of Penguin Group (USA) Inc.

First printing, June 2009
10 9 8 7 6 5 4 3 2 1

LIBRARY OF CONGRESS CATALOGING-IN-PUBLICATION DATA
Kersten, Jason.
   The art of making money: the story of a master counterfeiter / Jason Kersten.
      p. cm.
   ISBN 978-1-592-40446-9 (hardcover)
   1. Luciano, Arthur Julius.   2. Counterfeiters—Biography.   3. Counterfeits and counterfeiting.   I. Title.
HG335.K47 2009
   364.1'334092—dc22
   [B]

                                                                                          2009009407

Printed in the United States of America
Set in New Caledonia, with display in Engravers and AT Sackers Gothic
Designed by BTDNYC

FOR KRIS AND WILLIE

AUTHOR'S NOTE

To tell this story, I relied on interviews with primary sources whenever possible, reconstructing events and dialogue according to their memories. In instances where their recollections conflicted, I generally favored my protagonist's version of events unless other source material was convincing enough to override him. I also drew on numerous legal documents such as court transcripts, law enforcement reports and warrants, prison records, and wiretap transcripts. Historical and contextual material was obtained from books, newspaper articles, and interviews.

Some of the people quoted in this book consented to interviews on the provision that their names be changed. In other cases, I changed the names of minor characters myself or used established nicknames because contacting them was either impossible or impractical.

Other than a single interview provided to me at an early date, the United States Secret Service chose to remain secret, declining numerous requests for interviews. Quotes and scenes involving Secret Service agents appearing in this book are therefore reconstructed from official reports and interviews with criminal suspects.

THE ART OF
MAKING MONEY

"Modern man, living in a mutually dependent, collective society, cannot become a counterfeiter. A counterfeiter should be possessed of the qualities found only in a Nietzschean hero."

—LYNN GLASER, FROM
Counterfeiting in America: The History of an American Way to Wealth

PROLOGUE

I t took Art Williams four beers to summon the will to reveal his formula. We had been sitting in his living room, a few blocks from Chicago's Midway Airport, listening to jets boom by for the better part of two hours. I was there interviewing him for an article for *Rolling Stone* magazine, and he had promised to tell me the secrets that made him one of the most successful counterfeiters of the last quarter century. Understandably, he was reluctant.

"I've never shown this to anybody before," he finally said with a contempt indicating that I could not possibly appreciate or deserve what I was about to see. "You realize how many people have offered me money for this?"

Some men—he wouldn't say who—once promised him three hundred thousand dollars for his moneymaking recipe. They pledged to set him up in a villa anywhere in the world with a personal guard. It was easy to picture Art sitting on a patio above the Caspian Sea surrounded by bucket-necked Russian gangsters. With his high, planed cheeks, blue eyes, and pumped-up physique, he'd fit right in with an Eastern European operation. It was also easy to think that he was full of shit, because Art Williams was a born hustler, as swaggering as any ever found on the streets of Chicago. Later I'd learn that the offer had been real, and that he'd declined because he wasn't sure if his guards would treat him as prince or prisoner.

"My friends are going to hate me for telling you," he sighed. "They'll probably hate you for knowing." Then he shuffled off toward the kitchen. Hushed tones of an argument between him and his girlfriend, Natalie, echoed down the hall. It was clear enough that she didn't want him to show me. When I heard a terse "Fine, whatever," I was pretty sure that Natalie would hate me too. Then came the rumblings of doors and cabinets opening and the crackling of paper.

A moment later, Williams returned with some scissors, three plastic spray bottles, and a sheet of what looked like the kind of cheap, gray-white construction paper a kindergarten teacher might hand out at craft time.

"Feel how thin it is," he whispered, handing me a sheet. Rubbing the paper between my thumb and forefinger, I was amazed at how authentic it already felt. "That's nothing," he said. "Just wait."

He cut two dollar-sized rectangles from the sheet, apologizing that they were not precise cuts (they were almost exactly the right size). Then he sprayed both cuts with adhesive, his wrist sweeping fluidly as he pressed the applicator. "You have to do it in one motion or you won't get the right distribution," he explained. After he deftly pressed the sheets together and used the spine of a book to push out air bubbles, we waited for it to dry. "I always waited at least half an hour," he said. "If you push it, the sheets could come apart later on. Trust me, you don't want that to happen."

Another beer later, he sprayed both sides of the glued sheets with two shots of hardening solution, then a satin finish. "Now this," he said before applying the final coat, "is the *shit*."

Five minutes later I held a twenty-dollar bill in one hand and Art Williams's paper in the other, eyes closed. I couldn't tell them apart. When I opened my eyes, I realized that Williams's paper not only felt right, but it also bore the distinctive dull sheen.

"Now snap it," he commanded. I jerked both ends of the rectangle and the sound was unmistakable; it was the lovely, husky crack made by the flying whip that drives the world economy—the sound of the Almighty Dollar.

"Now imagine this with the watermark, the security thread, the reflective ink—everything," he said. "That's what was great about my money. It passed every test."

ART WILLIAMS WAS THIRTY-TWO YEARS OLD and already a dying breed. In an era when the vast majority of counterfeiters are teenagers who use ink-jet printers to run off twenty-dollar bills that can't even fool a McDonald's cashier, he was a craftsman schooled in a centuries-old practice by a master who traced his criminal lineage back to the Old World. He was also an innovator who combined time-tested techniques with digital technology to re-create what was then the most secure U.S. banknote ever made.

"He put a lot of work into his bills," Lorelei Pagano, a counterfeit specialist at the Secret Service's main lab in Washington, D.C., would later tell me. "He's no button pusher. I'd rate his bills as an eight or a nine." A perfect 10 is a bill called the "Supernote" that many believe is made by the North Korean government on a ten-million-dollar intaglio press similar to the ones used by the Bureau of Engraving and Printing.

Art would eventually reveal to me his entire process of making money, and I'd be awed by the obsession, dedication, and exactitude it had taken him to achieve it. But as extraordinary as his formula was, it defined his story about as much as a mathematical equation can capture the mystery and terror of the universe. Far more interesting were the forces that created and compromised *him*, and those could not be easily explored in a magazine article. Art had too many secrets to share, many of which he had hidden even from himself.

He'd spent half his life pursuing verisimilitude in an idealistic attempt to recapture something very real that he believed had been lost, or stolen, or unfairly denied. What enthralled and terrified me the most was that his pursuit had very little to do with money, and the roots of his downfall lay in something impossible to replicate or put a value on. As he would say himself, "I never got caught because of money. I got caught because of love."

BOOK ONE

I

SENIOR

"Yo' ole father doan' know yit what he's a-gwyne to do. Sometimes he spec he'll go 'way, en den ag'in he spec he'll stay. De bes' ways is to res' easy and let de ole man take his own way. Dey's two angels hoverin' roun' 'bout him. One uv 'em is white en shiny, en t'other one one is black. De white one gits him to go right a little while, den de black one sail in en bust it all up. A body can't tell yit which one gwyne to fetch him at de las'. But you is all right. You gwyne to have considable trouble in yo' life, en considable joy."

—WHAT THE HAIRBALL TOLD JIM ABOUT HUCK'S FUTURE, AFTER THEY PAID IT WITH A COUNTERFEIT QUARTER. *The Adventures of Huckleberry Finn*, MARK TWAIN

Stateville Correctional Center in Joliet, Illinois, sits back from the Des Plaines River on a low rise, its thirty-three-foot-high walls and ten guard towers a vision of medieval austerity amid cornfields and plains. Built in the 1920s and inspired by designs from the English social philosopher Jeremy Bentham, the prison's center-piece is a "panopticon"—a four-story circular cell block with a guard tower in the dead center. Bentham theorized that the layout would project a "sentiment of invisible omniscience" to the inmates, who would never know when the guards in the tower were watching. For guards and inmates alike it's a world out of Dante: a giant, clamorous cylinder hiving some of Illinois's most violent and deranged criminals.

It was in Stateville's visiting room, in the winter of 1978, that Art Williams Jr. had his earliest memory of his father. He was six years old, sitting on his daddy's lap, happy in the knowledge that he would soon be getting out.

By Joliet standards, Arthur Williams Sr.—inmate number C-70147—was a small fish. He'd been convicted two years earlier for robbing a truck in DuPage County. While the crime was nonviolent, it was part of a long line of similar offenses that stretched back to his teens, and so Judge William V. Hopf had rewarded Williams's felonious consistency with a stay in what one former warden called "the world's toughest prison."

That winter, there were some signs that Williams was finally getting the message. He'd been on good behavior throughout his term, and he was looking forward to resuming a normal life with his wife and three kids. Not that Williams had many positive reference points when it came to family life.

He'd been born Arthur Julius Luciano, the son of an alcoholic trucker from Sicily, and a mentally ill Irish mother. In his early years, the family, which also included his younger brother Richard, had lived in Bridgeport—one of the toughest neighborhoods on Chicago's South Side. When he was twelve, the Lucianos moved to the suburb of Lemont, a quarry town about fifteen miles southwest of Chicago. There they were among the poorest families in town. Their house lacked running water, and Luciano and his brother would lug their water from a nearby gas station, using it to drink and fill their toilet. On their beds were packing blankets from their dad's truck.

Things only got tougher. Within a year of moving to Lemont, Luciano's father died after driving his rig off an overpass on Chicago's Damen Avenue. His mother was ill-equipped to raise the boys alone. She was prone to spells of verbal fixation in which she would repeat the phrase *Lotti-fa-dotti* to herself, sometimes for hours. Within a year she remarried another alcoholic trucker, who had a tendency to go after the boys with a belt after a few whiskeys. Whatever mitigating influence their mother might have had on their stepdad's violence ended when she died of natural causes, when Luciano was only fourteen.

Poverty can always afford paradox, and the great one of Luciano's childhood was that somehow the family always managed to feed a pack of five or six dogs. Completely undisciplined, they were of every breed and bark and occupied the house with the same prerogatives as the children. They'd sleep in the beds with the kids, and Luciano adored them. "I can't say for sure that Art ever really loved anybody, but he definitely loved those dogs," says Bruce Artis, one of Luciano's childhood friends. "That was just the strangest thing about him, but maybe it wasn't so strange—given his folks, I mean."

By the time he was sixteen, Luciano had decided that home was not the place to be. He fixed up a broken-down '65 Ford that his stepfather had abandoned in the front yard and began road-tripping as far from Lemont as he could afford. On one occasion he stole some checks from his stepdad to fuel a trip to Florida. After he used one to buy some fancy shoes in Pensacola, a suspicious clerk called the sheriff, who picked up Luciano and called his stepdad, who made him ride a bus back to Lemont barefoot. When Luciano was nineteen, an acquaintance recently released from prison taught him how to be a short-range con artist. He'd take a twenty-dollar bill and buy something for a dollar at a gas station. After getting his change, he would say, "Know what, buddy? I didn't want to break that twenty. If I give you a five and five singles back can you give me a ten?" But Luciano would hand a five and four singles to the attendant, who would pass him the ten, then look at him and say, "You only gave me nine." That's when Luciano would respond, "Sorry about that. You know, I might as well just take back the twenty. You got nine, here's another dollar which makes that ten and here's another ten, so can I just get back my twenty?" By the time he was done confusing the attendant, Luciano would have an extra ten dollars.

Change raising was an ideal con for Luciano. It allowed him to make money on the road by using his natural charms. He was laid-back and funny, impossible not to like even though he was always on the make, whether it was fast money or women. With his high self-confidence, he began ranging farther afield, and to fuel his travels he graduated to paper hanging. He'd pull into a town, establish a residence and a checking account under a false name, and embark on a shopping spree. After a week or two, he'd return the goods for cash. By the time the checks bounced he'd be in the next state, on to the next scam.

It was during a ramble into Texas in the late sixties that he met Malinda Williams. She was a dark-haired beauty of seventeen who was waiting tables at a diner in Dallas. A country girl who'd grown up in the small town of Valley View, she'd moved to the city after her father got a job as a Dallas police officer. She'd been raised by conservative, evangelical parents, and was just beginning to taste her independence right at the time that half her generation needed little more excuse than rumors of a party six states away to leave home. Luciano regaled her with tales of the big city and his travels across the country, and within days she'd quit her job and joined him on the paper-hanging trail. Truth was, parts of Malinda were just as wild and unhinged as Luciano. Neither of them knew it then, but she suffered from bipolar disorder, and for the first few years there were a lot of highs. The couple latched on to the hippie movement, following the sun to places like southern California and Florida, then eventually gravitated back to Illinois and settled down in the Chicago suburb of Schaumburg, where Luciano worked various jobs in construction with his brother Richard. At some point, presumably either to avoid the draft or the law, Luciano changed his last name to his wife's—Williams. Whatever his motivation for the name change, in March of 1972 his draft number indeed came up and Uncle Sam found him. He was briefly stationed in Texas at Fort Bliss, but according to his military records he struck his commanding officer shortly after discovering that the army planned to ship him off to Vietnam. He spent the rest of his service, 533 days, in Fort Leavenworth. He was there on Thanksgiving Day, 1972, when Art junior was born.

He rejoined his wife and son after his dishonorable discharge. They moved back to Schaumburg and picked up where they'd left off. Over the next two years, the couple had two more children, Wensdae and Jason, and for a little while it looked like Art senior would reform. Then, in December of '77, he was arrested for robbing the truck in DuPage County and wound up in Stateville.

On the day he visited, Art junior was too young to think of his father as a "criminal"—a distinction that comes naturally only to those of us lucky enough never to have had a family member behind bars. In a vague way, little Art knew that his dad was "in a bad place full of bad men, but it was unfathomable that he was one of them." All he remembers was sitting on his daddy's lap in the visiting room, being perfectly happy that he indeed had a father, and ecstatically cognizant of the fact that in a few months his "pops" would be leaving Stateville to become, once and for all, a permanent presence in his life.

•   •   •

THINGS WENT ACCORDING TO PLAN at first. In March of 1978, Senior left Stateville to serve out the remaining six months of his sentence at a halfway house in Bensenville. During the day he worked at a wire-manufacturing plant, a job at which he excelled. Malinda visited him at night and on the weekends with the kids, and his reintegration into both his family and law-abiding society progressed smoothly. By the time he left the halfway house and rejoined his family, Magnum Wire was so impressed with Senior that the company made him a foreman, and he was able to begin anew his life as a father and husband in a three-bedroom home that was as respectable and as congruous as that of any workingman in town.

Art remembers that taste of normality with the possessiveness and incredulity of an old exile. "You wouldn't believe it, but there was a time when I was a kid when I had pretty much a normal life," he says. "I was a suburban kid. We had a nice home. We were a family. We did normal things like go to the movies. I remember my dad taking me to see *Superman,* you know, with Christopher Reeve, and holding his hand in line and thinking that was just the coolest thing."

Despite Senior's appearance of becoming a family man, what little Art and none of the other Williamses knew was that he had been seeing another woman even before leaving the halfway house. Her name was Anice Eaker and she was a lithe, blonde-haired, blue-eyed divorcée who lived on the other side of Bensenville with two kids from a previous marriage. From the moment she appeared she laid siege to Senior's affections with pythonic determination.

Malinda did not give in easily. She learned of the affair and insisted that Senior break it off. He did, but a few days later Anice came by the house looking for him. She even had the temerity to let herself in the back door, but instead of finding Williams she found

Malinda, seething and incredulous. Little Art was there, too, and watched wide-eyed as his mother proceeded to administer a beating as brutal as any he'd later see on the streets of Chicago. By the time it was over, she had broken Anice's nose.

Anice later called the police, claiming that Malinda had tried to kill her. Confronted by Anice's thoroughly battered face, they had little choice but to arrest Malinda. Senior bailed his wife out and convinced Anice not to press charges, but Malinda sensed that getting her husband away from the other woman would require more drastic measures. She told Senior that they either had to leave the state and head back to Texas, or she'd leave him.

Senior consented to the move, and within two weeks the family was packed up and headed south. They made a go of it in Houston at first, where Senior worked odd jobs, and when that failed to pan out they retreated to a mobile-home park in Pleasant Grove, a suburb of Dallas. Like many such marginal communities, it hosted a mix of blue-collar strivers, wanderers, the elderly, and religious zealots. The Williamses' next door neighbors were an older couple that consisted of a World War II veteran and a Santería priestess from the Philippines. The priestess, whose name was Connie, had long black hair that nearly reached the ground, and a beautiful smile. She babysat the kids, sang to them, and spoiled them rotten with cookies and milk. She told Art stories about the moody pantheon of Santería demigods, conversed with invisible entities, and told him that a powerful spirit dwelled inside of him.

Little Art loved her.

While Art was learning about the dark arts with his mystical nanny, his dad was spending days on the other side of the park with an evangelical minister. With no work, an unhappy wife, and a guilty conscience, Senior was reaching for Jesus. Things came to head one day when he dropped by his neighbor's place to pick up Art and found him kneeling in front of a Santería altar with candles ablaze. Harsh words, accusations of devil worship, and hexes ensued. The minister convinced Art senior to move his family to the other side of the park and organized a trailer-park exorcism, during which they held Art down on the floor of their makeshift church and commanded the devil to abandon the boy.

Needless to say, Art was terrified and hopelessly confused—a state that would only become more enhanced by what followed: Exhausted from all the moving, her husband's bad decisions, and finally the commotion surrounding Junior, Malinda had a nervous breakdown. It manifested itself as a near-catatonic depression and rages at Senior over the fact that they'd descended from a relatively good life to the status of trailer trash.

The obvious solution, he told her, was to return to Illinois and quickly reestablish themselves. And so a little more than a year after they left, they moved back to the Land of Lincoln. They stayed with Senior's half-brother Richard, who lived in Schaumburg—only eight miles from Bensenville and Anice Eaker. Senior's proximity to his old mistress was probably enough to doom his marriage, but the catalyst for his final break with Malinda proved far more destructive and tragic.

Senior and Anice's new plan was to enroll in bartending school, taking turns watching the kids while the other attended classes. One evening while Senior was watching the kids, Wensdae woke up and wandered into the kitchen, where she found her father at practice mixing drinks while the other kids slept. She was only five, but her memory of what happened next would stay with her like an immutable pathogen.

"What are you doing?" she asked her father.

"I'll show you," he said. He quickly left the house, returning minutes later with a bottle of red wine. He poured her a glass, encouraged her to drink it, and when she was happily dizzy, he led her into the back bedroom.

Malinda came home from class minutes later. She opened the bedroom door to find her husband lying naked on the bed with their daughter.

The fighting lasted most of the night. Senior tried to convince his wife that nothing had happened, but Malinda had seen. Her rage re-erupted the next morning even stronger. As they screamed and yelled at each other, Senior rounded up all three children and put them in the car. Malinda followed him to the driveway, demanding that he leave the children with her. When he refused and prepared to get in the driver's seat, she tried to wrestle the keys away from him. He shoved her hard to the ground, then jumped into the car. As he drove off, Malinda was still on her back in the driveway, kicking and screaming for him to return the kids.

Days later, the police would pick her up from wandering the streets and take her to Elgin Mental Health Center, where she would be diagnosed with severe depression and spend the next month undergoing treatment.

Art never knew what caused the fight. Because of their individual shames, no one ever told him the truth about what his father had done. In Art's childhood mind, everything congealed around the bizarre incident with Connie, and for years he'd harbor a vague shame that it had all been his fault—the work of the vengeful spirit inside him.

SENIOR DROVE STRAIGHT TO ANICE'S house in Schaumburg. She had a room prepared for Art junior and his siblings, and welcomed them in as if she'd been expecting their arrival for weeks. Senior told his children flatly, "This is your new mother, we'll be living with her from now on."

Art's first instinct was to not trust her; the last time he'd seen Anice, after all, his mother was pounding on her face. But he quickly grew to like her. Anice employed all the dialogical tricks that suggest coziness, calling Art and Wensdae "kiddo" and "honey" and even referring to Jason as "my baby." She was particularly affectionate when Art senior was present. Over the next several months she cooked for them, played games with them, and seemed remarkably unperturbed by the fact that she had gone from two kids to five overnight.

Anice's own children, Larry and Chrissy, were older than Art junior—Larry by four years and Chrissy by two. Larry, a budding jock who had always wanted a younger brother, duly drafted Art junior as his number one sports buddy, a role Art junior happily embraced. They'd play basketball at the courts at a nearby school on an almost daily basis, and Little Art beamed when the older boy began calling him "bro." Chrissy, a gabby little blonde, was less enthused by the three new "brats" who had taken over the house, but she eventually came to love them. Neither of Anice's kids had any relationship with their own father, and Art junior noticed that early on Anice encouraged them to call Art senior "Dad." Art junior called Anice by her name.

The kids were just adapting to the new arrangement when Malinda was released from the hospital. She quickly got an apartment in Arlington Heights and a job cleaning houses, then demanded that Art senior give her custody of the kids under threat of bringing in the law. Even though her mental stability was questionable, he made no attempt to resist.

ART JUNIOR AND HIS SIBLINGS didn't see their father for several months after rejoining Malinda. Senior called the house numerous times and spoke to the kids, but Malinda, horrified by what she had seen at Uncle Rich's, refused to allow him to visit. He swore to her that nothing had happened—he had experienced a moment of weakness, but her entrance into the room had prevented it from going further. He loved his daughter and would never let that happen again. Malinda experienced a moment of weakness too. She finally gave in and consented to let him have the kids for a weekend, stipulating that she did not wish to see his face. She would drop the kids off at her sister Donna's house on Saturday morning, where he'd pick them up and return them Sunday evening. She made sure that her eldest child knew the plan.

Everything began as it was supposed to. The kids waited at Aunt Donna's, then Senior showed up and took them out to lunch. They joked and teased each other over burgers, delighted to be spending two full days with Dad. After lunch, he told them that he had a surprise planned for them, and they piled back into the car with glee.

Art watched his father closely as he steered onto the highway, trying to divine where they were headed. All he knew was that they were not headed into the city. After an hour of watching off-ramps whiz past, shiftings of doubt moved through his stomach. His mom had never mentioned anything about a long trip.

After three hours, he began repeatedly asking his father where they were going. He wanted to go home.

Senior refused to tell him, and became short with him. He told him that they were taking a vacation, and that he shouldn't complain. Art junior started to cry, but it didn't do any good.

They drove 2,200 miles, all the way to Lobster Valley, Oregon. By the time they finally broke away from the highway two days later, Art junior and Wensdae knew that they were not going home. They were now farther away from it than they'd ever been, in a fascinatingly alien landscape of pine trees, mountains, dirt roads, and ranches.

Senior drove deep into the countryside, winding the car through hairpin turns until they finally crackled up a gravel drive to an A-frame house somewhere in the middle of a forest. As Senior killed the engine, from the front door of the house emerged the first familiar thing Art had seen in two days.

As always, Anice was smiling and expectant.

MALINDA CALLED THE POLICE, but they couldn't help her much. Kidnapping aside, Senior would not have been using his real name. Later on she'd come to believe that the entire time she'd been sequestering the kids from him, he'd been setting up camp with Anice in Oregon, waiting for the opportune moment to take them back.

By now Art junior had moved so many times that he was developing a feel for impending relocation, along with a sense of absolute powerlessness. Other than food and entertainment, his desires—to stay in one place, to be with his mother, simple regularity—were irrelevant. He controlled the only thing he could, his imagination, and latched himself to books and studies as a way of riding out the parental storms. No matter where he was, school was a sanctuary, and he consistently placed in the top of his class. "He was a little geek," remembers Wensdae. "He had these big glasses and he was always reading, usually stuff way beyond whatever grade he was in, almost like he was trying to stay ahead."

Art's childhood dream was to be a lawyer; he'd read that it had been the formative occupation of the founding fathers and it had the ring of accomplishment. On another level, it embodied the guiding structure that he was missing at home. Fair play, a governing set of rules and principles—the way things should be. Deep inside, he knew that he was at a disadvantage compared with the kids he'd meet in other towns whose fathers were not convicts, whose mothers were stable. He wanted to cross over into that realm, and his desire had not yet turned to anger.

THEY STAYED IN LOBSTER VALLEY for a few months, then it was on to Lebanon, Oregon, and later Mount Shasta, California. In each town, Williams, now aided by Anice, would hang paper just before departing. Art junior was learning to read the signs. The grown-ups would start speaking in hushed voices and appear preoccupied. The house would suddenly fill up with new goods that never emerged from their boxes—televisions, stereos, expensive suits. There'd be a celebratory night—a nice dinner out, a trip to the movies, or a few gifts for the kids—followed by a predawn exit. When they left Lebanon, Art actually saw the cash—a few thousand dollars on the kitchen table. He was excited until he realized that he wasn't getting any of it.

As the towns and months went by, the separation from Malinda and the itinerant lifestyle wore on Art and Wensdae, who increasingly complained to their father that they wanted to see their mother; but the more they bugged him about it, the meaner he became. Wensdae had it the hardest. Senior had of course lied to Malinda about nothing happening that day at Uncle Rich's—he had raped his own daughter. According to Wensdae, that was the only time he ever sexually abused her, but her psychic wound would only grow with her body. Shortly after Senior kidnapped the children, she started wetting the bed, and on her sixth birthday Art rewarded her with a large present, beautifully wrapped. She eagerly opened it to find that it was a box of diapers. She ran off crying. Art junior ran after her and tried to console her, but he was so miserable himself and shocked by his father's cruelty that he just ended up crying with her over the fact that they wanted to go back to Mom.

Anice's colors darkened too. Once it was clear that Senior had no intention of returning to Malinda, both Art junior and Wensdae got the feeling that they had become unwanted baggage. "She was completely fake," says Wensdae. "She'd ignore us when my dad wasn't around; then if he was she'd suddenly try to act like a mom."

The one place Art junior began to feel at home was Mount Shasta, a town of about three thousand tucked away among the mountains and redwoods near California's border with Oregon. Surrounded by national parks and graced with stunning views of an eponymous fourteen-thousand-foot dormant volcano, the town had the magical aura of a wonderland. He made fast friends with a local girl who lived up the road. Her name was Lisa Arbacheske, and during the summer of '82 he spent nearly every day with her.

"Her life seemed so perfect," he remembers. "She had a house down by the river, a big, beautiful log cabin. They had horses. She was the most beautiful little girl, with long, brown, curly hair. My first kiss was with her, on a log near her house. It was the happiest I'd been in a long time. She made me feel loved."

Art wanted to stay in Mount Shasta, but by then Wensdae's psychological rebellion had intensified beyond Senior's control. In addition to the bedwetting, she developed a habit of muddying her clothes after her father dropped her off at school, and sometimes removing them altogether. When school authorities complained, Senior and Anice panicked that he'd be discovered and arrested.

Toward summer's end Senior left town, taking Wensdae and Jason with him. He came back two weeks later driving a brand-new Ford Bronco, but the kids weren't with him. He told Art that he had dropped them off in Chicago with their mother, and to pack his bags because he would be joining them in a week.

"I didn't believe him," says Art. "I thought he had done something with them, and I freaked out. I remember fighting with him, and that was the first time he ever hit me, really hard in the face."

A few days later, Art said a tearful good-bye to Lisa, then climbed into the back of the Bronco, which was crammed with the family's belongings. He still didn't believe that his dad was taking him back to Illinois, and spent much of the next three days sobbing in the back while the rest of the family repeatedly told him to shut up. But he wasn't the only miserable child on the trip. "On the way back my parents ran out of money," remembers Chrissy. "So we stopped in these little towns, and my parents made us get out of the car and knock on people's doors to beg for money. I hated it; we all hated it. That's how we got gas money."

It was only once they crossed into Illinois that Art junior began to think his father might be telling the truth; when the Chicago skyline came into view, he was convinced. Senior drove all the way downtown, where he parked in front of a shelter for women and children on Sheridan Road. He told Art to wait, then went inside. A few minutes later he reemerged. Malinda was with him.

Over the years Art would scour his memory for clues and explanations for what happened next.

"He gave me a hug, and I asked him if I'd see him again soon," remembers Art. "He said he loved me and said, 'Yeah, I'll see you again.'"

It was a perfectly normal farewell, as if the nine months he had spent as a kidnapped child had really been a weekend after all.

IT WAS A ONE-TWO PUNCH that ended Art's childhood. The first was his father's leaving; the second blow came about a year afterward. The family had continued to live in Schaumburg after Senior's departure, and although Malinda found it a struggle to support three kids on her own, things hadn't gone too badly. The children were overjoyed to be back with their mother, and Art, now free from the constant moving, excelled at his new school, Eisenhower Elementary. He not only achieved the best grades in his class but became a star on the school's wrestling and baseball teams, his success on the latter no doubt thanks to many an afternoon spent practicing with Larry.

Malinda had gotten back to normal too. She'd had no more breakdowns since leaving the Elgin Mental Health Center, and had even begun taking an interest in her sister's seven-year-old son, Gregory, who had tragically developed a brain tumor. There was little hope for him, but Malinda did not believe that her sister was responsibly seeing to the boy's care. Donna had started dating a biker named Bobby, and Malinda was outraged that her sister was engaged in a romance with a leather-clad hooligan while her son was fighting for his life. And as siblings are prone to do, she reported the situation to her mother in Texas, who in turn chastised Donna.

Donna was furious. She showed up at Malinda's apartment with Bobby in tow. Malinda was out grocery shopping with the kids at the time, but upon their return Donna and Bobby were waiting by his motorcycle. As Malinda emerged from the car carrying bags of groceries, Donna intercepted her, and the two sisters immediately fell into a heated argument. Art was at first excited at watching the two adults fight, but the feeling quickly turned to terror.

Without warning, Donna reached into one of the grocery bags Malinda was carrying, snatched out a bottle of beer, and struck Malinda square in the temple. Malinda dropped as quickly as if she'd been hit by a sniper's bullet. Art ran to her.

"She wasn't moving," he remembers. "I knew it was bad. A neighbor called the paramedics and I could see by the looks on their faces that it was really serious. They tried to rouse her but they couldn't. They took her away fast."

Donna was long gone by then. She'd sped off with Bobby as soon as she heard the sirens, and the kids spent that night at the home of the neighbor, a kind woman who lived alone who had called 911. When she called the hospital for an update, she was informed that Malinda was in a coma.

The coma would last one month.

THE NEXT DAY, the neighbor turned the kids over to Child Protection Services. Unable to find a family willing to care for three children, CPS had no choice but to separate them. Wensdae went to a girls' home, while Jason and Art were sent to live with foster families. For the next three months, none of them would have any idea what was happening with the others, or the condition of their mother.

Art's foster family already had a real son, and the two boys didn't get along. He'd later theorize that the other boy was jealous of his arrival, but, in any case, after a month the family sent him back to CPS. He was then sent to a boys' home, which he ended up liking much better. At the home Art befriended an older boy whose name he no longer remembers, but he became the first in a long line of older males that Art would follow like a duckling chasing bread crumbs. He was ruddy, blond, and tall, and he spent all his free time bent over a sketch pad, drawing pictures of himself behind the wheels of muscle cars, usually accompanied by curvy and admiring women in bikinis. The boy was immensely popular because he'd do similar sketches for other boys he liked, thus keeping the rooms of the home perpetually blossoming with sexually empowering motor fantasies.

To get the older boy's attention, Art started carrying around a sketch pad too. He had natural talent, and the boy noticed. Soon they were spending long hours drawing together, and the boy taught Art the importance of perspective and drawing from life.

The only constant during this time was that Art was still able to attend the same school, Eisenhower Elementary. That year, the school held a student-art contest. Art drew himself trapped in a long, oppressive hallway that was a thinly veiled scene from the school itself. It depicted the kind of rebellious sentiment that every child feels against teachers and homework and institutional authority— the old school-as-prison lament. But within its execution there was a precision and attention to detail that the judges found startling.

He won.

2

BRIDGEPORT

Th' fact iv th' matther is that th' rale truth is niver simple.
What we call thruth an' pass around fr'm hand to hand is
on'y a kind iv a currency that we use f'r convenience. There
are a good many countherfeiters an' a lot iv th' contherfeits
must be in circulation. I haven't anny question that I take in
many iv thim over me intellechool bar ivry day, an' pass out
not a few. Some iv the countherfeits has as much precious
metal in thim as th' rale goods, on'y they don't bear the'
govermint stamp.

–*Dissertations by Mr. Dooley*, BY BRIDGEPORT
NATIVE FINLEY PETER DUNNE, 1906

I t was the fall of 1985 when Malinda was finally released from
the hospital. Art remembers the year because several months
later the Chicago Bears would annihilate the New England
Patriots in the Super Bowl, 46 to 10, and from his perspective, other
than rejoining his family, that was pretty much the only good thing to
happen that winter.

Without any notice, a CPS worker showed up at the boys' home,
told Art to get his things, and drove him to a Salvation Army family
unit on Sheridan Avenue. Like reunited refugees snatched from

four different camps, suddenly they were together again, and that was all that mattered at first. The Salvation home was clean and safe, and the families staying there were well-mannered. They were from every race, all in the same timid limbo, waiting more or less quietly for social services to find them public housing that would invariably be based upon the color of their skin. Still happily shocked from the reunion with his family, Art didn't realize that they had become completely destitute.

After three weeks at the Salvation home, one morning they piled into a social-services van and were driven south. The moment they crossed the Chicago River, they entered one of the most storied neighborhoods in Chicago, two square miles of tenements, brick flats, and light industrial warehouses known as Bridgeport.

Chicago's tough-town reputation rests on neighborhoods like Bridgeport, a place that both forges the flinty myth and keeps it from expiring. From its very beginnings as an American city, Chicago was based on a grand, connective dream: to link Lake Michigan to the Mississippi River. To do that, a canal had to be dug from the South Fork of the Chicago River to the headwaters of the Illinois River, ninety-six miles away. It was a distance twice as long as that of the Panama Canal, and when work began in 1836, there were no steam shovels or bulldozers—just thousands of Irishmen with shovels.

The canal's starting point was Bridgeport, which was originally named Hardscrabble after a local farm, then later Cabbage Patch because of the crops the Irish planted. The name later changed to Bridgeport after a span was erected across the South Fork of the Chicago River, but that didn't alter the fact that it was Chicago's first slum. Once the canal work began the Irish flooded in, and that was where they lived. Many of them had just finished digging the Erie Canal, and they labored for whiskey and a dollar a day. No one knows how many died building the canal, but when it was completed twelve years later, those who remained weren't so much workers as survivors. Many stayed in Bridgeport, where they built churches, schools, and—as the economic promise of the great conduit came true—the city itself.

But even as the Irish gained a foothold, Bridgeport remained an edgy place, as new waves of Germans, Poles, Lithuanians, and Italians all settled into the neighborhood, most of them drawn by work in the nearby Union Stockyards. The groups eyed each other distrustfully and segregated themselves to specific blocks. Ethnic strife was an almost daily occurrence, as gangs enforced the georacial boundaries and often battled each other in the streets. Carter Harrison Jr., Chicago's first native mayor, grew up in Bridgeport, and famously described it as "a place where men were men, and boys were either hellions or early candidates for the last rites of the Church."

The Bridgeport gangs were the city's most ruthless racial enforcers, and largely responsible for the 1919 race riots, which erupted when a black boy drowned in Lake Michigan after white youths threw stones at him because he was swimming off a white beach. As blacks began protesting, hordes of white Bridgeporters bent on "protecting" their community began roaming the South Side in a seven-day-long spree of violence that resulted in the deaths of fifteen whites and twenty-three blacks.

Despite all the tensions between its residents, for the first half of the twentieth century the neighborhood flourished. Five Bridgeporters went on to control City Hall—a mayoral legacy unmatched by any other Chicago neighborhood. But once the meatpacking houses started closing down in the 1950s, the fragile economic and social alliances that had held the neighborhood together collapsed. The more prosperous population moved out, low-income housing developments went up, and one of Chicago's most intransigent criminal cultures took hold. By the time the Williamses moved in, Bridgeport was as tough and as racially charged as it had ever been, with gangs composed of a hodgepodge mix of impoverished whites, Latinos, Italians, and Chinese fighting each other and the blacks for control of blocks, corners, drugs, and honor—a battle for the bottom that hit home with newcomers the moment they or a loved one were attacked by somebody who had been there first. Skin color, address, and income determined where you stood in the battle, and who your allies were, regardless of the fact that nobody liked or even comprehended it. You either played by the rules or, if you were willing to resort to violence, you made your own.

Place was preconditioning, and the particular patch of Bridgeport the Salvation Army set the Williamses down on was known as the Bridgeport Homes, one of the few "white projects" in the city. They comprised a square block of two-story brick row houses, eighteen units in all, with a total of about 250 residents. They were small compared with infamous Chicago projects like Cabrini Green or the Dearborn Homes, but what they lacked in size they compensated for in gloom. When they were built in 1943, they were hailed as stylish, low-income housing of the future, but the one future its residents looked forward to more than any other was the day they moved out. Unfortunately for many of the Homes' inhabitants, that day often got so obscured by the omnipresent traumas of poverty that it receded beyond the horizon altogether.

It took two days for the power company to turn the heat on. It was the dead clear of Chicago's winter when even clouds seem to hide for warmth. Malinda and the kids slept bundled up in their Salvation Army clothes, with blankets and some food from the local Pentecostal church. Later on, the church also brought some beds and a sofa and a table, but that just reminded Art that they were entirely dependent and in for the long haul.

Art hated the homes from the beginning and attempted to run away within days. For this twelve-year-old, that meant stealing off to find his father. He recruited Jason in the adventure, and one morning before his mom and Wensdae woke up they snuck out of the apartment and up to Canal Street. Having no idea where to go, they latched on to the one landmark they recognized, the iconic rise of the Sears Tower. They followed it all the way to its base and walked into the lobby. All morning long they rode the escalators and roamed the shops, then finally camped out in front of Alexander Calder's famous motorized mobile, *Universe*. They were still there when evening fell. Finally a security guard showed up and told them that it was time to leave.

"We can't leave," Art said, and in explanation he blurted out that they were waiting to meet their father. When the guard asked for their dad's name, Art gave it to him, and for the first time that day he realized they had a good plan after all. The guard told him to sit tight. He was going to make some calls and try to find their dad.

A few minutes later, two Chicago police officers approached Art and his brother. They informed him that their mom was terrified and had been looking for them all day. They led Art and Jason out front, put them in the back of a cruiser, and drove them back to the projects. It was the first and only time Art would ever be in the back of a police car without being a suspect.

A FEW MONTHS AFTER THEY MOVED into the Homes, Art ventured into the kitchen one afternoon and found the house totally bereft of food. Malinda explained to him and his siblings that they would have to wait. She left the house—Art suspects she went begging—and returned hours later empty-handed. By the following morning all three children were crying to be fed, and Malinda was crying hysterically herself. "My mother still didn't know how to adjust to the level of poverty we'd found ourselves in," Art remembers, "she couldn't feed her children so she was feeling helpless. She had a breakdown and didn't know what to do. This was all new to her."

Art once again grabbed Jason and left the house to see what he could do. He didn't consider going to the church or social-service agencies an option; he believed that if he did he ran the risk of being taken away from his mother again. With no money and no plan, the first monetary objects Art saw were the parking meters on Halsted Street: old-style, single-headed "Park-O-Meters" that probably dated back to the 1940s. He started hitting them with his palm in the vague hope that one of them would pour out change like a piñata. With each whack he heard the enticing rattle of coins. This caused him to stop and study the meters more closely.

They had a cylinder at the base containing two holes. He correctly assumed they accommodated some kind of twin-pronged key, and searched the sidewalk until he found a pliable piece of metal. He bent it, snakelike, so it could fit both holes at once.

"I stuck it into the holes like a pin and, what do you know, the cylinder began turning," he remembers. "The cylinder part popped out and inside there was a canister with change. Then we just went down the street, hit about two blocks' worth. It was really pretty simple. We got about fifty dollars and then we went to the grocery store."

Art knew in the abstract that he had committed a crime, but when he and Jason walked back through their front door with two bags of groceries each, the relief—and pride—in his mother's face obliterated any sense of shame. Malinda chastised him when he told her how he got the money, but she didn't hide her pleasure at his resourcefulness. The family had been starving, he had rescued them, and power had shifted. He kept the homemade key, using its rough design to make an even better one. Over the next six months he used it to buy more food, clothes, toys, and candy. To avoid repetition, he alternated blocks and went to other thoroughfares, but eventually the city caught on and began replacing the meters with a more secure model. He kept the key long after it was obsolete.

LESS THAN TWO WEEKS after the Williamses arrived at the Homes, Art, Wensdae, and Jason were walking down Lituanica Avenue, about a block from their apartment, when they crossed paths with a group of teenagers sitting on a stoop near the corner.

"Project killer!" one of them shouted, then he slugged Art in the stomach and pushed him to the ground. While Wensdae and Jason screamed, the others had at him, shouting, "Project killer! Project killer!" over and over again.

Beaten up and bewildered, Art returned home, and when his mother asked him why he'd been bullied he didn't even know what to tell her. He got his answer a few days later from a group of boys who also lived in the Homes and hung out in the project's playground. Noticing his shiner, they plied him for details about the fight, then explained the nuances. "Those kids who got you are Latin Kings," they told him. "Our gang is the Satan's Disciples. They figured you were one of us."

Art had never met anyone in a gang, much less been associated with one. He was surprised to learn that almost every boy in the projects older than fourteen was a member of the SDs, while younger boys like him were regarded as "peewees"—provisional members until they came of age. The gang had started on the South Side in 1964 and rapidly spread. There were more than fifty branches throughout Chicago and Wisconsin. Its supreme leader was said to be a guy named Aggie, its colors were black and canary yellow, and its symbol was the trident. The Latin Kings were their archenemies.

Art found the whole thing utterly weird. Raised a churchgoer and subjected to an exorcism, he had a visceral mistrust of anything with the word *Satan* in it, but, other than the word and the fork sign, the gang was less preoccupied with devil worship than the average church. Race wasn't a factor either; like the neighborhood, the SDs had originated as mostly white and Irish, then adapted to the changing demographics. Latinos stood alongside carrot-topped Irish kids and Italians, and the operative commonalities were that they were all stuck in the Bridgeport Homes, overwhelmingly lacked fathers, and they all hated the Latin Kings up the street, who differed in no way other than the fact that they were perhaps slightly less poor.

The gang kids teased Art at first. With his gawky glasses, small size, and bookish suburban outlook, he was a natural target. Art avoided them by staying inside, but one day as he was peering out his back door at the project's basketball court he saw three well-known neighborhood toughs confront and surround an older SD named José Morales. Compared with his assailants, Morales was small, and Art was certain he was about to get severely beaten.

"In the blink of an eye, José jumped in the air and did a spinning back kick," Art remembers. "It was like some shit out of a kung fu movie. The other two guys were so shocked they didn't have a chance, José went at them hard and fast. It was amazing. Here was this little Puerto Rican that just kicked the *shit* out of three bullies. After that day, there was no question. I wanted to be like *him*."

Art later approached José admiringly and asked the older boy to teach him how to fight. Morales took him under his wing, and there in the project playground he began teaching Art the South Side martial arts, which are pretty much the spiritual opposite of Asian martial arts. Bridgeport favors the offense, because attempting to talk your way out of a fight is often interpreted as a formal request to be victimized. With his natural athleticism and background as a wrestler in grammar school—not to mention his desire to avoid future beatings—Art was a star pupil.

Art's confidence in his ability to defend himself grew like a new skin that rejoiced in its adaptive freedoms. "I noticed then when José started teaching me how to fight, all the anger and frustration I'd been feeling for years, I started taking it out on people." His first strike at the world came when he was walking with two friends on Thirty-first Street. He stepped into an alley to urinate, and as he was conducting his business a fattish white man came out of a back door and asked him, "What the fuck are you doing?"

Art zipped up his pants and went right at him. He began beating him, kicking him, trying to destroy him. The man was bigger but Art was fast, chopping him down until cars on the street began beeping at him to stop. On another day in another alley, he encountered two drunks who began talking shit at him. Discarded nearby were some old golf clubs; he picked one up and answered their taunts by battering them until they were both bleeding, broken, and moaning.

"I'd gone from a kid from the suburbs who was really hoping life would get better to a kid who said, 'It's not gonna get better.' And I started losing it."

ONE OF THE ONLY BRIGHT SPOTS IN Art's new life was that, as usual, he was exceeding at his new school, Philip D. Armour Elementary—named after Chicago's most famous meatpacking magnate. This was despite the fact that he usually didn't have enough money for supplies. But he noticed early on that right around the corner from the projects was the printing house for the *Bridgeport News*, his local paper, and so he began showing up at the loading dock and begging for paper. The laborers on the printing-house floor invariably brought him inside, showed him around, and gave him whatever he wanted. That was how Art first came to think of printing as a friendly and fascinating endeavor. "The guys on the floor were really nice, and I remember the smell of the ink; I just loved it. There was a beautiful Heidelberg press in there, about thirty feet long, worth probably a hundred thousand dollars. I guess you could say that visiting that place planted a kind of seed."

At the end of his first semester at Armour, Art's teachers were so impressed with his performance and test scores that they recommended he be double-promoted, from sixth grade straight to high school. The downside of this was that his new school would be Thomas Kelly High, regarded as one of the worst schools in Chicago.

Originally opened in 1928 as a junior high, Kelly had all the architectural trappings that harkened back to a spirit of solemnity about education: arched double doors, a colonnaded peristyle, Celtic lettering above the gym. But in the ensuing decades its ornamentation had become icing on a rotten cake. By the time Art attended classes, the roof leaked, the bathrooms barely functioned, and the school had one of the highest truancy rates in Chicago, with more than five hundred out of about sixteen hundred students cutting classes on any given day. Sixty-six percent of its students were failing two or more classes, while less than half went on to graduate. Assaults on teachers and students were routine.

"You had people getting killed there," Art remembers. "Going from Armour to this shit school where teachers didn't care was such a shocker. It felt hopeless to the extent that I didn't want to be there. Studying no longer felt like a way out for me."

By the end of his freshman year Art had lost all interest in academics. In terms of survival skills and fulfilling his immediate needs, the Satan's Disciples were more pragmatic mentors. The SDs taught him to stop messing with the parking meters and instead break into the cars sitting next to them. He learned how to hotwire vehicles, where to sell the stereos and rims, and the locations of the chop shops, which were particularly abundant in Bridgeport. During thin times, the gang members would even chip in to help buy food for his family. "Once I saw that the gang could provide, moving up in it became the main goal," he says. "Food and money for the bills were immediate concerns, and the gang helped with those things. It was all bullshit, of course, but I was thirteen, and those good grades I'd gotten before got me nowhere. I was in the worst fucking school in the city."

Kelly High and the gang finally collided during the end of Art's sophomore year, when a rival gang known as La Raza began making inroads at the school. Tensions ratcheted up and erupted in a widespread brawl in the school's cafeteria; one student was knifed and the assistant principal had his head shoved through a glass food-display case. Although Art had no involvement in those particular acts, he was in the fight, and in the ensuing crackdown he was expelled from Kelly altogether. At fourteen, the eradication of a stellar academic future was complete.

That seems like a young age for a kid to wash out, but Art did have two siblings who were even younger. Right about the same time he was bashing his way out of high school, his little brother, Jason, was getting in trouble for acting up in grammar school. Jason enjoyed none of Art's academic advantages and had experienced even less stability. At ten years old, he was not only expelled from grammar school, but Malinda lost custody of him completely. The State remanded him to Maryville Academy, a boy's school in Des

Plaines, where he would languish until the age of eighteen and emerge with less education than Art.

Wensdae would fail to finish high school as well, but she would get a general-education degree. The only one of the Williams kids who never lashed outward, she would continue her interior battle, with consequences far more violent than any her brothers ever faced.

THE WILLIAMS KIDS were struggling with poverty, but there was another factor they had to contend with, one that haunted them in their own house. Art discovered it one day during his freshman year in high school after he forgot his key. Knocking on the front door, he called for his mom to let him in. He knew she was home because he could hear her inside, talking to someone. Malinda didn't respond, which he thought was strange. To the side of the front door was a little opaque window to a utility room, and through the glazing he could just make out the form of his mother crouched in the corner. He banged on the window and shouted at her.

"They won't leave me alone!" Malinda screamed back. She explained that she had gone into the utility room to look for supplies to build a spaceship, so she could escape them.

"Who won't leave you alone?" Art asked.

"The little people," she said. "They're all over me, they're driving me crazy."

Art didn't hear any other voices. He sat down beneath the little window, trying to talk his mom down and get her to open the door. He assumed she was on drugs, and figured they'd wear off, or if he could just calm her down she'd come out, but she didn't. After an hour, a neighbor came out to see what was the matter.

His neighbor, a Puerto Rican single mother, tried to talk to Malinda, too, but she just kept yelling about "little people" and "leprechauns." With no other recourse, and fearing for his mom's life, Art and the neighbor finally called the police. Minutes later, while half the Bridgeport Homes looked on in curiosity, the CPD kicked in the door and an accompanying paramedic unit entered the apartment, sedated Malinda, and carried her out of the projects strapped to a stretcher.

She was diagnosed with bipolar schizophrenia. The bipolar disorder, characterized by massive mood swings, had afflicted her for years. It was almost certainly rearing its head when she was institutionalized following the episode at Uncle Rich's. But schizophrenia, which typically includes hallucinations, intense paranoia, and the hearing of internal and often violent voices, was something frighteningly new. Although the cause of schizophrenia is most often genetic, recent studies indicate that a severe trauma to the head is also a trigger. Both Art and Wensdae flatly blame their aunt's assault with the beer bottle for what they refer to as their mother's "problem."

After that first "leprechaun" episode, Malinda's illness became a major destabilizing factor. Doctors prescribed her lithium, which was extremely effective at suppressing the symptoms—so much so that when Malinda was feeling really good she'd stop taking the medication altogether. Then it was only a matter of time before her brain realigned to its natural chemistry. When it did, the caring, affectionate, and fun-loving mother the children knew was replaced by a woman whose behavior ran on a roulette wheel numbered and colored with bad news.

To get an idea of the spectrum, on various occasions Malinda had declared that she was running for mayor of Chicago. She had perched herself in front of a bowl of collected pebbles and proceeded to silently suck on them for hours. She once wandered away from her home and turned up three months later in a field in Kansas, completely naked and showing signs of starvation. During a more recent episode, she told the FBI that she had been abducted by an Al Qaeda cell and held as a sex slave at an Oklahoma barn for a month. According to a friend familiar with the incident, the Feds were so convinced that she was telling the truth that they took her up in a helicopter in the hopes that she could pinpoint the location.

Those are the more exotic episodes. In the early days of her disorder, Malinda was either entirely uncommunicative or violently obsessed with the only other female in the house: Wensdae.

"Art had it easy with my mom," Wensdae says. "She doted on him and went after me. I got all of it."

The first incident Wensdae recalls came on the eve of a school dance when she was twelve, not that long after the leprechaun incident. It was her first dance, and like any girl that age she was eager to look her best. She put on lipstick, did her hair up, and wore a skirt. When she came out and asked her mother how she looked, Malinda told her she looked like "a dirty little whore." She then proceeded to grab Wensdae by her hair, punch her in the face, and tow her back to the bathroom. There, she forced her daughter to sit on the toilet while she took out scissors and cut off all of the girl's hair. By the time Malinda was finished, Wensdae looked like a concentration-camp inmate.

"You could see it coming with my ma," says Art. "She'd start chain-smoking and staying to herself. That could last a day or two, and if you couldn't get her to take the lithium, it was best to get away from the house."

That's what Art usually did. He'd go to McGuane Park or hang out with the SDs and hope that by the time he came home Malinda would be asleep. On some occasions he even crushed up lithium pills and spiked his mother's drinks. But most of the time Wensdae was left alone with Mother Hyde.

By the time she was fourteen, Wensdae had discovered her own escape: "wicky sticks"—marijuana joints laced with PCP and dipped in embalming fluid. Wickies were cheap and popular in the neighborhood, and the intense, brightly hallucinogenic high they provided was an instant, if temporary, vacation from the oppression of Malinda's rages, and the dread that, somehow, there really was something wrong with her, something that had caused everything to end up the way it was. "The wicky sticks were so *fun*. Everybody in the neighborhood did them. I didn't think they could hurt me, and if you do them in moderation they don't. But I didn't know what moderation meant when I discovered them."

One night in 1989 Wendz overdosed and went into seizures. She was rushed to the hospital, then later admitted into a rehab unit. Although she completed the program, her battle with addiction, and the conditional underpinnings that supported it, was just beginning.

ONE OF THE WAYS Wensdae coped with Malinda's episodes was to visit the house of her best friend, Karen Magers, who lived a few blocks away. No stranger to hardship herself, Magers had never known her father, a traveling musician from Mexico. Her mother, who was Bridgeport Irish, had been killed by a drunk driver when she was five, and her uncle had taken her in, doing the best he could to raise her on a nursing home attendant's salary. Though they had very little themselves, the Magerses fed and even clothed Wensdae, sometimes for days, until Malinda emerged from the storms of her delusions. "I don't know why, but it was Wensdae who always bore the brunt of her mom's episodes," says Magers. "I remember one time she accused Wendz of dressing like a tart, then burned all of her clothes. She came over in tears, and I had to give her some of my clothes."

The two girls were inseparable, and spent most of their free time at the Assembly of God church at Thirty-first and Poplar. They volunteered for fund-raising activities, youth groups, and appeared in all the plays and pageants. "It was the only place we felt safe, or normal," says Magers. "We weren't interested in the gangbangers."

Art wasn't much interested in his sister's friend either at first, but by the time she was thirteen Karen had blossomed into a stunning Irish blonde with faintly caramel skin. Whether it was more her emerging sexual transformation or his that sparked Art's attention, he was taken completely off-guard. "I remember one day just looking at her, and thinking, 'Wow. How could I have not noticed this really beautiful, sweet girl?'"

Soon the Assembly of God church had a new member—a Satan's Disciple no less—as Art made a point of attending Sunday services. He'd plop into the pew next to his sister and Karen, and during the sermons his eyes would lock on the flaxen cascade of Karen's hair and the lustrous sweep of her thighs. "I wasn't going in there for spiritual enlightenment," he says.

Magers had sized up Art long before that, of course. She'd been impressed by his intelligence, but he, too, had a new body. At fifteen, his skinny arms and knobby shoulders now showed bowling-pin curves, while his jawline had come in square and firm. All of his prior delicacy was vanishing, as if the inner armor he'd adopted after moving to Bridgeport was expanding skinward and sounding out as a swarthy, hard handsomeness.

"He was really cute, and when you're young you go for looks," Magers says. "He always thrived on his looks; he was always a charmer. It also might have been an opposites-attract thing. I was always the good girl, and he was the bad boy. I didn't like the fact that he was in a gang, but in those projects boys basically had to join the gang. It was either that or get the shit beat out of you on your way to school."

When Art finally worked up the nerve to ask Karen out on a date, she accepted, and they quickly became a regular item. During the winter they'd go to movies, and in summer they'd laze around at a beach off Lakeshore Drive, then grab a meal at one of the tourist spots on Navy Pier. Parental loss was their unspoken bond, but like most teenagers, they rarely spoke about the past and even less so the future. On the occasions when they did talk about their dreams, Art would throw any number of pies into the sky; one day he'd want to be an inventor, the next a real estate developer. Karen, however, was magnificently consistent. She intended to follow a Bridgeport path almost as well-worn as the one that Art would take, and he was so smitten by her that he never considered that it made any future with her problematic at best. "I only ever had one dream. Maybe it's because when my mom died, the man who broke the news and comforted me was a cop, but I knew since I was five that one day I would become a Chicago police officer."

Karen's dream would have to wait. Six months after they began dating, she learned she was pregnant. At fourteen, she was about to become a teenage mother, while Art—with no high school diploma, no job, and few connections outside of the street—had at best dim prospects of supporting a child. "I didn't know what I was gonna do," he says. "I was a kid myself. I knew I didn't want to be like my father and just avoid responsibility—that wasn't going to be a possibility. Somehow I had to find a way to make it out of there."

3

THE APPRENTICE

We are all bastards;
And that most venerable man which I
Did call my father, was I know not where
When I was stamp'd; some coiner with his tools
Made me a counterfeit. . . .

—WILLIAM SHAKESPEARE, *Cymbeline*,
Act II, Scene V

Ed's Snack Shop had been around for twenty-one years when Malinda took a waitressing job to help prepare for the baby. Owned by a local named Ed Thompson, it was a Bridgeport fixture, an old twenties-style diner with a bar counter and a long line of windows overlooking Halsted Street. It was a familiar world to Malinda, easily navigable, and Ed was sympathetic to her condition. As long as she was on her meds, which was most of the time, he let her work the day shift. Since it was right across the street from the Bridgeport Homes, she was never far from her children. Art and Wendz dropped by on a daily basis, a ritual she always looked forward to. She'd sit them at the counter, feed them burgers and soda, and pry them for details about their lives while they pried her for tip money.

Years later, Ed's son, Gary, would find himself writing a small memoir about Ed's, then posting it on an Internet blog devoted to Bridgeport memories:

> Ed's was a hangout for greasers, dopers, city workers, teenie-boppers, blue-haired bingo ladies, cops, winos, gangsters, gang-bangers, lonely old men, horny young men, college students, ex–cons, and families. You never knew what kind of crowd you'd see in there. We knew them all. We didn't even try to remember all their names, so we gave most of them nicknames. I'm guessing that a lot of the nicknames were given because some people would rather no one knew their name. I knew people with names like: "Bloomers," "Fallin' Eddie," "Pennsylvania Eddie," "Bridgeport Eddie," "Pete the Cop," "Blonde Headed Sharon," "Fuck Chuck," "Mugsy," "Crazy Charlie," "Puerto Rican Sammy," "Sarge," "Large Marge," "Cavey," "Stormy Weather," "Little Joe," "Indian Joe," "Billy Moon," "Size Ten Mary," "Mother Mary," "Pollack Paul," "Mr. T," "Cono," "Li'l Bit," "Guy Guy," "Big Mickey," "Slick," "Red," and "Ronnie the Preacher." Sometimes we just called them what they ordered every day, like "Boston with three sugars" or "Raisin toast no butter."

Pete "da Vinci" was an easygoing Italian who usually perched by himself in a booth up front, across from the counter. At about five seven, he was short, but striking thanks to his deeply tanned skin, and eyes so yellow they were almost gold. He was in his mid-forties but looked much younger, and unlike most of Ed's characters, who tended toward the blue collar, da Vinci had a bohemian air about him. His defining accessory was a black leather beanie. Unless he was asleep, in the shower, or at church, it sat on his head with the permanency of a tattoo.

Like all the other characters at Ed's, da Vinci was not his real

name. It's a street name that Art later gave him because of his fond-
ness for drawing and painting. "I liked him from the beginning," says
Art. "He had class. He didn't curse, he didn't raise his voice. But
most importantly he treated my mom really well, better than any
man ever did."

Art first noticed him as a regular presence about two months after his mom starting working at Ed's. He'd show up and Pete would
be nursing a coffee, cracking jokes with Malinda. He had a naturally
sunny disposition, and he'd see Art come in and shout, "Hey kid,
how ya doin' today!" and he always had a huge grin that went ear to
ear. Art never once saw him complain about his life, and when Pete
was around, Art could see in his mother shades of the happy-go-
lucky country girl who had been cowed by abandonment, poverty,
and a crippling mental disease. And after a few months, Art and
Wensdae were no longer asking Malinda for spending cash. "There
was just this point where he'd insist," remembers Art. "We all knew
my mom didn't make any real money there, and he was just going to
give it to her in tips anyway. So he'd lay a little cash on us, nothing
big, nothing more than she would have given us."

Pete's stated occupation was that he was "in construction,"
Bridgeport's oldest and most ubiquitous occupation. It meant that
he was either really in construction or a criminal—probably both.
Da Vinci certainly didn't dress like a foreman or crewman, and if he
was overseeing some nearby development, then its dust never pow-
dered his shoulder or interfered with his quality time at Ed's. He
drove a white Cadillac, and Art simply assumed that he had some
kind of a racket going, but he could never glean what it was, and in
Bridgeport you do not ask questions.

Criminal or not, da Vinci was generous and warm, and that was
what Malinda noticed. After about four months, Pete was dining
with the family at the house, watching a bit of TV, then discreetly

slipping out before bedtime. He also began taking the family out to the movies, or on weekend trips to Indiana Dunes, a magnificent stretch of rolling sand hills along the shores of Lake Michigan. The excursions, and the presence of a kindly, older male in the house, was a welcome change to Art, but he didn't invest too heavily in Pete's long-term presence.

ART HAD OTHER THINGS TO WORRY ABOUT than his mother's love life. Karen gave birth to a son on August 28, 1990. Few things are more telling about Art than the name he insisted on calling him. Of the all the shoes in the world a boy can be asked to fill, he picked the ones made biggest by their emptiness: Arthur J. Williams III.

To raise money for the new arrival, Art, like his mother, took a job. It came to him one morning shortly after Karen became pregnant, when a young man driving by in a pickup truck spotted him and a friend throwing a football around in the project's parking lot.

"You guys want some work?" he asked. All he told Art was that he'd be working at a construction site. The pay was low—$3.25 an hour in cash—but Art needed the money, so he jumped in the back. He was taken to the North Side, where a crew was reroofing an old woman's house. There, he met his new boss, Morty Bello.

Morty was infamous in Bridgeport, though Art was too young to have heard of him. He was short, fat, and charming, with dark circles under his eyes and a deep Romanian accent—a bona fide gypsy. Morty made his living by looking up the addresses of elderly people—usually women—then sending crews to their houses to knock on their doors. They'd point out problems with their roofs or siding and offer to fix everything for a bargain rate. By the time Morty's crew was done, half of the old women's savings—along with various heirlooms—would be in his pocket. He paid poor kids like

Art chicken feed to create the pretense of labor, doling out platitudes and encouragement to hide the fact that he was exploiting them. He was the first in a long line of paternal misfires that Art would glom on to.

"I really liked Morty," says Art. "He definitely liked me, or at least acted like he did. Sometimes he'd take me to his home and feed me dinner. He had a nice house on Parnell Avenue, a big family, and he treated me like a member of the family. He did all that to make it easier to use me."

Sometimes Morty wouldn't even pay Art; he'd cry poor and promise to reimburse him come the next job. But whether Morty paid or not, Art wasn't making anywhere near enough to support his girlfriend and their child. After consulting with a few Disciples, he opted for a side job that was almost as conventional in Bridgeport: auto theft.

Halsted Street was Chicago's chop-shop capital, and since the age of thirteen Art had been hotwiring vehicles for fun. It wasn't a big step to simply drop the cars off at a garage, and depending on the make and model he could earn up to two thousand dollars per vehicle. Cars were usually insured, he rationalized, and in the event of discovery the stolen item itself offered a mode of escape. Best of all, at seventeen he was also too young to go to prison; if caught, he faced no more than a few months in juvie. And every bit as enticing as the fast money was the excitement and a chance to prove his manhood.

About four months after Karen gave birth, Art hotwired a Buick Regency on Poplar Avenue, a long block from the projects. As he was pulling away, his jittery teen reflexes got the better of him and he clipped a nearby parked car, smashing the Buick's front. He quickly abandoned the Buick, then sprinted back toward the projects. But an elderly woman, drawn by the noise of the crash, had seen him. By now Art was well known to the Ninth District, and the woman's description of him was good. Twenty minutes later, two Chicago PD officers knocked on the door of the Williamses' apartment.

Pete da Vinci answered.

Art's delinquency had been a story to Pete until that moment, told by an aggravated mother to a sympathetic ear. While Art hid in his room upstairs, he listened to Pete talk with the cops. The tone he took was something Art had never heard in Pete before—that of a concerned and irate father. "It was embarrassing," Art remembers, "I knew that he knew I was up to stuff, but now he was actually seeing what a shit I was." Malinda was right there at his shoulder, and she was convinced that it was high time that Art was taught a lesson.

"Arty! Come down here!" she shouted.

Art sheepishly made his way downstairs, knowing full well what was coming. The officers arrested him and drove him to the district house, where the elderly woman identified him. A juvenile court judge later sentenced him to three months in a youth detention facility. But a little over a month later, just as he had calculated, he was free.

Pete and Malinda were waiting for him at the release center. It was a happy occasion, but Pete was somber and preoccupied. They took Art out to a celebratory lunch at Ed's, and when Malinda excused herself to go to the bathroom, Pete looked him directly in the eye.

"I'm not here to lecture you," he said evenly, "but if you keep up with the stealing, your baby's going to have a crummy life."

It certainly sounded like the beginning of a lecture to Art.

"I understand that you're under a lot of pressure," Pete contin-ued. "You're still a kid, but you're also a father. Did you know that kids whose fathers abandoned them are much more likely to abandon their own children?"

"Really?" Art said snidely. He was thinking that Pete didn't know anything about him.

"I know you're a smart kid. I know all about your achievements in school, and I know that the last few years haven't been easy on you. I know you don't want your own son growing up in these projects, and if you give me a chance, I'd like to help you get out."

Art was now intrigued, but Malinda returned from the restroom before Pete could continue. "We'll talk more later," he said before she sat down.

Later that night as Art lay in bed, he heard the muffled tones of an argument taking place across the hall. He couldn't make out the words, but he had the distinct feeling that they were arguing about him, and that Pete was trying to convince his mother to allow him to do something. Later on, he realized that Pete had probably been asking her for permission. The argument cooled down and Art drifted off to sleep, assuming that it was a typical spat between a mom and a boyfriend giving her unsolicited advice on how to raise her son. But when Art awoke the next morning, Malinda was nowhere to be seen. Pete was downstairs sipping a cup of coffee.

"Remember what we talked about yesterday?" he said. "If you're up to it, there's something I'd like to show you. So get dressed. We're going for a ride."

Based on the look in Pete's eye, Art knew that they were not headed off to a construction site.

THEY DROVE SOUTH, which in that part of Chicago is back in time. They passed the eastern railroad approaches to the Union Stockyards, where generations of Irish, Italian, Lithuanian, Polish, and Slavic immigrants once labored in the largest concentration of slaughter-houses in the world—an industry immortalized in Upton Sinclair's *The Jungle*. Later on the area became a haven for bootleggers, who could mingle in with the packing and storage facilities without drawing much attention. How many criminal operations had set up shop in Packingtown since then was anyone's guess, but its industrial anonymity was daunting. As da Vinci wheeled the Cadillac deeper into blocks of buildings bracketed by vacant lots and truck parks, neither of them spoke.

Pete finally parked next to an old stone quarry. For the briefest of moments Art wondered if maybe he was legitimate after all. "I try not to park right in front of my business," the older man explained. "A block away is fine."

They continued on foot to a three-story, nineteenth-century brick building with a loading dock in front. Once inside, they made their way down a long hallway to the back of the building. There, Pete plugged a key into an elevator call box. A few moments later, a pair of double doors reeled back to reveal an old-style, top-gated lift. After they entered, Pete pushed the down button, taking them below ground level, where he unlocked another door, revealing a space that was almost pitch-black except for a few block windows. Pete flicked on a nearby switch, blasting the space with fluorescent light that emanated from long, buzzing bulbs. And as Art's eyes adjusted, he was surprised to encounter a familiar scene.

Spread out before them in a large room was a full-service offset print shop, a smaller version of the sort of setup he'd seen next to the *Bridgeport News*. Immediately to the left was a photography alcove, which was followed by a light table, a platemaking station, and then the offset press itself—a beautiful, six-foot-long AB Dick. After that came an industrial paper cutter.

"It was a perfectly kept setup," remembers Art. "Everything was in order, each machine placed right where it should be in the overall process. You could work clockwise through the room, and by the time you came to the end you would have a finished, printed product."

Da Vinci remained silent as Art walked around and inspected the shop, giving him some time to figure out the situation for himself. At first glance, it struck Art as a completely normal, "camera ready" print shop, the kind neighborhood printers used to make flyers, posters, and pamphlets for local businesses. But if that was the case, then why all the secrecy? The first odd detail that caught Art's eye was a steel cabinet filled with ink canisters. Aside from a few yellows and reds, the vast majority of the cans were forest green, charcoal black, and white. Even sitting on the shelves, the colors brought to mind only one image. When he saw a shrink-wrapping machine sitting at the very end of the print line, he moved from suspicion to conviction. He could picture the small rectangles coming off the cutter, then being wrapped into neat little bricks of plastic, ready for sale.

"Is this what I think it is?" Art gasped.

Pete answered with a simple, "Yeah."

"You're a *counterfeiter*."

Art had barely ever used the word. He immediately recalled an encounter he'd had about a year earlier, when he'd been taken to the precinct house for questioning after a street battle with some Latin Kings. Waiting with him in the holding cell was a kid in his late teens who told him he'd been picked up for "copying." He was dressed in a suit, and he was wired up and smiling like he'd just won the lottery. He explained to Art that while working as a janitor at the Sears Tower, he had seen a cutting-edge color copier in one of the offices and snuck in after hours to run off dozens of twenty-dollar bills.

He'd spent the next two days on a wild spending binge, buying clothes, expensive meals, and drugs, until a suspicious cashier at a shoe store ran an eraser across one of his bills and the ink blurred. She called the police, who picked him up running down the street with a pocketful of bills. The kid had had so much fun that he was planning to print more bills as soon as he got out of jail, and Art had always wondered what became of him. The idea that people could print their own money astonished him, and it struck him as the ultimate crime.

Da Vinci was obviously way beyond amateurish larking with color copiers. Based on his equipment alone, Art could tell that Pete was a professional, a far higher grade of criminal than anyone he had ever met. All this time, his mother had been dating a man who held the keys to his own bank.

"Come over here and sit down, Arty," da Vinci beckoned. Art joined him at some chairs he had set up near the light table. He could not believe what was happening. Were they going to print money right *now*?

"This has been in my family for a long time," da Vinci began. His tone was serious, but not threatening. "I learned it from my father when I was young, right about your age. He learned from his uncle. The man who taught my great-uncle was not a relative, and I don't know much about him. I know that he was from Italy, and somebody certainly taught him. It probably goes back hundreds of years. If you're interested, I'm willing to teach you. It's safer than stealing cars and there's more money in it, but it's also harder. It's also a federal crime, and if you're stupid enough to get caught, odds are you'll be convicted. You won't get out in a month like you did yesterday. You'll do years, up to twelve for just your first offense. Are you interested?"

"Yes."

"All right, but there are some rules," da Vinci continued, and began a list that would grow longer than Art ever imagined.

The first rule was that Art could tell no one, not even relatives. "Once people realize what you do they will ask you for money," Pete explained. "If you refuse to give it to them, they will hate you. If you give it to them, they will get caught and probably turn you in."

The second rule was to never spend counterfeit money in the area where he lived. For reasons that Art would learn later, every counterfeit bill inevitably triggers an alarm, whether it's in the hands of a grocery store clerk or a sophisticated bank counting machine. And once counterfeit bills are identified, they can be fingerprinted, forensically analyzed, and plotted and traced on a map that the authorities—namely the United States Secret Service—will use to close the geographical noose until it tightens around the counterfeiter's neck.

The third rule was the most general and the most important. "Never be greedy," da Vinci said. "If you're cautious, you can have a good life. But if you print too much, you will be caught."

Art swore to follow all the rules.

"Do you have any questions?" da Vinci asked him.

"How much do I get to keep?"

"You don't get to keep any," Pete said. "That's not how this works. Passing counterfeit is a whole different ball game from making it, and if you got caught your mother would murder me. Every time we print, I'll pay you seven thousand dollars in real money. Does that sound good?"

"Yeah." It was more money that Art had ever made in his life.

"Any other questions?"

"What happens to the money after we make it?"

"It will go to clients."

"Who?"

"That's none of your business, and you'll never know. That's for your own good, Arty. Another rule is that you never reveal who your clients are."

Da Vinci gave Art no more instruction that first day. After spending less than twenty minutes in the shop, he stood up and said that it was time to go. Just before they left, he spoke two final words.

"He told me to 'get ready' with that little devil smile he had," remembers Art. "I was so fucking anxious, I couldn't sleep. I stayed up all night long thinking that I was gonna make some money."

COUNTERFEITING HAS SOMETIMES BEEN CALLED the world's second oldest profession. Its conceptual birth, predicated on the simple notion that people will accept what you give them if it looks and feels "real," is as ancient as rocks in a rice sack, but when it comes to money, most numismatic historians agree that counterfeiting probably dates back to very shortly after the invention of money itself, sometime around the year 700 B.C. in the ancient kingdom of Lydia. Enterprising craftsmen quickly learned that few people bothered to weigh lead and copper coins coated with a thin veneer of gold or silver as long as they bore the king's stamp. The archeological record tells us that from that moment on, in virtually every society making coins there were also people faking them.

From the beginning it was a crime of legacy. Doing it successfully required an intimate knowledge of not only how real money was made and defended, but how to replicate it—specialized knowledge that could be passed on only by a mentor. One of the oldest accounts of counterfeiting comes from the third century B.C., when a Greek named Diogenes was banished from the city of Sinope, on what is now the Turkish coast, for "adulterating in coinage." As the city gate closed behind Diogenes, he trudged off toward the horizon with an accomplice, the old man who had taught him how to counterfeit. His name was Tresius, and he not only happened to be head of the local bank, but was also his father.

Diogenes would have been forgotten had he not gone on to become one of the greatest philosophers in Greek history. He gave us such pearls as "We have two ears and only one tongue in order that we may hear more and speak less," "Man is the most intelligent of animals—and the most silly," and "He has the most who is most content with the least." Diogenes is considered the king of the Cynics—no surprise considering that prior to his reformation he spent a lot of time passing fake for real.

Diogenes and his father got off easy. Throughout most of human history, the typical punishment for counterfeiting has been death. Rome fed its counterfeiters to the lions of the Colosseum, while in various medieval European nations they were drawn and quartered, burned at the stake, or—in the Netherlands—boiled alive. In the early days of the United States, counterfeiters were hanged, and the crime was considered so heinous that the first American currency, the continental, even bore the ominous warning "'Tis death to counterfeit." Up until 1994, it was still a capital crime in Russia, and it remains so in Vietnam, China, and most of the Middle East.

Although the crime is nonviolent, it undermines the very basis of every economy—and therefore threatens governmental authority. One of the founding fathers of modern economics, the Englishman Sir Thomas Gresham, best summarized the threat in what is known as Gresham's Law: "When there is a legal tender currency, bad money drives good money out of circulation." We've all heard that old philosophical query, "If all the money in the world were fake, what differentiates it from the real?" Without an agreed-upon and vigorously protected standard of "real" currency, modern trade would not exist. The heart of the world's economy, which over the last hundred years has revolved around the American dollar, would suffer a terminal attack.

Such a fiduciary meltdown has come close to happening before. In the decades just after America won its independence, national mints did not exist. Each bank hired engravers to scratch bill designs onto copper plates, then printed however many notes they needed. Thousands of different kinds of bills were in circulation, and for counterfeiters it was a golden age. The only way people could tell a real note from a fake was by reading broadsheets, which printed pages of warnings describing false bills on a daily basis. Bills deemed credible one day could be banned the next, and the situation became so bad that by the end of the Civil War as many as half of all bills in America were counterfeit.

Up to its ears in war debt, and with only worthless paper to pay it off, the federal government decided to act. On the day of his assassination, Abraham Lincoln directed the secretary of the treasury to form an organization to hunt down counterfeiters and bring them to justice: the United States Secret Service. Initially staffed by Civil War vets and private detectives, the Service employed what were then revolutionary methods—undercover infiltration, heavy use of informants, and the playing of counterfeiters against each other to bring down large networks. At the same time, the Service harassed anyone who came too close to trampling on the sacred turf of U.S. currency design. In one instance, they confiscated the molds and cookies of a Philadelphia baker because he was selling cookies designed to look like an Indian-head penny, then threatened him with a fine and jail time if he baked them again. In another famous case, agents ripped a rug out of a department store window because it had been stitched to resemble a dollar bill.

The Service's zealotry, along with the unification of all currency production under the Bureau of Engraving and Printing in 1877, produced dramatic results. By 1903 the amount of counterfeit currency circulating had fallen to one dollar out of every hundred thousand—a phenomenal reduction. The Service was so effective that in 1901, following the assassination of President William McKinley, Congress informally requested that they protect his successor, Theodore Roosevelt, and within a year presidential-protection duty became the other of half of what remains the Service's joint mission. Throughout the twentieth century, improved law enforcement techniques and the Service's expansion would cut into counterfeiting even more. Today, an infinitesimal three one-hundredths of one percent of the roughly seven billion bills circulating is counterfeit. At the same time, seventy-five percent of all counterfeit currency is confiscated before it hits the streets.

By the time Art entered da Vinci's shop, in other words, counterfeiting had long been a dying art. Skilled practitioners like da Vinci who made a steady living at it were virtually extinct. He was the last of his line, a lone wolf offering to hand off what he knew to Art, who at seventeen could barely appreciate the gesture or understand the danger of the knowledge he was about to receive.

ART'S FIRST LESSON in the criminal craft of counterfeiting began when da Vinci placed a cassette tape into a boom box, and the velvet strains of an Italian opera swelled through the print shop.

"Oh, my God, can you please turn this crap off," Art moaned.

"Crap is the stuff *you* listen to," Pete told him. "This is beautiful music. It's old, what we do here is old, so this is what we'll listen to."

As the first overtures filled the basement, they embarked on the process of platemaking, a skill that Art was vaguely familiar with from his tour of the *Bridgeport News*'s printer. The easiest way to think of a plate is as a stamp; it's a thin, rectangular slab of metal— usually aluminum—that carries a raised image of whatever is to be printed. Chemically conditioned and wrapped around a spinning cylinder on an offset press, the plate first picks up water, then ink, with each revolution; as the two substances repel each other, the ink clings to the raised portion of the plate, then transfers its image onto a second roller that is usually made of rubber. This second, or "off-set," roller in turn transfers the ink onto paper. When an offset press is rolling at full speed, it can produce hundreds of images per minute. Almost every printed item you read, including this book, is de-rived from a plate and an offset press. Invented in 1843 by a New Yorker named Richard March Hoe, the process is responsible for more wars, revolutions, bureaucratic forms, pornography, economic booms and busts, and minds both educated and subverted than any other invention on earth.

Art watched as da Vinci pulled out three crisp hundred-dollar bills from an envelope and mounted them in front of a process cam-era—an accordion-like device designed for capturing flat images.

"Take a look," da Vinci said, offering Art the viewfinder. The bill, magnified and illuminated by studio lights, like a painting, filled the entire field of view. The detail was incredible: Franklin's hair looked like rolling surf, while the lines on his coat resembled plowed fields coursing gently over hillsides. Based on a 1778 portrait by the French artist Joseph-Siffred Duplessis, Franklin's face appeared se-rene and slightly amused.

After they photographed the bill fronts three times and the backs once, they developed the negatives in a closet that da Vinci had converted to a darkroom, then brought them over to the light table. He inspected them with a loupe, then masked out the serial numbers and seal on one front, leaving nothing *but* the serial num-bers and the seal on the others.

The next step involved utilizing one of the more magical devices in da Vinci's print shop: an arc-light burner. About the size of a refrigerator, it used high-intensity light to burn the negatives onto the metal plate. Like a modern copying machine that prints on metal instead of paper, the light passes freely through the clear parts of the negative and burns away a thin layer of the plate beneath, leaving only the lines of the negative intact and raised—a stamp carved by light. Once they burned four plates, they scrubbed them clean in a chemical wash, until all that remained on their surfaces were intricate, raised images of all the components of a hundred-dollar bill.

The plates took the better part of two days, and Art was steadily awed by da Vinci's precision and attention to detail. He emphasized precise measurements and timing, warning Art that if he burned the plates too long the bills would come out too dark; burn them too briefly and they'd come out light. He explained the reason behind everything he did.

However formidable da Vinci's skill at platemaking was, it was nothing compared with what Art witnessed over the next four days, as da Vinci schooled him in the art of mixing inks and running the press. "The difference between a bill that passes and one that draws attention can sometimes come down to drops of ink," he told Art. "Unless you constantly watch your colors, a whole print run can be ruined."

Williams observed as da Vinci mixed gray for the bill front, then armed the paper intake of his four-color press with a pale green, linen-based paper. Art would later learn that the paper had come from one of Chicago's many printing houses, and that da Vinci had bought it straight from a connection at the loading dock, no questions asked. Like the paper genuine currency is printed on, it was thin and durable, and another feature that made it distinct was that it contained tiny fibers that simulated the red and blue silk security threads that have been woven into U.S. currency since 1869.

Once da Vinci had the paper ready, he attached the plate to the offset's cylinder and fired up the press. As the machine rumbled to life, Pete poured his ink into the trough, engaged his cylinders, and let the press roll. Once he had finished with the bill fronts, they cleaned the press, switched the plates, and mixed their next colors: mint green for the back, and stoplight green for the seal and serial numbers. In this way they "built up" the bills, adding different visual elements with each print run.

"The smell of the ink became addictive," remembers Art. "Watching him take the ink out and throw it on the palette, it was amazing how quick he was. Just like that, he'd snap it on and mix it." Counterfeiters say that the act of creating money can evoke an intensely pleasurable, almost sexual, rush. Williams felt its full force for the first time watching the finished sheets spill from the press. "Orgasm is a good comparison, but there really aren't any words for the feeling," he says. "And it never went away from me. Every time was as powerful as that first time."

On the final print run, sheets of mint-condition hundred-dollar bills emerged from da Vinci's press, like Christmas cookies from an oven. In all, Art and Pete's first run together came to about a hundred thousand dollars in counterfeit. As Art cut the bills and stacked them in neat ten-thousand-dollar piles, he felt an overwhelming urge to take some. There are always extra bills after a print run, so when Pete wasn't looking he slipped a few into his pocket, despite the promise he had made to his mentor.

Later the same day, he visited a local gas station, where he asked the cashier for a pack of Kools and handed him one of da Vinci's notes. Instinctively, he apologized for not having a smaller bill, and half expected security gates and sirens to activate the moment the attendant took the bill.

Nothing happened.

The cashier gave him back ninety-six dollars in real money, and he left the gas station as free as he had entered. But every bit as real as the change in his pocket was the buzzing through his brain as he made his way back to the projects.

"When I saw him take the money and give me back the change, I felt a huge sense of power, more power than I had ever felt in my life," he recalls. "As a young kid from the South Side, that wasn't something I was used to. I was used to the opposite feeling. And I was instantly addicted."

DA VINCI NEVER CAUGHT ON that Williams had pocketed some of the bogus bills. True to his word, later that week Pete handed Art seven thousand dollars in real money. It was more cash than Art had ever seen, much less possessed, and it had an instant, opiate effect on the sense of struggle he'd been feeling since he was twelve. He gave some of the money to Karen for the baby, telling her that he was now making good money "working construction" with da Vinci. Then he proceeded to blow most of the rest on a used black Grand Prix. Overnight, he had the nicest car in the projects, and had no worries about saving any money; he knew that soon they would be making more.

By the time da Vinci called Williams in for their second print run two months later, he was broke and had forgotten almost everything he'd learned. Or, more accurately, he had barely assimilated anything to begin with. "That first time he showed me, I was in awe, and I don't think I even paid attention to a word Pete said, my heart was racing so fast. But the second time I was a like a hawk. I knew I had to learn this."

This time da Vinci allowed Art to do much of the work himself while he stood silently over his shoulder, supervising. He'd watch closely as Art shot negatives and burned plates, offering tips and quizzing him on the process. As Art became proficient in the technical aspects of the craft, he began grilling da Vinci on some of the broader aspects of the crime. One of the first things he wanted to know was what other useful items they could counterfeit. Pete explained that you could also fake bearer bonds, checks, titles of ownership, food and postage stamps, posters to sell at the county fair—almost everything of value sooner or later comes down to paper and ink. Da Vinci had dabbled in all sorts of items over the years, but he considered most of them a waste of time.

"There's nothing better to print than money," he said. "Everybody wants cash. A guy selling drugs is selling it to get cash. A guy stealing jewels is stealing jewels to get cash. We don't have to do anything but print it."

The Secret Service was a frequent topic of conversation. Pete had tremendous respect for the Service, almost to the point where he considered other law enforcement entities minor nuisances. One morning as they were driving to the shop, they spotted two Chicago PD cruisers prowling through the neighborhood. Pete piloted the Caddy and parked in his regular spot like they weren't even there.

"Aren't you worried?" Art asked.

"Not about the cops I can see," Pete told him. "I'm worried about the ones I don't see. When you don't see them, that's when you have a problem."

Pete taught Art what he knew about the Service's infamously sneaky methods and tactics. As the original undercover agents, they pride themselves on infiltration. They are also infamously ruthless when it comes to using divide-and-conquer tactics to break up counterfeiting rings. The Service's annals brim with cases in which they've turned family members against each other. Once they catch someone passing counterfeit, they will threaten and pressure them and their families in an effort to turn them into informants against the maker. In recent decades their best weapons have revolved around their surveillance abilities. They can infiltrate counterfeit rings remotely, wiring up informants, phones, and computers to collect evidence from afar. Since it is the same force that protects the president of the United States, it is well funded and possesses the most cutting-edge technology, including an electron microscope capable of analyzing bill components on a molecular level. In a broad sense, the Service's greatest strength is that it enjoys the benefit of an unambiguous mission.

"They only have two jobs," Pete explained. "Protect the president and protect the currency. And they protect the president pretty well, don't they? Well, they do the same with the money."

No matter how hard Art pressed, there were questions that da Vinci refused to answer. How and where to pass counterfeit money in the marketplace was a subject that Art brought up so frequently that it became a running joke, as Art tried different ways of getting the "old man" to reveal his secrets. "What's the most you've ever passed?" he'd ask, or "Is it better to hit a small store or a place like Macy's?" But da Vinci never bit. "Passing, to him, was a very low-level way of operating," says Art. "He'd get annoyed at me for even asking, and say 'C'mon, Arty, you know that's not what we do. You'll learn that in time, but you need to be patient.' He was always telling me to be patient."

The biggest mystery of all to Art was how da Vinci sold his money. How did he find his clients? How should a deal go down? What was the most he'd ever printed? Da Vinci surrendered only the most rudimentary details. His main clients were not from the United States, but overseas—somewhere in Europe. He wouldn't reveal how the money got there or who was involved, but he did tell Art that he charged thirty to thirty-five cents on the dollar—the top rate—and he decreased his rates for amounts over one hundred thousand dollars. At the same time, he was extremely reluctant to produce batches over a hundred grand, and did so only if he was satisfied with the way a client intended to distribute the bills.

"Always find out where the money is going," he explained, "because if too much winds up in one place, you'll be in trouble. Counterfeit spreads like a virus once it hits an area, with bills popping up everywhere, in banks, shops, bars, people's pockets. It moves outward like an explosion, occupying a bigger and bigger space. If your space gets too large, you'll attract way too much attention. That's when the Secret Service puts your case on the top of the pile."

It was a lot to assimilate for a sixteen-year-old: advanced printing techniques, abstract concepts of monetary "space," law enforcement tactics of one of the world's most elite agencies. Art started to feel a bit like James Bond, an adopted persona that he would embrace and never quite get over. "Years later, I would think back on how I had learned from the best, telling myself that I knew what I was doing, and the arrogance it would inspire was ridiculous."

At the time, of course, he quickly learned that the act of counterfeiting itself is less than glamorous. Eliminating evidence was essential to Pete, and Art came to loathe the endless precautions. They never began work in the shop without first applying superglue to their fingertips to avoid leaving prints. A stray print on a bill spells instant doom for a counterfeiter, especially if it can be linked to a shop or a press peppered with the same prints. Pete was militaristic when it came to cleanliness, and one of Art's prime responsibilities was to rub down every surface at the day's end, then throw the rags in the washing machine—an act he thought unnecessary since they'd be right back at it the following morning. But Pete was insistent that the Service could very well raid or conduct an extralegal visit to the shop while they were away, and if that happened they had to make it as sterile as possible. When Art was finished, the master counterfeiter would inspect the job, grousing about a stray ink stain here or a paper shred there.

Gardeners have "green thumbs," and Williams learned the hard way that counterfeiters get them too. To clean the press, Pete insisted on using a powerful, alcohol-based degreaser. "Never let this get on your skin," Pete had warned Art, but one day during the middle of wiping down the press he went to the bathroom still wearing rubber gloves. He was instantly crippled by a tremendous burning sensation. "It burned like a motherfucker, but that wasn't the only bad part! I had green money ink all over my dick. And then I had a hard time getting it off. I couldn't use the degreaser, because that's what made it sting. Basically I just jerked it off over the next couple days—that's one way to clean it! I was too embarrassed to tell Pete about it. I still had cleaning to do and the whole time my penis was burning. It was the worst."

Every bit of garbage had to be burned, and at the end of each day Art carried piles of chemical-saturated paper towels and printing stock to the back lot, threw it all into a fifty-five-gallon drum, and tossed in a match. He'd watch it burn as the far more captivating lights of Chicago's skyline brightened in the dusk. He'd gaze at the city from the industrial hinterlands, no different from any American teenager daydreaming of bigger things while engaged in a shit chore.

If anything, he was far closer to obtaining those dreams. During the print runs, the garbage often included money—hundreds of bills that da Vinci had determined were flawed due to bad color, alignment, or just an odd feeling he had when looking at them.

"How much money have you burned?" Art once asked him.

"Oh, man. There have been runs when I've burned as much as I've made," Pete replied.

After it got colder, on several occasions Pete took Art back to his house and they burned money in his fireplace, warming themselves by it while watching football. Pete's house was the most refined home Art had ever seen, a collector's home crammed with old books of English poetry, tall, exotic lamps from China, and oil paintings of cities and landscapes, many of them done by da Vinci himself. Away from the shop, they'd slip out of counterfeit talk.

"What's it's like to be a father?" Pete inquired one time.

"It's weird," Art said. "I can't believe I actually am one. I want to be a good one, but I don't feel like I'm qualified. I love my son, but look at what we do, where I am."

"Have you ever heard of Epictetus?"

"No."

"He was a slave, a Greek slave brought to Rome to serve a very powerful adviser of the emperor Nero. But he was also a writer, a poet, and a philosopher. He said beautiful things, and even though he was a slave, the people loved him. At parties, people would gather around him. They wanted to hear everything that came out of his mouth because he was wise and funny. They didn't think of him as a slave. But his master always did.

"Over the years Epictetus's body betrayed him. He became a cripple, ugly and disfigured. Some said that it was because his master was jealous and beat him when nobody else was around. But the interesting thing was that older and more ugly Epictetus became, the more beautiful were his thoughts and words, and the people loved him even more. 'How can you have such a positive outlook on life when you've suffered so much?' they asked him. And his reply was that even though it might appear that life had made him ugly, it was only an appearance. Throughout all his suffering, his insides had become only more beautiful—and that was the true reality, what made him a great man.

"It's not your fault that your pops left you," da Vinci told Art.

"You can still be a good pops yourself. It's not your fault that you're in the projects, and you'll get out of them. Just don't give up."

It had occurred to Art earlier that maybe the reason da Vinci was teaching him in the first place was because he didn't have any kids of his own. Did da Vinci think of him as a son? He wasn't an emotionally demonstrative man. The one time Art had seen him blush had been in the print shop when, feeling frolicky, he had snatched Pete's beanie off his head and run around the shop, refusing to return it. "Now I know why you never take it off!" Art had shouted. "You're bald!" Pete had grumbled, demanding his beanie back, then halfheartedly chased him around the shop until they both tired of the game.

"I kind of think of you as my pops," Art blurted out that day by the fire of burning bills. He will never forget his mentor's response. Pete's "eyes bugged out" and he didn't say anything for a long time. Art threw the rest of the bills into the fire and they joked and talked more as a cold night fell down on Bridgeport. It was one of the last times he ever saw Pete da Vinci.

A FEW DAYS AFTER THEIR THIRD PRINT RUN, Art noticed that it had been a while since Pete had dropped by the apartment to visit his mother. When he asked her about it, she began to cry.

"I don't know where he is," Malinda said. "He hasn't called or come by the snack shop. Nobody there has seen him. I've called his home and office and nobody picks up. I'm worried."

"Did you guys get in a fight?"

"No, no fights. That's why I'm worried."

"I'm sure he'll turn up," Art consoled his mom, but he was bothered himself. The last time he had seen Pete, nothing had been out of the ordinary. He told Art that they'd been doing another run in six weeks and jokingly admonished him not to forget everything he'd learned. He'd made no mention of any impending trips, and Art had assumed he'd see him around the house as usual. If Pete had known he'd be leaving, it would have been completely out of character not to say good-bye and offer an explanation.

At the same time, Art understood that Pete wasn't in the kind of business that benefits from predictability and informing others of your actions. If Pete had a reason for staying away it was probably a good one. Had he been under surveillance by the Secret Service or even arrested, Pete would not have risked exposing Art and his mother by calling. Thinking that might be the case, Art avoided sniffing around da Vinci's print shop or his house.

He did start swinging by Ed's on a daily basis. He'd stick his head in the door, scanning the usual crowd of heads in the hope of spotting the beanie. He figured that Pete would be back any day and have one hell of a story about why he had left town. But as the days turned to weeks and the date of their appointed print run passed, Art started getting a bad feeling. Unable to contain his worry any longer, he began driving by both the house and the print shop, hoping to spot the Caddy. When it never appeared he even knocked on the door and peeked in the windows of Pete's house; no one answered, and although Pete's stuff was still there, the place had an empty aura, as if it hadn't been inhabited for weeks. Art finally began wondering about another explanation, one he'd forced himself not to consider.

It happened all the time in Chicago. He pictured Pete pulling the Caddy up to a hotel or an out-of-the-way lot. The client would have been someone he knew well, a regular who he felt comfortable with. He exited the car carrying a satchel filled with the same bills Art himself had helped create. For some reason—greed or paranoia—the buyer had decided that this would be the last deal, but

Pete didn't know that. He would have greeted his executioner the way he greeted everyone, with that happy-dog smile.

Art thought about making a few inquiries to some of the local associates of the Outfit—Chicago's Italian Mafia—then thought better of it. If Pete had met his end at the hands of the mob, a search for answers could easily take him on the same trip Pete had made, into the suffocating darkness of a car trunk and the illimitable voids of Lake Michigan.

"I'd like to think that he's still alive and out there somewhere," Art says. In his heart, he still wants to believe that Pete never would have left both him and his mother without an explanation.

ESCAPE

> The American dream is, in part, responsible for a great deal
> of crime and violence because people feel that the country
> owes them not only a living but a good living.
>
> —DAVID ABRAHAMSEN, CRIMINAL PSYCHIATRIST,
> QUOTED IN THE *San Francisco*
> *Examiner & Chronicle*, 1975

Art's hopes of becoming a master counterfeiter disappeared with his mentor. He was still a kid, and the discipline, financial resources, and equipment necessary to start his own operation seemed unobtainable. With three printings under his belt, he had a solid understanding of the basics, but he didn't possess the intuition and experience that separates fiddler from master. Most of all he lacked patience, and as he looked around for new options he saw his friends making faster money the Bridgeport way—by their wits and their balls.

Many of the SDs were now dealing drugs, cocaine mostly, while others had gotten deeper into auto theft. Art dabbled in both, but fresh from da Vinci, those crimes didn't fulfill his sense of craftsmanship or excitement. He had become something of criminal snob, a condition as common to counterfeiters as inky fingers.

Art had been spending a lot of time hanging out on Taylor Street—Chicago's Little Italy. Unlike his own neighborhood, Taylor Street was solidly middle class, a world of cafés, bakeries, pizza places, Italian-ice shops, and some of the best restaurants in the city. At the same time, it had its own criminal sect, which was much less visible but by far the most successful in the city. The Outfit had ruled the neighborhood since the turn of the century, when its predecessors, known by the old Sicilian moniker *La Mano Nera,* or "Black Hand," carved the names of their enemies on a poplar tree that stood at the intersection of Taylor and Loomis. "Dead Man's Tree" was long gone by the time Art started hanging out in Little Italy, replaced by progress and more subtle methods of influence, but the Mafia itself was still firmly and quietly rooted there. It was a street where kids hanging out in front of a coffee shop might suddenly be hailed by a man driving a black Crown Vic, handed two hundred bucks and a gas can, and told to drive the car somewhere out of the way and burn it to the ground—something that Art himself did on one occasion.

Unlike the boys from the projects, the crime-oriented kids he knew from Taylor Street were making good money as bookmakers, debt collectors, or by selling stolen merchandise. Art wanted to make his own fast bucks, too, and since he was no longer interested in the classic Bridgeport routes of stealing or selling drugs, he opted for a combination of both: robbing drug dealers.

Like everywhere else in the late eighties and early nineties, in Chicago cocaine and marijuana were rampant. Spotting the dealers was easy; they carried beepers, tended to drive flashy vehicles with gaudy accessories like blinding rims, and of course everyone knew who they were anyway, because just about everybody Art's age in Bridgeport did drugs.

His favorite technique was to either buy or steal a Chevrolet

Caprice, preferably black or white, and outfit it with a long, squiggly police antenna and a cherry dashboard strobe. He and two other crew members would tail a dealer all night, until his stash box was full of cash and, hopefully, more drugs. They'd wait until he was on a side street, then flip on the cherry and pull him over. They'd rush out of the Caprice wearing black nylon Windbreakers, brandishing pistols and Maglites, and "basically scare the living shit out of the dealer." They'd go through the whole routine, screaming profanities, pegging the dealer to the asphalt, cuffing him, then searching his vehicle until they found the cash and the stash. When they were finished, they'd knock the dealer upside the head, walk back to the Caprice, and speed off, screaming and laughing and floating on adrenaline.

A good drug-dealer hit could earn Art up to fifteen thousand dollars, and it appealed to his sense of justice and his flair for drama. He felt, in his own words, "like a bad motherfucker." Over the years it would be a crime he'd have a hard time resisting, even when times were good.

With Art's resurgence as a street criminal, he was once again on the fast track to either prison or death—fates that by now were visiting his friends with morbid regularity. His first, horrifying taste of the perplexing speed with which the projects can snuff out a life had come one day in the summer of '89. That afternoon, he was doing nothing more than standing next to a brick wall and chatting with his friend and fellow gang member Peter Friegel. He was looking his buddy right in the face when a bullet ripped into the left side of Peter's head. He was killed instantly.

The police attributed Friegel's murder to a gang hit. Art, who never saw the shooter, assumed it was the Latin Kings, but gangs weren't the only the killers. On another occasion, his friend Darren Frandelo walked into a Dunkin' Donuts on Thirty-first and

Halsted—after just having attended the funeral of yet another friend—and got into a minor argument with a man inside. After picking up his crullers and coffee, Frandelo walked back to his car, where his young wife and daughter were waiting. Moments later, the offended man emerged wielding a double-barreled sawed-off shotgun. He strolled up to Frandelo's car and unloaded both rounds into the driver's seat. Just before he was hit, Darren begged the man not to hurt his family.

Other than poverty, the common denominator behind many of the deaths was simply guns, which in the late eighties hit Chicago like a medieval plague. "It was just one summer and suddenly guns were everywhere," Art remembers. "It was scary. Something happened and then everyone had a gun. They were easy to get, almost like somebody planned it and brought them in by the crate. It wasn't just my neighborhood, but the whole fucking city."

By the time he was nineteen, Art had lost five friends to gun violence. In terms of American lives lost, Bridgeport had become as much a war zone as Baghdad later would, and similar death traps were sprouting up all over the country—South Central Los Angeles, Detroit, Harlem—anyplace where people were poor, angry, and looking for fast power.

It sounds trite to say that Art's number was bound to come up—violence is never inevitable until someone decides it is—but it did early one morning in the summer of 1990 as he was walking home from a party. It was about three A.M., and he had just crossed into the basketball courts at the Homes when two young men stepped out of the shadows and accosted him.

Their faces were covered in bandanas and Art never got a good look at them. They were black, and one was in his late teens and the other didn't look much older than eleven. They started asking Art questions: "Where you from? This is our court. What you doin' here?" in that tone people use when you know there's no right answer, because they're just fishing for a verbal response as excuse to hurt you. Art got out a "What are you talking about?" before they both raised pistols at him and opened fire.

He wheeled around and started to run, dropping his chin down close to his chest. He got about twenty yards away, then felt a sharp push on his left hip and tumbled to the cement. He'd been hit by a .25 caliber round. The shooters screamed with glee and chased after him, but he got up again and kept running. As he did so, another bullet from a 9mm struck him on his right thigh. Flying on adrenaline and knowing that he had no choice but to keep running, he rounded the corner onto Thirty-first Street, where a *Chicago Tribune* deliveryman was unloading stacks of the early edition. He collapsed next to the van and asked him to call an ambulance.

LUCKILY ART'S GUNSHOT WOUNDS were superficial; paramedics took him to Mercy Hospital, where surgeons removed the bullets and released him in less than twenty-four hours. The shooters were never caught, and in a macabre way, getting shot was a good thing for Art; it crystallized the literal dead end he'd been heading down since arriving at the Bridgeport Homes. Lying incapacitated in his bedroom, he knew that the moment he recovered he would be right back where he had been. He had hated the Homes from day one, then the Homes had become home, and for the better part of a decade they had defined him and then nearly killed him.

"After I got shot, I thought a lot about the things da Vinci had told me about getting out of the projects," Art says. "I knew that I'd die if I stayed there. I didn't know how I'd get out, but I decided that I would."

It turned out the decision would be made for him. About three weeks after he returned from the hospital, he awoke one morning to the sound of his mother in his doorway.

"Arty! Get up! There's a fire downstairs. We gotta get out of the house. Hurry up!" she shouted until she saw Art's head pop up from his pillow, then whisked back downstairs.

He groaned plaintively, naturally thinking that his mom was experiencing another delusional episode. But a few seconds later, he smelled smoke. He lifted his head off the pillow, saw a black cloud pouring through the heater vent, and ran to the doorway. When he looked downstairs he saw the living room half engulfed in flames. Malinda and Wensdae were nowhere to be seen.

Art snatched up some jeans and a T-shirt and ran out to the parking lot, where his mother and sister were waiting. The three of them watched as the Chicago Fire Department moved in and tried to save the home they loathed. The firefighters were able to contain the flames to just their apartment, but it was a total loss. Fire investigators later attributed the blaze to a cigarette butt that Malinda had left burning on the living-room sofa. Interviews with the neighbors and records checks confirmed that Malinda was certifiably crazy and a heavy smoker. Case closed.

Art wasn't so sure. "I asked her about it later and she was cagey," he says. "I agree with the fire department in that she started the fire, but I don't think it was an accident. I think she did it because it would be the only thing that would force us to find a way out of the projects. It was right after I got shot. I don't think she wanted to live there anymore. I think something snapped in her mind, and I think she fucking lit the house up. I mean, my mom was a *smoker*. She may have been crazy, but she knew how to smoke."

And that was how they finally got out of the Bridgeport Homes. Accident or not, Malinda had initiated one the most desperate jailbreak gambits in the book: She'd lit her own cell on fire.

• • •

TWO DAYS AFTER THE FIRE, one off the local churches found the Williamses a new apartment ten blocks away at Thirty-first and Wells. Although just a short hop from the projects, it was another planet. There were brick town houses with little iron gates in front, well-lit streets, trees—and none of the gunshots and gangbangers that had made the simple act of coming and going from home akin to navigating a siege zone. Rent was a few hundred dollars more than it had been at the Homes, but Art had saved enough to tide them over for the first few months. Once the family moved in, the collective mood soared as they realized that they had spent the last seven years stuck inside a trap from which they were now free. Art wished his mother had set the fire the day they moved in.

The Williamses spent a year in the Wells Street apartment, which became a base that each of them would use to embark on their next stages of life. Wendz was the first to move on; she took a job at Ed's Snack Shop, and there she met and fell in love with Dr. Samos—a dentist from Greek Town who was fifteen years her senior. He not only treated her well and fixed her teeth for free, but he also paid for her to attend both junior college and modeling school. Wendz eventually moved in with him, and a year later Art would attend her first fashion show at a club on State Street. He had always thought of his little sister as a rag doll, but the young woman he saw striding down the catwalk was stunningly beautiful. "She was wearing a white outfit. Slacks with a white shirt, and a white coat. And I didn't even realize it was her at first. I thought, 'Wow, that's my sister.' A whole crowd of cameras went off, *click click click*. I remember her looking at me when she came to the end of the runway. She turned and the jacket dropped to her arm; it was beautiful. I remember how proud I was of her, because she just *had it*."

Once Wensdae moved out, Malinda quickly followed suit. Sick of the city altogether, she headed back to Texas, leaving Art enough room to bring in Karen and the baby. For the first time since becoming a father, he finally had his own family under one roof, but he soon learned that escaping the Bridgeport Homes would require more than geographical separation.

The Thirty-second Street Satan's Disciples were not enthusiastic about Art's move. Now twenty years old, he had risen to become one of the top lieutenants and moneymakers. At first he continued to visit his old friends at the Homes and show up for the Friday meetings, but after Karen and the baby moved in he decided it was time to end his involvement in the gang. Knowing that the gang's leader, Marty Arbide, wouldn't be too happy about one of his top lieutenants jumping ship, Art chose a passive exit strategy: He simply stopped attending meetings in the hopes that everyone would understand his new situation. But a few days after he failed to show up, he ran into two SDs on the street and realized it wasn't going to be so easy. They immediately asked him where he'd been.

"You know I love you guys, but I'm not about this anymore," he told them. "I have to look after my family now."

"You gotta show up, Arty," one of them replied. "Even if you're not out there anymore, you gotta pay your respects."

"Hey, I respect you, but I don't know what else to tell you, man. I'm steppin', I gotta move on," he said, and told them he had somewhere he needed to be.

After Art failed to attend the next meeting, he started missing the camaraderie of the Disciples, and decided to drop by the playground the following Friday for a visit. Marty was there, along with his three biggest attack dogs: Danny, Porky, and Redhead Jerry. When Art greeted them with his normal enthusiasm, he realized right away that he had made a mistake. "They kind of rolled up on me, gave me the silent treatment," Art says, "and I knew something was going down."

"You have a violation coming for not attending the last two meetings," Marty flatly told Art. In Disciple-speak, that meant that he was now expected to submit to three gang members as they beat him for thirty-two seconds—because they were from Thirty-second Street. If he resisted, more seconds would be added according to Marty's whim.

"I'm not taking it," Art told him. "If you start swinging, we're fighting."

"That's the way it is, then," Marty said, and before Art knew it Marty and his lieutenants were charging him.

Art was standing with his back to a brick wall, and the first to reach him was Danny, who opened up with a wide, wild right. Seeing it coming, Art sidestepped left and ducked. An instant later, he heard a crack followed by a scream, and was amazed to see one of Danny's wrist bones sticking out from the skin of his right hand; he had struck the brick wall instead of Art. That turned out to be the only heroic moment for Art, because after that the other three boys moved in and beat him senseless. As he lay on the ground, knotted up and bleeding, they reminded him to be at the next week's meeting.

The indignation of the beating only solidified Art's determination to get out of the gang, and sure enough, he refused to turn up the following Friday. He didn't hear anything from the Disciples for three weeks, and then one evening he heard a knock on his front door. Thinking it was probably one of Karen's friends, he opened it, and the next thing he knew Marty and two Disciples bum-rushed their way into his apartment and began beating him in his own hallway.

Art covered his face and scrambled to get a footing, but in moments they had him on the floor. He heard his wife and son yelling hysterically in the next room, then suddenly all three Disciples were running for the front door. When he looked up, he saw Karen pointing his 9mm at the gangsters, screaming at them to get the fuck out, and looking very much on the edge of justifiable homicide.

"I never really talked to any of them after that for a long time," says Art. "They left me alone. I think they were more afraid of Karen than they were of me."

That was the final straw for Art. With scenes of pissed-off drug dealers and gangbangers invading his home and killing his family boiling through his dreams, he resolved to get out of the robbery business as well. In the relativity of his world, he had matured, and with it came an epiphany.

"I remembered what Pete had told me about having a nice life," he says. "He had showed me that stuff for a reason, because he wanted me to have another avenue out. I had no idea how I would do it because frankly I had forgotten just about everything, but I knew that I was going to become a counterfeiter, like him. And, well, you know me. Once I set my mind to something, I'm obsessed. I took what he taught me and amplified it a hundred times over."

5

THE DUNGEON

So I fixed up the basement with
What I was a-workin' with
Stocked it full of jelly jars
And heavy equipment
We're in the basement,
Learning to print
All of it's hot
All counterfeit

—B-52'S, "LEGAL TENDER"

Starting a counterfeiting operation from scratch is a formidable task for a crew of men; for a single man, it's a protracted logistical battle in which a hundred items must be acquired, prepared, and studied—all before ink wets paper. Four years after learning the basics from da Vinci, Art possessed the maturity and patience to pursue the endeavor, but as he set about his mission it was no less daunting. Pete had taught him only everything that took place in the shop, and production is only part of counterfeiting. Art didn't know where the old man had gotten supplies, how he found clients, or how to conduct deals.

By necessity, Art's first acquisition had to be a safe house, or what the Secret Service calls a "printing hole." Like the song says, counterfeiters like to operate in basements, and for good reason: Chugging along at full speed, even a small electric offset press generates vibrations rivaling an off-balance washing machine full of shoes. Ideally, the press should have solid ground beneath it and thick walls around it, or be located far from any other building. With limited resources, Art didn't have the option of renting an isolated space somewhere in the sticks or even an industrial spot like da Vinci's. He needed to stay as local as possible.

Luckily, it turned out that one of his friends, Chris Bucklin, was the son of a local real estate baron. Chris's dad lived in Ireland and delegated the management of his properties to his son. After a few vague descriptions, Art was able to pay Chris cash for a three-bedroom basement apartment on Halsted Street, the kind of gloomy subterranean den that few people passing on the sidewalk above ever notice.

He called the apartment "the Dungeon," and immediately went shopping for equipment. Offset printing supplies are easy to find in most large cities, but Chicago in particular offers a bountiful hunting ground. Just like the meatpackers, printers were drawn to the city by its central location, and by the early twentieth century it hosted the greatest concentration of printers in the world. Companies like RR Donnelley & Sons grouped along Chicago's South Loop in an area that became known as Printer's Row, eventually spreading their industry outward. To this day, the graphic-arts industry remains the city's largest single employer, and the heart of America's printing industry still lies within a two-hundred-mile radius.

State-of-the-art small-sized presses can cost upwards of ten thousand dollars, so Art focused his search on used presses. He checked the For Sale sections of local newspapers and called local print shops, asking if anyone had a press they wanted to unload. At a going-out-of-business sale, he picked up an old AB Dick for five hundred dollars. "It was the lowest end of the line," he says with a tinge of embarrassment. "It was literally something out of the nineteen seventies, sitting abandoned in the corner of the print shop."

Adding on the process camera, plate burner, hydraulic cutter, inks, lights, tables, tools, and chemical solutions, he stocked his shop for about five thousand dollars. It was a bare-bones setup befitting the name of Art's hideout. But in one regard it was also advanced: In addition to the other equipment, Art also picked up an Apple computer, a scanner, and a diazotype blueprint machine—a high-end architectural printer.

In 1992, less than one half of one percent of counterfeiters used desktop-publishing equipment, but Williams had long wondered if there was a way to integrate the new technology into a counterfeiting operation. Wired into a Macintosh computer running the image-editing program Photoshop, he'd have the option of playing with bill images and cleaning them up on the screen, then printing them out on the diazotype. He had no idea how well the technology would work and decided to stick to the tried-and-true method Pete had taught him, but he wanted to experiment in the future—an inclination that would later define his criminal career. "Da Vinci never messed with computers and printers—he was strictly old school— but I knew they had possibilities," says Art. "It was just something I wanted to play with."

At the same time Art was accumulating all his printing supplies, he set aside one room in the apartment for a new "hobby"—a hydroponic marijuana grow room. On the streets "Dro," as it was called, was becoming all the rage. It was selling for $350 an ounce, and Art figured that the weed operation would be a good fallback, with the added benefit that he'd be able to smoke as much as he wanted, for inspiration. He needed to rig a fan and duct system to get rid of the smell of printing chemicals anyway, and it would also work just as well evacuating the skunky-sweet stench of a roomful of Dro.

Two months went by before he had all the equipment ready, and by then he was missing the one crucial counterfeiting element that can't be easily obtained: the paper. United States currency is printed on a paper composed of 25 percent linen and 75 percent cotton. Da Vinci's Royal Linen had done a good job of mimicking the material, but the old man had never told Art where he got it. All Art knew was that it was lightweight newsprint, the kind of industrial publishing paper that generally comes in refrigerator-sized rolls that often weigh several tons.

Knowing that da Vinci had used a connection at one of the many local printing houses, Art improvised a plan for acquiring paper. After running through a list of larger printing houses in the Yellow Pages, he targeted one on Dearborn Street, a low-lying redbrick monster that specialized in printing trade magazines, brochures, and newsletters by the millions. He dressed up in khaki slacks and put his glasses on, then drove over to the printing house in a pickup truck borrowed from a friend. After walking in through the loading dock, he asked to see the manager.

A few minutes later Art was a greeted by a short, jocund man with white hair, bright blue eyes, and a round face. Drawing on his days of begging paper for school, Art told him that he was a student who was working on a presentation that would cover a whole wall of the gym. He needed a roll of light newsprint, but he didn't have much money. Specifically, Art asked the manager if he had any "butt rolls." Also called "stub rolls," they're the unused cores of the huge industrial rolls—the publishing equivalent of those last, untappable sheets on a roll of toilet paper, with the exception that butt rolls typically weigh a couple hundred pounds. Too small for a large-scale print run and too large to throw away, most printers send them to the recycling bins. For a flourish, Art told the manager that he was also interested in becoming a printer someday. The manager, who was South Side Irish to the core, perked right up.

"Look, if I got some in the bins, you can take 'em," he told Art, "but since you're interested in becoming a printer, wouldn't you like to take a look around?"

Art said yes.

The manager proceeded to give him a tour of the whole building, from their computerized design studio to their roaring, forty-foot-long presses that devoured ink by the barrel. As they came to each machine, he'd tap a supervisor on the back, introduce Art as an aspiring printer, and have him explain the details of his post. Art peppered them with questions, and enjoyed the tour so much that he almost forgot why he had come, until the manager pointed out the recycling bins.

Rummaging around inside the bins, he found three butt rolls of light newsprint that fit his need to a tee. Not only did the manager give them to him for free, but he even shouted a couple workers over to load them into the pickup.

He drove off waving to the manager, with enough paper to print millions of dollars.

WITH HIS SHOP FULLY EQUIPPED, Art hunkered down in the Dungeon and began the exacting process of re-creating everything da Vinci had taught him. Like a pilot attempting his first solo flight four years after his lessons, he was shaky and tentative, operating mostly on guts and general memory. Time's dulling flow had softened his appreciation of the crime's fundamental truth: Counterfeiting is immensely difficult.

He didn't even consider printing da Vinci's preferred product—hundred-dollar bills—because they were the most scrutinized denomination. His plan was start with twenties, working his way up as his bills improved.

To his surprise, his plates came out okay. Not quite as crisp as da Vinci's, but his mentor had drummed into him the importance of taking precise measurements before shooting the negatives, and this had stayed with him. It wasn't until he moved to the offset press that he realized his education was woefully incomplete.

Art did everything the way he remembered—mounting his plates on the roller, mixing his inks, and firing up the AB Dick—but as his first batch emerged on the delivery tray he didn't see the bright, fine rectangles of mint that he remembered from the da Vinci days. Instead, he had a batch of purple bills. He turned off the press and went back to the ink palette, adding more green and yellow. But his next batch of bills was almost chartreuse and looked like they had been exposed to radiation. Again and again he'd adjust his color and run off a few hundred sheets, only to find he'd created some new perversion of the twenty-dollar bill, like a mad scientist with a labful of mutants.

"I got discouraged," says Art. "When I was with Pete, I never got to run the press or mix the inks. I just watched him, so I tried to go off what I had watched. I knew how to turn the press on, raise the paper, put the plate on, get it to run, but I didn't know how to do it all by myself."

He took a week off and spent the time hanging out with his friends from Taylor Street, mulling over what had gone wrong. The problem, he knew, was one of attention and patience: Rather than letting the press rip away and hope for the best, he needed to control the pace. So on his second attempt he began stopping the press every fifteen or twenty sheets, then adjusting his colors and alignment. He did this dozens of times, losing himself in the process.

After hours of tweaking, he went to the tray and saw something that made his heart pound: All of a sudden he was looking at money. A little dark, but it was there.

Like a roughneck striking oil, he quickly turned the press back on and ran off more than two thousand fronts. Then came the seals and serial numbers. From experience, he knew that the backs— which consisted of only one color—would be far easier, and they were. In a matter of a few more hours of printing and cutting, he was sitting at the kitchen table in the Dungeon, exhausted. In front of him was twenty thousand dollars in counterfeit.

"There were a lot of feelings going through me. I felt really good, but I also felt alone, like I was in this all by myself because Pete wasn't there. I remember thinking, 'Man, I wish you could see me now, Buddy. You never got to finish teaching me, but I went ahead and finished for you.'"

DESPITE HIS ELATION, Art was now confronted with a much bigger problem than the mechanics of making money. Obsessed with re-membering the details of how to counterfeit, he'd given little thought to what he'd do if he actually succeeded, and when it came to the second half the business—unloading it—da Vinci had provided him no training whatsoever. And so he went to the one person he knew who would have a plan.

Back when he was learning how to counterfeit, Art hadn't ex-actly kept his promise to da Vinci about not telling a soul. "I had to tell *someone*," he admits with embarrassment. "It was too intense to keep all to myself. So I told one person."

His confidant had been Michael Pepitone, a nineteen-year-old from Taylor Street who was one of the most peculiar specimens of Chicago criminal Art had ever met, beginning with his looks. With a lithe build, bright blue eyes, a crew cut, and light Mediterranean skin, Pepitone was by no means unattractive, but he had a gawkish tendency to carry his head out in front of his chest, sometimes moving it in a herky-jerky pivot when he spoke. This little head-dance placed him squarely in the odd-bird family—an image that was bolstered by his unnatural obsession with details. "Every morning, the first thing Mikey did was change his voice mail," says Art. "He'd say, 'Hello, this is Michael Pepitone. The date is Tuesday the twenty-second. . . .' If you called him the next day he would say exactly the same thing, but it would be the twenty-third. It didn't matter what day you called, he'd always have it current. He's a fucking madman. But I like that about him."

Long after his childhood, Mikey would learn that he suffered from attention deficit disorder. But what was truly bizarre about Pepitone was that although he showed definite strains of geek, he was one of the fiercest boys on Taylor Street. A lifeguard by day, he spent his nights working as a debt collector for independent bookmakers, who knew him as Mikey "Bad to the Bone" Pepitone, one of the most successful amateur boxers in the city. At six two and 175 pounds, he had a nasty left hook and would end his amateur career with a 19–2 record. The bookies took notice and offered him thirty to fifty percent of everything he could collect, depending on the age of the debt. He'd show up at a debtor's doorstep, try to gab his way to the money, and if that failed he'd go from zero to Nero almost instantaneously. "I wouldn't say I *liked* roughing people up," explains Mikey, "but you have to understand where Arty and I came from. If somebody gets over on you and you let it happen, that's on you. When I was collecting, those guys knew why I was there. Once he paid, a guy might invite me to sit down and have a coffee with him. Yeah, that was weird, especially if he had bandages. But they didn't blame me. They blamed themselves."

Williams and Pepitone actually met during a street fight. One day while Art was walking down Taylor Street, two kids from the nearby Jane Addams Homes stopped him and demanded his shoes, a brand-new pair of high-tops. Art immediately started swinging, and as he struggled to hold his own, he suddenly found Mikey fighting alongside him, whipping his fists with such speed and ferocity that the two assailants quickly backed off. Pepitone's fearlessness earned tremendous respect from Williams, and as the boys came to know each other better they discovered that they had more in common than the ability to use their fists. Mikey was yet another paternal amputee. He had never met his dad, who had abandoned his mother before he was born, and she'd raised him with the help of a stepfather who came along later. "Arty's life and my life were very similar, and we recognized that right away," says Mikey. "The only thing I was thankful to my dad for was that he made me a hundred percent Italian."

Unlike many other street criminals Art knew, Mikey rarely boasted when it came to his exploits as a shakedown man, and Art sensed that the older boy was cautious and enterprising when it came to crime. It had been all these factors—Pepitone's street smarts, his courage, cautiousness, and spiritual brotherhood—that led Art to break his second promise to da Vinci and tell Mikey that he was learning an esoteric criminal art.

"We'd been shooting some hoops at Sheridan Park and afterwards Art pulls me aside," Mikey remembers. "He told me he had learned this new trade, then he showed me one of these hundred dollar bills, and my penis became erect. I couldn't believe it. That was a rare thing he was learning, and he was just a kid. Where we come from, learning something like that was almost a privilege. We call the stuff he made by its Italian name, *fugazi,* and guys who can do it well are rare. I said, 'Don't be a jagoff and pay the fuck attention to everything this guy is showing you.'"

Now three years on, Art approached Mikey at the basketball courts once again, this time handing him a bill made entirely by him. Pepitone's nose for profit immediately kicked into overdrive.

"How much do you have?" he asked.

"Twenty thousand."

"That's it?" was Mikey's response. Art would hear similar complaints from many friends and associates over the years. No one would ever appreciate the effort it took to create a convincing bill, or the dangers of making too many. Everyone but the counterfeiter himself assumes that if you can make a thousand, then the logical thing to do is to go ahead and print a million.

Despite his great expectations, Mikey was happy to help Art unload the twenty large. A week later, he called Art and presented him with his first "deal." There was a pot dealer, a young guy who was growing hydroponic weed in his home, who would take the whole batch in exchange for six pounds. But there was a catch: The dealer, Mikey told Art, would have no idea that the money was counterfeit. Art felt like he was headed right back into the racket he'd been trying to escape, but he needed the money.

"By the time he realizes the money is fake, we'll be long gone," Mikey assured him. "And if he does realize it, fuck him. What's he gonna do? Call the cops?"

"Where's he from?" Art asked.

"Kenosha," Mikey replied with a smile.

And that sealed it. Everyone on the South Side knew that guys from Kenosha were "soft"—suburban kids unaccustomed to having to fight for their meat. A few days later they met the dealer in the parking lot of a local gas station.

Art had stashed the money in a large-sized manila envelope. When the dealer opened it and flipped through the bills, centuries passed between the beats of Art's heart.

"Go ahead and count it," Mikey said amicably, but after running his thumb through the two-inch-thick bricks, the dealer was satisfied. By the time they got back to their own car, Art was uncharacteristically nervous, insisting that they speed away immediately. He still thought the bills were too dark, and was certain the dealer would recognize this.

"Relax," Mikey told him. "The money will pass."

The dealer called Mikey two hours later.

"Your guy gave me counterfeit bills," he said. Mikey played dumb and told the dealer he wanted to come over and inspect the bills himself. The dealer was hesitant, and gave Mikey vague warnings that there'd be "repercussions." Unfortunately for the Kenosha Kid, it was just the kind of threat that Pepitone's inner thug delighted in answering. Mikey had a cop friend run the Kid's license plate for an address, then went to his house and popped him over the head with a tire iron. "It was too bad it ended that way," says Mikey, "because I was looking forward to establishing a relationship with him so I could fuck him again."

They never heard from the Kenosha Kid again. Art split the six pounds with Mikey, and within two weeks he had unloaded most of his half for a profit of twelve thousand dollars. He kept a few ounces for himself and stuffed it in the Dungeon's freezer.

Although the pot deal had been lucrative, Art cringed at the fact that a bumpkin had identified his bills as fake after a mere two hours—a vulnerability that could have gotten him killed by a more streetwise dealer. It was also the kind of reckless, bottom-dwelling deal that his old mentor would have sneered at. "Da Vinci would have been appalled," says Art. "Something like that was way beneath him. And I wanted to do the kind of deals he had done, big batches with deep-pocketed clients."

The only way to do that was to improve his bills, so he went back to the print shop. And this time he threw out the rulebook.

Part of the reason his bills had been too dark had to do with his press. Thanks to its advanced age, it lacked agility when it came to registering fine lines off a plate. To compensate, Art had darkened his colors, sacrificing detail for the illusion of substance. He guessed that the dealer in Kenosha had been convinced enough in the dim light of a car ceiling bulb, but once he'd taken them home and counted them in good light, the faces caught his attention. His suspicions piqued, the dealer probably then compared serial numbers and noticed the same four again and again—the final tell.

The only way to eliminate the darkness and improve his lines was to buy a better press, but Art was curious about the computer equipment. He scanned some bill fronts and started experimenting with the Photoshop program, which at the time was only a few years old. It didn't take him long to realize that by spending hours touching up a scan he could boost the output on the ink-jet printer to the point where it surpassed the level of detail he was getting from his old AB Dick. "Right away I saw that the computer could take care of my darkness problem and give me fine lines," says Art. "Even back then you could get the ink-jets and computers to do amazing things. In fact, some of the older printers will do things new ones can't."

At the same time, Art saw the limitations. There were things the digital equipment just couldn't do well: the faint, almost imperceptible green background of bills, the sharpness of the seals and the serial numbers, and the minuscule red and blue silk fibers all looked pixilated and artificial. Every advantage the computer technology gave him came with a weakness. The solution he came up with was almost unheard of at the time: a hybrid bill that utilized both offset *and* digital. He employed the offset for his background, seals, serial numbers, and fibers, then moved his sheets to the inkjet to print his faces. Overall, it was no more or less time-consuming than purely sticking to the offset, but it gave him more control, and the results were immediate and dramatic. "I don't want to say that they were as good as da Vinci's bills . . . ," Art hems. "They were different. He probably wouldn't like them because he was old school. But they were infinitely better than that first batch. I was pretty sure I could get thirty cents on the dollar, in daylight."

ART KNEW that if he wanted to sell a hundred thousand dollars in counterfeit at thirty cents on the dollar, then he needed clients with both the cash to pay for his product and a network to distribute it. That meant he really had only one choice.

Organized crime loves counterfeit money. Since their own businesses are illegitimate, their patrons are usually in no position to complain. If you're running gambling rackets, you can mix counterfeit into the payoffs and people are not only unlikely to protest, but they won't be in a hurry to seek the police. If you're smuggling, the fakes go abroad, where a third-worlder is as likely to stuff American dollars under his mattress as he is to deposit them in a bank. It's even better if you're running drugs, because then you're dealing with so much cash that a hundred thousand dollars in counterfeit may well be a drop in the pond. And there are always the middlemen, the ones who buy counterfeit for thirty cents on the dollar and sell it downstream for fifty cents to guys without connections.

Fortunately for Art, Chicago was about as bountiful in Mafia as it was in printers. The most accessible group was the Outfit, which had dominated the city since the days of Al Capone. Having grown up in Bridgeport and made a second home of Taylor Street, Art personally knew Outfit associates from two of the six different "crews" that ran the city much in the same way that New York's Five Families divided up their turf. The Twenty-sixth Street or "Chinatown" Crew was right there in Bridgeport and specialized in truck hijacking, gambling, extortion, and juice loans. Some of its members even lived on his street (albeit on a nicer block) and he knew them on a first-name basis. Art was even better connected to the Taylor Street or "Ferriola" Crew, which was heavily involved in gambling and bookmaking. With one phone call, he could have arranged a meeting with a made man who was sure to want hundreds of thousands of dollars.

But there were problems when it came to doing business with the Outfit. As every crook in Chicago knew, once a crew had you on their radar, you risked becoming their personal ATM. If they didn't try to run Art's operation outright, at the very least they'd force him to pay a "street tax" of twenty-five percent on everything he made—under penalty of death. For this reason, Art not only discounted doing business with the Outfit, but also refused to have any direct contact with it.

That still left an entire city in which virtually every immigrant group had a criminal adjunct, and Bridgeport, whose sociocriminal intricacies were as familiar to Art as the run of a backyard stream, was home to many of them. One of the groups that impressed him the most was the Chinese Mafia. Better known as the On Leong organization, the group had a long history in the city, evolving out of a traditional Chinese secret society, or *tong*, of the same name. It operated out of Chinatown's most iconic structure, the On Leong Merchants Association Building, a traditional pagoda-style edifice on

Wentworth Avenue. From there, the organization ran a small criminal empire that included gambling, prostitution, auto theft, human trafficking, and selling heroin. To keep the Italians off its back, On Leong paid a street tax that constituted one of the Outfit's biggest cash cows.

Art had gotten to know an On Leong member a year earlier through Carlos Espinosa, a half-Chinese, half-Mexican acquaintance who ran a chop shop in Bridgeport. Knowing that Art occasionally stole cars, Espinosa had approached him with an unusual job offer: The Chinese were looking for someone to steal Corvettes, and claimed to have not only the addresses of every car, but an electronic key that would open all of them. Art thought the story about the key was "full of shit," but he said he'd at least meet with the On Leong guy and hear what he had to say. His contact's name, Espinosa told him, was the Horse.

"Why's he called that?" Art asked.

Carlos smiled. "Believe me, dude. You'll see."

A few days later, Art went to the corner of Thirty-fourth and Wallace, where a Chinese guy pulled up in a white Corvette. When Art hopped into the car, he was transfixed as the driver, speaking from a face that could have graced a Palomino, introduced himself as the Horse.

In a thick Chinese accent, the Horse explained the job. He wanted only Corvettes, and he would pay Art five thousand dollars for each one. He handed Art a key chain with a small plastic box attached to it, along with a list of addresses where he could find the vehicles. Art signed on dubiously, but when he visited the first address, the car was right where the Horse had said it would be, and the little magic box, which emitted a radio signal that was the equivalent of a master key, worked flawlessly. Over the next week, he stole seven 'Vettes for the Horse for a total of thirty-five thousand dollars.

It was the easiest and best money he'd ever made at crime. On Leong was clearly all about conducting business with as few surprises as possible, and to Art that made them the ideal potential clients.

Hoping that the Horse might be interested in purchasing some counterfeit, Art gave him a call and arranged a meeting at Ping Tom Park, a pleasant patch of green on the edge of Chinatown that skirts the South Branch of the Chicago River. As they once again sat in the Horse's 'Vette, Art handed him a bill and explained, proudly, that he was its maker.

"I thought you were a car thief!" the Horse said after scrutinizing the bill. "You're full of surprises."

The Horse told Art that he was impressed and interested, but first he had to consult his superiors in Chinatown and do a background check on the street. Two days later, the Horse offered him twenty cents on the dollar for a hundred thousand dollars. Art asked for thirty and they settled on twenty-five.

"It's none of my business what you do with the money and I don't care, but there is one thing," Art explained as they went over details. "If my money will be distributed in the Chicago area, I need to know. It helps me understand my risk. You know what I'm saying?"

The Horse thought about it for a moment and nodded his long face.

"Sure, I understand. This money will stay here," he said. It wasn't the answer Art had hoped for, but at least he knew. He made a mental note to not sell locally bound bills again too quickly. Let the money pop, let the Service sniff around, then give the trail time to dry up before executing another deal. And make sure the next batch is different enough to raise doubts about its origin.

They met in a South Side hotel room three weeks later. Art brought along Bill Barcus, a six-foot-tall, 280-pound Lithuanian friend that he knew from Taylor Street, who was better known as "Big Bill." Art was really beginning to like the Horse, but with that much cash and counterfeit in play he had no intention of walking into a deal without an insurance policy, which in Barcus's case also included a 9mm.

The Horse, who brought two of his own men with him, was nonplussed by Big Bill's presence and got right down to business. They both brought out their goods. Art's satchel was filled with shrink-wrapped counterfeit hundred-dollar bills, and the Horse's backpack contained twenty-five thousand genuine dollars.

The exchange was flawless, casual, and precise—everything Art had hoped for.

The Horse was so impressed with Art's money that he ordered another batch two months later, once again explaining that it would circulate locally. When he called the Horse to arrange delivery, Art assumed that it would be in another hotel, but this time, the Horse had other plans.

"Why don't you come to the On Leong Building," he told Art. "We can have a good time."

Art was astonished. Being invited into the On Leong Building was a privilege reserved for only the highest echelons of Chicago's criminals and businessmen (distinctions that, incidentally, have a long history of fuzziness), and there was a very good reason. Deep inside the building was a massive, windowless gambling den with a swanky bar, high-end Asian prostitutes, and table service that included drugs—an inner sanctum and playpen for both the Chinese Mafia and the Outfit. Like everyone else in Bridgeport, Art had heard stories about the den, but when he set foot inside, it defied his wildest dreams. There were gambling tables everywhere, dozens of them—blackjack, mah-jongg, poker, roulette, craps—and because it had been partially designed by men who had investments in Vegas, it looked like Vegas, without the meddlesome influence of government regulation. As Art made his way onto the floor, following the Horse, he looked to his right and saw a VIP section filled with Sicilians, faces that members of the city's organized-crime task force probably stared at on a peg board all day, wondering how to get as close to them as Art now was. They were Outfit guys, doing their thing, and there he was, a kid from the projects, walking right past them with a satchel as he did his own thing.

The Horse led Art to a booth where they ordered drinks, then they stepped into a private side room to quickly exchange satchels before returning. Art spent the rest of the night partying with the Horse, his friends, and some of the most beautiful women he'd ever seen. At the end of the evening, one of the women led him downstairs to a room in the Chinatown Hotel and gave him the "executive treatment"—on the house, of course.

WITHIN SIX MONTHS of rolling with the Chinese, Art secured two more clients from organized-crime groups. Like the Horse, both of them were close to his own age, young men with whom he'd had dealings during his earlier days as a street criminal and who were now trying to expand their operations.

The first, Pedro "Sandy" Sandoval, was Mexican. Art had known Sandy since age fourteen, when he started hanging out on Taylor Street. Short, laid-back, and tattooed up his legs with depictions of various Aztec and Mayan gods and geometry, Sandy was from the west side of Taylor Street, an area long known as Pilsen. Once home to thousands of immigrants from Bohemia as well as Eastern and Northern Europe, it was now mostly Latino. Sandy's uncle was a member of the Mexican Mafia, the most powerful Mexican crime group in the nation, with origins dating back to a California prison gang in the 1950s. Though relatively new to Chicago, the Mexican Mafia was expanding rapidly, in no small part due to its cocaine-smuggling connections. Sandy was dealing cocaine for his uncle, who was a major supplier for the Chicago area. Given the tremendous amount of cash that the cocaine business generates, Art figured that his friend might be able to put the *fugazi* to good use as "padding"—counterfeit cash mixed into large shipments of genuine currency.

Sandy liked the idea from the first moment Art showed him a bill, a reaction that Art thought was hilarious because it was well known that Sandy had vision problems. "Sandy was blind as a bat," Art says. "He had glasses and contacts but he didn't like to wear them if he wasn't driving, so he'd go around squinting all the time. I could have given him Monopoly money and he would have said it looked great. With him, it was all about trust, and he trusted me implicitly."

Just to test the water, Sandy started out slow, ordering twenty-five grand from Art to see how the money played once it left his hands. When no one made a stink, he quickly upped his orders to a hundred thousand dollars—the maximum amount that Art agreed to make per da Vinci's rules. Art didn't ask Sandy many questions about where the money was headed; he knew that Sandy's uncle got his cocaine from out of state, and given the quantities of cocaine he'd seen at Sandy's house, it was safe to assume that his uncle was moving much larger quantities. Although Sandy offered, Art had no interest in meeting his uncle. "I never want to see his face," he told his friend.

Art's other client, Dmitri Kovalev, was a Russian he met at a party thrown by one of his Italian friends from Taylor Street. Thick-chested, with brown hair and a heavy accent, Dmitri was a party animal who Art liked from the moment he saw him sitting at a table surrounded by friends and slamming five shots of vodka in a row. "This guy was the biggest party animal I'd ever seen," Art remembers. "There aren't many people I know who can outdrink me, but he could every time. He was one of those guys who seems to get more sober the more they drink. He liked booze and girls, but he wasn't obnoxious. He was extremely polite and polished, a classy guy. And he was very Russian. The one way you could tell he was getting drunk was because he'd never shut up about how great Russia was and how much he missed it." Dmitri was from St. Petersburg, which is perhaps best known for two things: its magnificent architecture and its Mafia, the latter of which is the most resilient and powerful in all of Russia. He liked to praise the merits of both. "He'd tell me that the United States was a pain in the ass. He'd say that in Russia, no one had to worry about cops or crackdowns because everyone was paid off. They could do anything they wanted. He always told me that one day he'd take me there."

Dmitri was evasive about why he was in the U.S., and Art suspected it had to do with mob trouble. He ran a social club on the North Side, and after a few all-night visits, Art gleaned that gambling and prostitution orbited there. Each time Art came, Dmitri treated him like an old friend, and on a hunch Art decided to lay a note on him to see if he was interested in buying.

"Falshivki!" Dmitri declared with a smile as he fondled the bill. "Pretty good. But in St. Petersburg we make better."

"So you don't want any?"

"I didn't say that. How much?"

"Thirty cents on the dollar."

The Russian said he'd think about it. Once again, within a week they had negotiated a hundred-thousand-dollar order, this time for the requested thirty-cent rate. And when Art posed his question about the direction his money would take once it left his hands, the

Russian's response was music to his ears: "Don't worry, Arty," Dmitri told him. "It will leave the country fast."

AS THE DUNGEON TOOK OFF, Art realized that his apprenticeship with da Vinci had probably been more than a generous criminal scholarship; satisfying multiple orders for counterfeit is heavy work for a lone operator. He soon enlisted some help of his own, drawing on friends from Taylor Street and Bridgeport who were willing to risk federal time for a quick profit. He intentionally kept them largely ignorant of each other's activities, but each man played a role, and together they formed a colorful crew.

Along with Mikey, Art's most trusted associate was Giorgi Munizzi, a Bridgeport native who'd grown up just four blocks from Art, but in terms of advantages, they may as well have been miles apart. Giorgi was Bridgeport royalty, the grandson of one of the Outfit's most powerful and legendary bosses. "Out of respect for other family members, I won't say my granddad's name," declares Giorgi, "but everyone knows who he was. I mean, he was *the boss*. People would tremble when they saw him, that's how mean he was." One hundred percent Sicilian, with dark skin, curly black hair, and a laid-back air, Giorgi had grown up surrounded by men who feared and served his family, but he never joined the organization and insists he was never pressured to—he didn't have to, because he already enjoyed all the privileges of being associated by lineage. "It was crazy," Giorgi says of his status. "My whole life, people have come up to me and given me money. For nothing. For being somebody's grandson. It's bizarre, but I'd have to be stupid not to appreciate that."

Art had witnessed the power of Giorgi's family firsthand at the age of thirteen, when he unwittingly stole a Cadillac belonging to Giorgi's dad and was quickly arrested. Giorgi accompanied his dad down to the station, where he saw Art, who was three years younger than him, sitting in handcuffs and locking eyes with him. Giorgi knew Art from the neighborhood as a tough little kid from the projects who had it rough. He told his dad that Art was okay, and the cops released Art right then. After that, Giorgi was the only kid who wasn't an SD who was allowed to walk through the projects by himself. He was also one of the few people close to Art who had known da Vinci, thanks to a bookmaking operation he later ran out of Ed's Snack Shop. "He was a genius," Giorgi says of Pete. "I didn't realize it until Art showed me what he learned, but I always sensed that about him. And it didn't surprise me that Art was the one he picked to teach."

All these connections made Giorgi a natural confidant for Art, who was quickly amazed by the Mafia prince's gift as an acquisition specialist. With his connections to the Outfit, his hands were on the pulse of what was coming in off the trucks and trains, and if he heard about something he thought Art could use—computers, ink, paper stock—he'd set it aside and deliver it to Art factory-fresh.

Once a batch was ready for delivery, Art usually called Tony Puntillo, a garrulous cabdriver he'd known since his teenage years. A wiry Italian who loved nothing more than trash-talking, Tony was Art's wheelman. Whenever Art needed to move money and material, or avoid tails, he'd call Tony on his beeper and leave him a number between 1 and 15. Each number represented a different location in the city, and unless he was stuck in traffic Tony would pull up within half an hour, ready to turn his cab into a race car or bury it in a sea of other yellow taxis if needed. "Art used to make five-dollar bills just for me," Tony remembers. "It's no secret that I like to talk, I like people. But if you've just come in from out of town or from a bar and you're in my cab, you won't know what hit you. I'll be talking your ear off so much that you won't notice that I've given you two of Art's fives back as change. If you're an asshole, I'll give you four."

Along with providing security at drop-offs, Big Bill helped with production, running errands for ink and other supplies that constantly seemed to be tapping out. And of course Mikey remained Art's primary dealmaker and counselor. Even if Art arranged a deal himself, he'd usually consult Mikey for a second opinion. "Half the time I was teaching him things," Mikey recalls. "Where was the deal? Is it in a public place? If it is, you show up an hour early, park in a dark spot, and watch so if somebody is planning to fuck you, there's a good chance you'll see it coming."

Like da Vinci, Art was willing to teach his friends the secrets of how he made counterfeit, but few had the inclination. They were happy to help him with piecework, but when it came to the details and artistry, they quickly lost interest. "Oh, we all said we wanted to know how he did it," laughs Mikey. "Lots of people bugged him. I probably knew more than anybody. I could tell you the steps, but I still don't know how he did it so *well*. He was gifted. I know I could never have done what he did."

Despite such praise, Art is dismissive about the counterfeit he made during his Dungeon days. "It was caveman stuff," he says. "Compared to what came later, I don't even like to think about it." But his cohorts have a different opinion.

Chris Sophocleus, a Greek social-club owner who was a close friend of Art's, had so much faith in the "Dungeon dollars" that he put them to the ultimate test one night when Chicago PD and the FBI raided his club. Art was in the club at the time, and carrying about five thousand dollars in counterfeit—bills that would surely be scrutinized once the officers and agents began searching patrons.

"Give me whatever you're holding," Chris whispered to him. "I can mix it into the cash box."

Art quickly passed Chris the bill roll, and a few minutes later both he and Chris watched as an FBI agent proceeded to count out the contents of the box, including Art's five grand, on the hood of a CPD cruiser.

The agent gave every single bill back to Chris.

AS HIS OPERATION FELL INTO PLACE, for the first time in his life Art had more money than he knew what to do with. Having been raised with a scarcity of dollars, he might have taken a conservative approach to spending, but the knowledge that he could always make more overrode any parsimonious instincts. His outlook, certainly not uncommon to criminals, was purely feast or famine, almost as if the money would expire if he didn't spend it first. "We'd do a deal and Art'd have five thousand dollars in his pocket," remembers Pepitone. "We'd hit a bar and he'd go in there and the first thing he'd do was buy everyone a round, the whole bar. Then he'd just spend and spend. By Monday morning he'd be asking *me* if he could borrow twenty bucks."

"No one could spend money like me," Art proudly admits. "If I had it, I spent it. I was stupid, because if I had invested the money I made I'd never have to work again. But that's the criminal attitude: You live from one crime to another." Art wielded his cash the Bridgeport way: He carried a fat roll in his right front pocket, small notes shelling the large so no one could see how much he had. Wallets were for squares, people who didn't understand that the best way to get anything done was to whip out that wad at a moment's notice, crack out a C-note, then get the roll back in your pocket and next to your cock as fast as possible. All day long the roll came out; for groceries, smokes, cocaine, alcohol, oversized tips, strippers, new clothes, bets, valet parking.

Art's favorite exuberance was to rent limousines for a night out with friends. For this, he'd call a driver in his sixties who went by the name "Mr. U." Despite or perhaps because of his age, Mr. U. loved nothing more than taking the kids for a night out. He'd drive with the partition window down so he could be one of the boys, breaking balls and telling stories about his own days as an outlaw. "He was Irish mob straight to the core: red in the face with only two fingers on his left hand. People said he got the other two shot off doing something back in his younger days." A typical night would start out with Mr. U. meeting Art, Mikey, and Giorgi on Taylor Street, then they'd pick up a few more friends and head for a steak dinner at Gibson's or the Chop House. After that, they'd hit the bars and clubs. If Art was feeling particularly elated over a deal, or if he was just plain drunk and happy, he'd pony up the bar round. "People would freak out because that's something you only see in movies. You drop a grand in one shot. But the best thing about it is that the women see shit like that and they just swarm in."

The vast majority of money Art spent in Chicago was real. Da Vinci had warned him of the dangers of spending locally, but he also found it distasteful to lay counterfeit on doormen, bartenders, and waiters from his hometown who were sweating out legitimate jobs. "My ma worked in a restaurant; service jobs are brutal. So I didn't like to hand out counterfeit when I was partying. To me, that would have ruined the whole experience. It made me feel good to give them real money. And I'll tell ya, pretty soon I didn't wait in lines. I got in for free."

Beyond the disposable spending, there were the goods and toys, like a high-end Kenwood stereo system for his car, new computer equipment, and Armani shirts, which he had tailored because he was big in the shoulders. An unwritten rule of criminal masterminds is that they must also have a collection, the more bizarre the better; Escobar had a zoo, Capone had jewelry, and though Art wasn't exactly an underworld emperor he wasn't about to be kept out of the club. He took to collecting antique money, especially notes from the "Golden Age" when each bank printed its own currency. He bought hundreds of bills from dealers and fences that he knew; old Wells Fargo notes from the California gold rush, silver notes with portraits of Indian chiefs, and bills with tall ships, locomotives, and intricately engraved scenes from Americana. He cared less for their market value than for their aesthetic impression. His prize pieces were a set of three immaculate "fractional notes"—five-, fifteen-, and twenty-five-cent bills that the Union printed during the Civil War because of metal shortages. "I told Karen they were quite valuable, so what does she do? She takes them and has them laminated, thinking she's doing a good thing. They were completely ruined."

HIDING HIS CRIMINAL ACTIVITIES from Karen became an increasingly high-stakes game for Williams. Each weekday he would eat breakfast with his wife and son, put on a Windbreaker bearing a "Bello Construction" logo, then Karen would drop him off at one of Morty's construction sites. He'd kiss her good-bye, throw in a workingman's sigh at the prospect of another day of manual labor, and wait until she turned the corner. Afterward he'd make his way to the Dungeon or over to Taylor Street. If he wasn't printing, he'd meet up with his pals for cappuccinos, then head to the basketball courts at Sheridan Park, the horse track at Arlington, or maybe a White Sox game. Or they'd just spend the day partying at a bar or a friend's house.

"I never knew what he was up to, but I had my suspicions," says Magers. "He always had money, and I'd ask him how he got it. He'd say it was payday, then I'd ask him for a stub and he'd have another excuse. I was always the investigator trying to crack the case! But then I'd just get tired of arguing with him."

Williams found the double life exciting, Karen's inquisitions a turn-on. "I'd tease her," he says, "I'd tell her she was a wannabe cop." Their fights, which were frequent and fierce, often led to explosive sex, and as long as it didn't interfere with his new lifestyle, Art was content to let the loop play out and reset indefinitely. He attributed Karen's outbursts to jealousy over the fact that he was happy with his life, even if it was a lie.

"I *was* jealous," she admits. "Here I am taking care of the baby, and he's doing whatever the hell he wanted, lying to me about it. Things always came easy to him. I didn't know he was counterfeiting, but when I found out years later I wasn't surprised. He was good at anything he set his mind to. If he put half the energy into just a job, he'd probably make good money anyway."

But pretending to be a cop was more than a game to Karen. The baby had merely put a hold on her dream. When Art III was four years old, she placed him in day care and took a job waiting tables. And just as Art's own mother had fallen in love with a criminal by serving him coffee, she met a cop.

His name was Ned Fagan. He was a Chicago PD lieutenant, in his late forties and on the verge of retirement, and ran a security company on the side. He didn't laugh when Karen told him about her dreams, but instead offered her an office job at his firm. She took it, and suddenly Karen was not only talking about becoming a cop again, but she and Art were hanging out with them at weekend barbecues. At first Art was supportive; he thought becoming a cop would be good not just for her, but for him as well. Cops could be useful. One of his friends, Cyrus, was CPD, and back in his drug-pirate days Cyrus would run plates and names for Art. That usefulness, however, extended only as far as their friendship, and the more Art saw of Ned Fagan, the more he became convinced he was a facing an enemy.

Spoken or not, Fagan's name seemed to pop up in every conversation Art had with Karen. He would have been a perfect antithesis except that in Art's experience, half of Bridgeport cops were dirty. Art asked around and heard stories that Fagan's side business sheltered corrupt cops who'd drawn too much attention on the force. When he told Karen about the rumors, she interpreted it as another attack on her dreams, which of course it partially was. In the ensuing fight, she took the baby and moved out, but according to Karen, the irony was that she still loved Art. "He was so paranoid about Ned Fagan that he couldn't see it. Nothing was happening between me and Ned. I loved Art, but all of a sudden he became fixated, convinced that he was losing me to Ned. And it became a self-fulfilling prophecy."

The rivalry came to a head when Fagan called Karen's apartment one day while Art was visiting. Art answered the phone, and when he heard Fagan's voice he decided it was time to draw a line.

"I don't care if you're a cop or not, motherfucker," Art hissed. "If you don't stay away from my family we'll both go down, you and me together." Fagan hung up without responding.

Art's threat completely backfired: Karen banned him from her apartment, and within a few weeks she was seeing the only man who seemed to understand her, Ned Fagan. Incensed with jealousy, Art began tailing Fagan, studying his patterns the way he used to surveil drug dealers. He noticed that the cop passed a dark stairway on his way to his apartment—and began planning an ambush. He went out and bought some piano wire, then looped the ends through two wooden handles he made in the Dungeon. His plan was to hide under the stairway by Fagan's apartment, and as soon as the cop passed by, he'd drop it over his head, tug him back into the shadows, and quickly strangle him, leaving a minimal crime scene. He'd then throw the piano wire into the South Branch of the Chicago River and it would be done.

Art was on the verge of executing his plan to garrote Fagan when he received a phone call from his mother in Texas. Word had reached Malinda that Art was on the verge of losing it, and when she spoke to him she was at her best, with a lucidity and compassion that was worthy of the crisis. She was terrified for her son and would not take no for an answer. "She told me, 'Listen, baby, will you please just come to Texas? Just come here and give it a shot, leave the city today. I feel something bad going on with you, please come.' And I listened to her. I went, packed my clothes, went to the Greyhound bus station, and took a bus to Texas."

6

TEXAS

Things haven't worked out quite liked we planned, but
that's all right, because there's no better place than Texas to
start over. . . .

—JOHN CONNALLY, FORMER GOVERNOR OF TEXAS

Art sold off his printing equipment and vacated the Dungeon prior to leaving Chicago. In his anguish over losing Karen, he wanted to cut all ties to his old life. Counterfeiting and crime, he realized in a depressive epiphany, had caused him to lie, and lies were a major reason why his relationship had failed. Like that of a smoker throwing away a full pack, shutting down the Dungeon was a gesture intended to help propel him into a new life without temptation.

For a big-city criminal, Valley View, Texas, was a desert monastery. An eyeblink of a town about sixty miles north of Dallas, it consisted of about a hundred buildings, most of them one-story ranch homes hugging Interstate 35. The town's population was about seven hundred, the majority of them blue-collar workers or dairymen who had farms in outlying plains. There was a bank, a couple of small stores, and one bar.

At the time Art arrived, Malinda was dating Evan Wright, a local who kept a small farm on the outskirts of town and also ran a construction firm. One of the ways she had enticed Art to come down to Texas was by convincing Wright to give Art both a construction job and a place of his own to live—an unused trailer on the side of Wright's house. Since Art had construction experience from his days working with Morty Bello, he took to the work quickly. Young and pissed off at life, he could lug siding all day long, pushing for that moment when his anger momentarily dissipated through his sweat glands. He'd spend his days framing houses in nearby towns like Frisco and Plano, and at night he'd return to the trailer exhausted, sit outside on a lawn chair, and pound beers until he felt himself falling up toward the stars. He'd gone from inner city trash to trailer trash and it wasn't so bad. The stars were lovely, and Texas had other, more earthly distractions as well.

One of Wright's next-door neighbors was a blond, country-bred girl named Lucy Rasmussen. Art first glimpsed her when she stopped her car to say hello to Wright as they passed on the road. Evan introduced them and her Lone Star hospitality kicked right in. She dropped by a day later with some food, and after a few more visits he finally confessed some selective yet emotionally honest details of how Karen had shattered his heart beyond repair. He was convinced that it was a hopeless situation. If true love, the only good thing in the world, could be broken, then what was there left to believe in? Lucy sympathized completely and, with a solemn sense of purpose, set out to restore femininity to its rightful place.

"Oh, God, was she something," Art muses. "A wild-ass country girl who knew how to have fun. Blond, big tits, slim waist, a deep drawl. She was always happy and really, really sweet. She'd even wear Daisy Dukes with her shirt tied up and everything." Evan Wright's ranch was ten acres, and on one corner of it sat dozens of old cars—a real redneck garden. Art's favorite activity was to take

Lucy out among the Chevys and Fords at the end of the day, when the cars had cooled and the sun was setting. She'd let her Daisy Dukes slip into the dust, perch herself her up on one of the hoods, and they'd go at it like demons while the glass and metal around them glowed gold.

Moments like those snapped Art back into the present, but Lucy quickly realized that Art's broken heart was beyond even her capacity to heal. A few weeks after the rehabilitation project started, she confessed that she already had a boyfriend, but wanted to introduce him to some friends of hers from the nearby college town of Denton, home to Texas Women's University. At a party later that week, he found himself sitting with Lucy and three new women, all of them Texans. The new girls—Janet, Susan, and Natalie—had not only also been raised in the comparatively Spartan cultural confines of North Texas, but had the added insulation of having been brought up as conservative Christians, ingrained with the kind of sensual and moral taboos that Art happily violated on a regular basis. At the party, sensing their curiosity, he doled out generous portions of South Side grit and tales of his urban adventures. "We'd never met anyone like him," says Natalie, the youngest of the three girls. "You gotta understand that I was raised in the middle of a bunch of pastures, I'd never left the country, and I'd only left the state a few times. He starts going on about Chicago and gangs and getting shot, plus he's really cute. I mean, he was *different*. His world was like an alternate universe."

To Art, so were the girls. Their accents, naïveté, and country breeding were delightfully new, and they were much less psychologically serrated than the South Side warrior women he'd grown up with. All three were beauties. Janet was tall and fair-skinned, with bright blue eyes and reddish brown hair, while Susan and Natalie were petite, curly-haired brunettes with blue eyes and fruited lips.

Their personalities were markedly distinct: "Lucy was wild, Janet was very conservative and kind of snooty, Susan was real artsy, and Natalie was the quiet one."

He went for Janet, the snooty one, first. She was a student at TWU, and Art sensed that much of her attraction toward him was based on the fact that he was precisely the sort of man that her parents had sent her to a women's college to avoid. Although she let him kiss her at the party, he pursued her for weeks before she let him go further—not that she was an obstacle to maintaining periodic visits to the car yard with Lucy. "I couldn't help it. Lucy was just . . . I loved her in bed. She wasn't one of those girls who would just lay there. She was too much fun and she lived too close to me."

School was just getting out at the time Art met the girls, and that first summer in Texas became the most idyllic season of his life. On weekends he and the four girls would meet up at the north end of Ray Roberts Lake, a sprawling man-made reservoir created by the Army Corps of Engineers that includes two state parks. They'd park in a remote public lot, then hike down to the water and set up camp. "I had this place, my spot that I found that I used to love," Art reminisces. "No one would ever come there. It had this real big cliff that you could dive off into the water. We'd go out there with rafts, throw them out into the water, and the girls would be laying on the rocks with their bikinis on. We'd have the grill out there, we'd have grass to smoke, and all that water. And I'd be the only dude with four girls, just fucking loving life!"

After six months, Art had had encounters with all of the girls, as they passed him off to each other not unlike a beloved puppy who, though fun to play with, proves too hard to housebreak. "At one point I tried to talk three of them into it at once, but they didn't go for it," he says with a laugh. He kept things casual through a combination of charm, well-selected lies, and somber reminders that he had a family back in Chicago, although he was in no hurry to return.

"He'd call once a week," says Karen. "He sent me five hundred dollars one time. I know that Art loved our son, but he wasn't around much. He was hurt." Art's failings as a father would almost rival that of his own dad, but his early days in Texas had all the appearances of a man who was getting off the criminal path. Pot smoking aside, he went nearly a year without committing so much as a misdemeanor. More importantly, he was content with his new life. "I thought about getting a ranch, maybe buying a few horses, setting up my own construction firm," he says.

It's a nice vision to entertain. Current quantum theory supports the idea that every choice we make or don't make generates an infinite number of parallel "multiverses," meaning there could indeed be one in which Art Williams is sitting contentedly on a corral fence this very moment, chewing the hay and watching the sunset under the wide Texan sky. The choice was always his. Farther off in the bushy ramparts of space-time, there may even be a universe in which he's a district attorney or a successful businessman. One of Art's most endearing traits is that he has never lacked for imagination when it comes to envisioning the majestic peaks of a straight-and-narrow future. He just has serious deficiencies when it comes to the dirty act of scaling them.

ABOUT NINE MONTHS after he'd moved to Texas, a magical date rang out in Art's memory: June 4, 1994. Nearly a year earlier, Morty had informed him that his daughter Risa was getting married that day, and Art had filed the date away in his mind—not that he planned to attend the wedding. For him, it was significant because he knew that on that day Morty Bello and everyone in his household would be gone.

Working construction in Texas had inflamed Art's resentment toward Morty for paying him so little during the two years he'd toiled for him. He calculated that if Morty had paid him merely minimum wage, he would have had tens of thousands of dollars more, but what really angered Art was that he had allowed his feelings for the gypsy to make him vulnerable to exploitation. That anger, along with the date, had hibernated in his head for months, and when May rolled around, his criminal alarm clock started clanging as surely as Big Ben. Having gone all that time with barely a thought of crime, he was now confronted with a decision: stay clean, or rob the most despicable man he knew. "As the calendar got closer and closer, I couldn't stop thinking about it," says Art. "I was really enjoying my time with these girls, and I knew if I went back to Chicago I'd be taking a risk. But that date . . . it was really the only opportunity I'd ever have to get revenge on this guy."

He called some of his old robbery crew members and, on Friday, June 4, drove the marathon 940 miles from Valley View to Chicago. Sure enough, on the following morning Art watched from a car up the street as Morty and his retinue filed out of the house, boarded cars, and left for the wedding. He waited a few minutes to make sure nobody was left in the house, then broke in through the back door. Inside Morty's bedroom closet, Art found a steel lockbox, which he opened with a pry bar. "We got the box and pulled about sixty thousand in cash out of there," Art remembers, "but that wasn't everything. We also pulled diamonds and emeralds! They were folded real nice in rice-paper envelopes, and there was also a little box inside the big box. Inside that there were earrings and jewelry and watches and gold necklaces."

After dividing the take with his crew and fencing it, Art returned to Texas with about forty grand. "I figure it was about as much as Morty had shorted me over the years," he says. As usual, he began burning through the cash with a vengeance. "I was taking all four girls out, partying a lot," he explains. "I was still working, but construction pay in Texas was low because there you're competing with Mexicans. But the thing about the Morty job was that, when I did it, all the thrill came back."

That thrill was fresh in his mind a few months later when his first Texas criminal temptation presented itself. By then, Art and Janet had broken up and he'd started to pursue Susan—the artsy brunette. Art sensed that Susan was more infatuated by his bad-boy image than any of the other girls, and he put it to the test one day after she came home from a shopping spree loaded up with new clothes and jewelry.

"Where'd you get all this stuff?" Art asked her.

"A friend of mine took me shopping," Susan said. "Her boyfriend's a huge drug dealer in Denton, and she was telling me he's got like stacks of money underneath his bed. She just goes in there and snatches some whenever she wants to shop."

Art's clean future in Texas disintegrated as she spoke. Up until that point, he hadn't really given the girls many specifics about his criminal activities. He'd mentioned that he'd been in a gang and even the counterfeiting operation, but he had billed it all as a dark past that he was trying to put behind him, which had been true enough when he'd said it.

"Back in Chicago I used to rob drug dealers like him," he told Susan. "I made good money at it."

"Really?" Susan said, fascinated. "How'd you do it?" He told her a few stories from his drug-pirate days, watching her eyes get bigger as she realized that he wasn't kidding. Once she was immersed in the criminal contact high, he engaged her in playful interrogation.

Within ten minutes he knew where the dealer lived, what he drove, and what he sold. Susan had no criminal background, but by the time he was done with her she was helping him plan the job.

The dealer's name was Clayton. He lived in an apartment complex on the other side of town. He drove a black Mustang and peddled pot and Ecstasy. Susan didn't know which apartment was his, so Art hid in some woods across from the complex and waited until he saw him leave. Once he had the residence pinned down, he began forming a plan.

Deeming it too dangerous to enter the dealer's house alone, Art enlisted Jason, who after eight years had recently been released from the boys' home in Des Plaines. Art had visited Jason many times over the years with his mother and sister, and had never held any illusion that the home was helping him. By the time he finally left, Jason could barely read or write, and at the time, he was living with Wensdae and looking for work. When Art asked him if he was interested in making a fast buck, Jason jumped at the opportunity and flew down to Dallas the very next day. If there was any doubt among the girls that Art was serious, one look at his brother eliminated it. "When we picked him up at the airport, he had this big Chicago Bulls jacket on," Art remembers. "He looked like a straight-up thug from the South Side."

ART'S PLAN WAS STRAIGHTFORWARD: While he and Jason waited in the woods near Clayton's, Susan would call the dealer and ask him to deliver some marijuana. Once Art and Jason saw him leave, they'd emerge from the woods, break in, and rifle the apartment for cash and drugs. Their getaway driver would be Natalie, who'd be waiting up the street.

"Things went perfect at first," remembers Art. "Susan called,

Clayton came out and left, and me and my brother jimmied his sliding-glass doors and went right up in there." In Clayton's bedroom, the brothers found about seventeen thousand dollars in cash, a vacuum cleaner bag stuffed with hydroponic weed, and five prescription bottles filled with Ecstasy. Art was feeling so comfortable inside Clayton's that he even dallied to liberate some of Clayton's high-end cologne off his bureau. "That's how much of a jagoff I was," he muses. But they ended up paying for every extra second: When they opened the front door to leave, the first thing they saw was Clayton, holding his key in his hand, about to insert it into the lock.

"He looks up, and the look on his face!" Art recalls. "Can you imagine? I covered my face and started walking real fast. My brother's behind me and he says, 'Who the fuck is that? What's going on?' I'm like, 'That's *him,* walk!' And the dude freaks out and starts following us." As soon as Jason realized Clayton was following, he wheeled around to confront him, but rather than take on two men, the dealer backed off. Art and Jason took a side street, circled around, and met Natalie. But a minute after they pulled away Art spied the black Mustang behind them. Clayton was on his cell phone, undoubtedly rounding up friends to come help him take back his drugs and money by force. Art had no intention of being around when that happened.

"When we get to the next stop sign, Jason and I are jumping out," he told Natalie. "Then you turn around and get the fuck out of here, go home. He's gonna follow us because we're carrying all the bags."

Natalie, who was terrified of being left alone, didn't like the idea at all, but by then she had already reached the next stop sign. Before she could protest, the brothers were already out the door. The ruse worked. After the brothers bailed out of the car, Clayton backed up and tried to follow them, but they quickly lost him by jumping fences. The problem was that they weren't familiar with Denton, and soon found themselves slogging through a swamp on the outskirts of town. As the day wore on, the dejected brothers started arguing, then wound up getting into a small fistfight right there in the muck. By the time they finally found their way back to Susan's apartment, hours later, they were both covered in mud, shrub-cut, and exhausted.

Natalie, Susan, and Lucy were crying when they arrived, terrified that Art and Jason had been killed because Clayton had called and threatened as much. Art calmed the girls down and assured them that the dealer was simply talking tough. But Clayton did do something: He found the phone number and address of Art's aunt Donna, then called her house and threatened to burn it down unless he got his money and drugs back. That was as far as Art was willing to let it go. He and Jason hid in the woods again, waited for Clayton to leave his home, and gave him a South Side beating. By the time they were done, he not only promised to leave them alone, but left town altogether.

CRIME SO OFTEN POISONS RELATIONSHIPS that it's easy to forget its power to feed them. Although the Clayton robbery was a fiasco, for Art the episode's most surprising aspect wasn't getting caught: It was the women. "They were frightened, but they stood strong," he says. "And in spite of everything, they had a taste for it. I blame myself for that. I think in order to be a criminal, to a certain extent one has to have it in them, but I was the catalyst that brought it out. I straight-out corrupted them."

Art wasted little time devising a way he could use two of the women, Susan and Lucy, to hit drug dealers. On a trip across the Mexican border to Nuevo Laredo, he obtained a bottle of Rohypnol—

better known as the "date rape drug"—and starting taking the girls to honky-tonks. The group would perch themselves at a table where they could watch the bar, and Art would scout for cowboy drug dealers. Except for the boots and hats, they were as conspicuous as Chicago dealers. They carried the fat billfolds and beepers, and came and left the bar every ten minutes. After Art zeroed in on a mark, one of the girls would sidle up to the bar, take a nearby stool, and chat him up. Over the course of a few hours, the girls would let the dealers buy them drinks, growing increasingly flirtatious until coyly suggesting that the dealer take them back to his place. And when they'd pull out of the parking lot, Art and the other girls would be sharking right behind them.

Once a girl got inside a dealer's house, she'd fix him a drink and drop in the Rohypnol. The drug was infallible and magnificently fast, usually about fifteen minutes before a dealer passed out. The girl would open the front door and Art and the others would breeze right in. With the dealer out cold, they'd leisurely rifle the house until they found the drugs and cash, then drive away. "It was so easy it almost wasn't fair," Art muses.

Now fully back in the criminal life—and with a harem for a crew no less—Art wasn't so sure that staying straight was his best move. "There was too much opportunity in Texas. These rednecks were just clueless, the girls were down, and it wasn't like we were robbing nice people. These guys were dirtbags and we were kinda their reckoning." After getting into an argument with a coworker at a construction site, he quit his day job, rationalizing that the wages were too low anyway thanks to an overabundance of migrant workers from Mexico.

Not long after he and the girls began pulling the Rohypnol gambits, Art met Dave Pettis, a local from Denton who rode a motorcycle and seemed to share Art's appetite for excitement. Like Art,

Pettis talked big when he had a few drinks in him and came off as fearless, though in his case it was mostly a front. He had very little criminal experience, but Art took him under his wing, thinking that it might be useful to have a male crew member around. And within a week of meeting him, Pettis approached Art with a potential score. Pettis had a girlfriend whose father was a struggling jeweler. Times being tough, he was looking to liquidate his business, and figured the fastest way was to cash in on theft insurance. All he needed was someone to break into his house and steal his inventory; he'd report the theft and file his claim, and the hired thief would get to keep about twenty-five thousand dollars' worth of gems and precious metals. "I'd do it myself," he told Art, "but you have more experience with this than me, and we'll still have to break in and be smooth about it. He works from his home and he has neighbors and everything."

Art was not only flattered, but it sounded like a dream opportunity. Even if they somehow got arrested the jeweler wasn't going to press charges, and there'd also be no need for surveillance since they'd know exactly when he'd be out and for how long. The jeweler was leaving town the upcoming weekend, and he had told Pettis that he wouldn't report the theft until Sunday night.

On the designated Saturday, Dave and Art bought some gloves and a pry bar, then cased the house, a one-story home on the outskirts of Denton. Once it was dark, Art dropped Pettis off on the closest corner, then joined him after he'd pried his way in through the back door. Just as Dave had said, the house was dark and deserted, and he led Art straight to the jeweler's workshop. It was then that Art started to have misgivings. Even for a home business, the shop seemed little more than a tinkerer's den—a few power tools, a work lamp, some plastic bins of beads, and a file cabinet. When they pawed through the cabinet's drawers they found about thirty gold and silver chains and semiprecious stones, but nothing close to as valuable as what Dave had described. "It was like we were robbing somebody's artsy-and-craftsy grandma," Art says. "There was maybe five thousand dollars' worth of shit."

Dave seemed confused and dejected. He wanted to search the house more but Art insisted that they leave immediately. Whoever the jeweler was, he had either lied about his inventory or Dave had misled him. After Art threatened to leave him there alone, Dave reluctantly followed him back to the car. On the way back to Valley View, Dave drove fast and nervously, weaving in and out of traffic as Art chastised Pettis for lying to him about the merch. And it was smack in the middle of that harangue that the red and blue strobe lights of a cruiser from the Denton County Sheriff's Office graced the rearview mirror.

Art suspected that the deputies were pulling them over for a simple traffic violation, and he urged Dave to pull over and play it cool. But Pettis's nerves were overloading, and when one of the deputies approached the driver's side and asked him for his license and registration, he fumbled and failed to find them, then stammered as the deputy quizzed him as to where he was headed. Suspicious, the deputy requested to search the car—and Dave refused so adamantly that the cops went ahead and searched it anyway on the grounds that they had reason to believe there were drugs in the car.

They had placed the jeweler's goods into an old bowling-ball bag they'd found in the house, and when the police opened it and saw the chains and stones their suspicions were immediately aroused. The bag was monogrammed with the jeweler's name, which they used to look up his address. While Dave and Art waited, a unit was dispatched to the house, where officers quickly discovered signs of a break-in. The pair were arrested and taken to the Denton County Jail. A day later, they were both charged with burglary of a habitation—a first-degree felony that, under Texas's infamously harsh penal code, can carry a maximum sentence of twenty years.

Dave had lied about the whole enterprise—a nervous novice, he'd invented the story about the insurance scam as a way to enlist someone with more experience to commit a genuine robbery (though Art's familiarity with crime hadn't helped much when it came to assaying the trustworthiness of a fellow criminal). The only truth was that the jeweler had indeed been the father of Dave's girlfriend, but it turned out the two men hated each other, meaning the jeweler had every intention of pressing charges.

Having been caught with the stolen goods, Art knew that he had little chance of beating the rap. He could have attempted to cut a deal by testifying that Pettis had been the mastermind behind the burglary, but in his mind he was still in Bridgeport, where the only certain honor is resisting the opportunity to become a rat. Unhampered by any such code, Pettis told prosecutors that the burglary had been Art's idea and agreed to testify against him, winning himself probation. On the advice of his court-appointed lawyer, Art pleaded guilty to second-degree burglary of a habitation.

On January 12, 1996, a Denton County judge sentenced Art to six years in prison. With time served and good behavior, he and his lawyer calculated he'd do only three. But that would be plenty of time to reflect on the fact that he'd lost his freedom over a crime that, compared with his earlier stint as a counterfeiter, was low-rent, lowbrow, and high risk. Perhaps in that regard the reformatory powers of Texas's prison system would work; Art would never rob from an individual again, drug dealer or otherwise. From that point on, only one crime would consume his thoughts. What he didn't realize was that the rules of the world's second oldest profession were about to change.

BOOK TWO

7

BATTLE OF
THE BILL

Scarcely was the ink dry on the first note from the press of
the Treasury, before its bogus counterpart appeared in
circulation.

—LA FAYETTE CHARLES BAKER, 1867

On April 30, 1999—three years, two months, and nine
days after his robbery arrest—Art Williams stepped out
from behind the security gates of the Holiday Unit in
Huntsville like a man preserved in ice. He was dressed in the same
pair of jeans and white T-shirt he'd worn on the night of his arrest,
and in terms of his plans for the future, he hadn't evolved much
further. He had spent most of his time coping with the present reali-
ties of one of America's worst correctional systems.

While serving out his sentence, Art had gotten the grand tour of
Texas's penal system, which at the time was the second-largest in the
country and the fastest-growing system in the world. After riding
the merry-go-round through transfer and processing units like Gur-
ney, Moore, and Huntsville, he finally wound up at the Lopez State
Jail, which was both geographically and spiritually the ass end of the

system. Located at the southernmost tip of Texas in the town of Edinburg, it sat twelve miles from the Mexican border, in a parched, three-hundred-acre parcel that the twelve hundred prisoners farmed for vegetables while shotgun-bearing guards on horseback watched over them like extras from every bad prison movie ever made. During the summer, temperatures routinely broke a hundred degrees Fahrenheit while humidity from the Gulf of Mexico turned the whole place into a soul-sapping sweatbox. Although the unit was brand new, it was brutally Spartan: there was no air-conditioning to speak of, and prisoners often had to boil their own water to make it drinkable. The running joke among the inmates was that they were no longer in the United States. "We're in fucking Mexico," they'd say, and invent stories about how then-governor George W. Bush had struck a deal under NAFTA to export Texas's prisoners south of the Rio Grande.

"It was just hell," Art remembers. "It was a hundred degrees in a tin box, and people were so angry because of the heat. At different times of the season we'd have billions of mosquitoes and they had to cancel rec because people were getting eaten up. When you could go to the rec yard, there were also rattlesnakes. You're hitting iron, and fucking baby rattlesnakes are coming up behind you!" The social ills weren't much better. Statistically, Texas was the state where an inmate was most likely to be raped, and most likely to die in prison. A few years after Art was sentenced, a federal judge (who was aptly named William Justice) declared that Texas's penal system was rife with "a culture of sadistic and malicious violence." Art participated in it firsthand. Early on, another inmate had demanded he hand over some of his commissary goods, a brief exchange that resulted in the other inmate winding up in the hospital and Art spending a month in solitary confinement. That was the only time he was attacked, but on numerous occasions he faced

down other inmates, mostly blacks and Mexicans, who are dispro-
portionately represented in Texas. Having come from Chicago,
where race is less important than your gang affiliation, Art found the
self-segregation utterly weird. Most of the time he read books and
kept to himself. As one of the few inmates who could read and write
well, he ended up working in administration, which was considered
a cushy job.

Throughout it all, the one bright spot in his life was the quiet
girl he'd barely gotten to know before he went to prison: Natalie
Silva. Prior to his arrest, he'd had a couple romantic encounters with
her, but after he went to jail she'd had a brief fling with another man
that resulted in a son, Alex. Art naturally assumed she'd fade away,
but she'd surprised him by visiting him early on, then followed up by
writing him letters. She was the only one of the four girls who stayed
in contact with him once he was sentenced, and over the years the
letters never stopped, nor did her visits. She trailed him throughout
the system, filing her name on visitor-request forms and driving
hundreds of miles to whenever he was transferred. "I was in love
with Art the first moment I saw him," she'd later confess, "but I
would have been stupid to tell him that. I was young, he was dating
my friend, and he definitely wasn't husband material. But he was
unlike anyone I've ever met. I have very little tolerance for stupid
people, and the thing about Art—other than the fact that he is very,
very good-looking—is that he has brains. Yeah, he was a criminal,
but to me that always came second."

For both of them, Lopez—576 miles from Denton—was the
ultimate test. Art would have understood if she'd visited him once a
year, but once a month Natalie would hop in her Toyota on a Friday
and set off on a ten-hour drive. She'd pop Metabolife diet pills to
stay awake and sleep at rest stops when they wore off. After washing
her hair and doing her makeup in a gas station restroom, she'd show

up in Lopez's visiting room on Saturday afternoon looking like she'd just stepped off a private jet. The permissible visiting time was four hours, and when it expired she'd turn right back around to be at her ticketing-agent job at Dallas–Fort Worth International Airport by Monday morning.

Natalie was right outside the gate when Art was released. She drove him back to her place, made love to him, and over the next few weeks offered him encouragement as he looked for a legitimate job. "Initially he had a positive attitude about going straight. He got up early every day and found a job framing houses, like he did before. And he went to work. But after a couple weeks he became quiet, depressed. And then he started complaining about the jobs not paying enough."

Art was earning seven dollars an hour for backbreaking labor. Since the work itself was intermittent, and he was wrestling to help support his nine year old son up in Chicago, he began to slip into the old victim's mind-set. "I know every criminal says this," he says, "but it's almost like the system *wants* you to commit another crime. Since you're a felon, nobody wants to hire you, and those who do are paying you shit because they know they can get away with it. At the same time, most prisons don't do shit to give you skills. They get the more educated inmates to teach classes. Needless to say, they aren't the best teachers. I know it sounds lame, but if you've never stood in those shoes, you don't know. You start thinking about how much money you used to make as a crook. And once you start thinking like that it's hard to stop. Then that opportunity comes along, and suddenly you're back in it."

A few weeks after Art was released, he and Natalie visited a local Barnes & Noble. Feeling depressed about his work situation, he wanted to pick up a copy of the *Tao of Jeet Kune Do* by Bruce Lee, who he'd found inspiring ever since he was a kid. Art hadn't been paid yet from his construction job, and as they stood in line Natalie gave him a brand new C-note to pay for the book. He had barely gotten a look at the bill before handing it to the cashier, but in those brief seconds his curiosity ignited with the shattering alacrity of buried ordnance.

The hundred-dollar bill, he was astonished to see, had changed.

AMERICA'S CURRENCY had already begun to change as early as 1990, the year the Bureau of Engraving and Printing instituted the security strip and microprinting. Hold any bill except a dollar note in front of a light source, and the strip appears as a vertical line, with "USA," the denomination, and an American flag running its length. Made of a 1.4mm-wide polyester thread, the strip is embedded in the bill and invisible unless it's backlit. It foils counterfeiters who use copiers because the flash bulb exposes the strip, leaving a jarring black line across the copy. If exposed to ultraviolet light, the thread will also beautifully fluoresce: red for a hundred, yellow for a fifty, green for a twenty, and so on. Microprinting, the second change, installed the words *The United States of America* in the window framing the portraits, in letters six to seven thousandths of an inch wide—too small for most copiers or scanners to register without blurred results. Over the ensuing three years, the measures were extended to all but the dollar bill.

Both of those changes—neither of which affected the look that U.S. currency had maintained since 1929—had been instituted to combat rapidly developing reprographic technology, which by the mid-1980s had become so good that even nine-to-fivers were increasingly flirting with counterfeiting. Every month newer, more advanced color-copiers, printers, and scanners were entering offices, where one of the first things curious employees did was lay a twenty on the glass, press start, and see what came out of the dispenser—call it the counterfeiting reflex. For the overwhelming majority it was an innocent game that resulted in a momentary thrill followed by a trip to the shredder. But by 1985 the copiers were becoming so advanced that the Treasury Department commissioned the National Materials Advisory Board to research ways of making U.S. currency more secure. The resulting report recommended sweeping changes to the currency, including the institution of a watermark, more complex printing patterns, and an invisible "security thread" specifically meant to foil color copying machines. In the best bureaucratic tradition, Treasury shelved the report, only to commission another study two years later that reached virtually identical conclusions. But the department worried that radical aesthetic changes in the currency would undermine the distinctiveness and continuity of the dollar—and therefore the value of the dollar itself. Compromising, they ignored most of the second report and adopted the two least intrusive changes.

The 1990 modifications failed dismally. Despite an extensive publicity campaign, few people ever knew the strip existed, and since the average lifespan of a hundred-dollar bill is about seven and a half years, counterfeiters simply continued running off older bills. People were equally oblivious of the microprinting because all but the most hawkeyed needed a magnifying glass to see it. Treasury had been so obsessed about preserving the continuity of the greenback's appearance that they had effectively minimized their anticounterfeiting improvements. Back in his Dungeon days, Art hadn't even bothered with the strip because he'd never seen anyone look for it, and he'd found that as long as he could approximate the size and spacing of the microprinted words, no one closely inspected those either. "I was far more worried about the pen," he says.

The counterfeit-detector "pen"—patented only a year after the security strip was introduced—was a felt-tipped marker with a yellow, iodine-based ink that turned dark brown when it reacted to the starch binding agent contained in most paper. Since currency is starch-free, the ink stays yellow on cash—a fast, apparently simple way to test a bill. By 1995, a company called Dri Mark was selling about two million pens a year for approximately three dollars each, and promoting them as a pen "that detects authenticity of U.S. currency instantly." Major chains like 7-Eleven were using the pens to test all hundred-dollar bills. The pen was so effective and popular that, toward the end of his Dungeon days, Art had started printing twenties and tens on specific occasions just to avoid it.

By 1993, only three years after the Series 1990 note entered circulation, the amount of counterfeit bills produced using electro-photographic equipment was doubling every year. Scanners, ink-jet printers, and computers were developing so fast that they were even beginning to replicate microprinting. Many of the new counterfeiters were teenagers, natural masters of new technology who wanted spending money. They'd run off a few twenties and try to pass them at music stores or McDonald's. The Secret Service dubbed them "digifeiters," a name that offered little consolation to elite agents who were now spending much of their time chasing kids. Under pressure from both the Service and the Federal Reserve, the Treasury Department decided to take drastic measures. America's currency, it concluded, needed a complete overhaul. For the first time in sixty-six years the almighty dollar was going to change.

Treasury formed the New Currency Design Task Force, a group of a dozen men and women led by a bright, career BEP official named Thomas Ferguson who had been skeptical of the 1990 changes as being too moderate. With free rein to design a completely new currency, Ferguson immediately went about implementing security measures the likes of which Americans had never seen. The final product, which Art first glimpsed that day in the bookstore, was the Series 1996 hundred-dollar note, and it was so unlike every other bill before it that Treasury simply called it the "New Note."

The first change—and the most visually dramatic—was Franklin's portrait. Using the original Duplessis painting as a guide, BEP engravers enlarged it by fifty percent. The new, "supersized" portrait accommodated much greater detail and line count, making it far more difficult for scanners to render. A straight scan would also produce a "moiré pattern"—an optical effect that turned the portrait's otherwise muted background into a jarring mess of geometric waves upon printing. Even Franklin's lapel was microprinted with the words *United States of America.*

The denomination marks were the next most notable change. As in the portrait, the BEP enlarged them to include fine lines, but the mark on the lower right-hand corner boasted something truly space-age. It was now a bright, metallic green, which changed to black depending on the angle you looked at it. The technology behind it, optically variable or "color-shifting" ink, was based on the same protective film that coats the windows of the Space Shuttle.

There were also many small, less noticeable changes as well. The back of the note—which had long been easy prey for counterfeiters because of its uniform color—also featured fine line, moiré-producing printing in the oval around Independence Hall. There was an extra serial number, a new Federal Reserve indicator, a universal seal, and numbers indicating which plate had been used for production, but these were mostly for internal tracking purposes. Out of all the changes, the one that turned out to be the most effective was one of the oldest printing techniques in the book.

Hold any U.S. bill above a dollar in front of a light source, and as in the moon letters of fantasy novels you will suddenly see a smoky image paralleling the portrait. This is the watermark, a printing technique invented by Italian papermakers in the thirteenth century. Although it was otherwise invisible, unlike the security strip it smacked of mystery, a secret image that was not only incredibly difficult to replicate, but also harkened back to something runic and old-world. There was a little bit of magic in the watermark that caught people's interest—and that, by far, would be its greatest power.

The New Note was released to the world on Monday, March 25, 1996—less than two months after Art Williams disappeared into the rabbit hole of Texas's penal system. On that day, hundreds of armored trucks set out from the nation's thirty-seven Federal Reserve offices. In a wondrous system that has gone on almost every weekday since 1913, their holds were filled with bills meant to satisfy America's $125-billion-a-day appetite for paper currency. There's no other word for it but *circulation*. Like blood cells from the heart, the bills had been pumped out from the BEP's presses in Washington, D.C., and Fort Worth, then distributed to the Fed offices, which in turn trucked them to roughly 7,600 commercial banks. From there, they were destined for the pockets of 280 million Americans, the vast majority of whom—for lack of a more exchangeable medium—considered the greenback both the means and the embodiment of attaining their very dreams on earth.

Despite an intensive publicity campaign under the Treasury Department's "Know Your Money" program, Americans greeted the new bills with almost universal skepticism. The off-center portrait of Benjamin Franklin, whose head had ballooned overnight, bore the brunt of the derision. "Big Head Ben," people quickly nicknamed him, and that was about as flattering a description the bill received. Newspapers relished printing articles about just how ugly the New Note was. A stockbroker in Fort Lauderdale told the *Florida Sun-Sentinel* that the new bill looked like "Monopoly money," while Primo

Angeli, a San Francisco graphic designer, called it "tacky" and declared to a *Washington Post* reporter that the note was "the cheapest hundred-dollar bill I've ever seen." One *Post* columnist advised people to hang on to their old currency and cited the New Note as the beginning of "an era of Ugly Money." Some cashiers refused to accept the bills altogether. A resident of Kenosha, Wisconsin—the same town where the pot dealer who took Art's first counterfeits lived—was forced to return to the bank for change after clerks at both a grocery store and a gas station deemed the bill "too suspicious-looking" to honor.

What the media failed to recognize was that, for the first time in sixty-six years, Americans were assimilating the components of their cash. In bars and banks and restaurants, they held the weird new bills up to the light and discussed the changes with their friends. Even as they ridiculed the new design, they learned more about the security features of their currency than any previous generation.

For counterfeiters, it all meant very bad news.

ART HAD READ AN ARTICLE about the new currency while in prison. At the time he'd been intrigued, but the ennui of life inside had all but drained any recollection that he would be seeing a new bill upon his release. And when he finally did see it there at the checkout line in the Barnes & Noble, like everyone else, he had to take a closer look.

"You got any more of those hunds?" he asked Natalie the moment they cleared the counter. They sat down in the bookstore's café and she dug another bill from her purse. He held it between his thumbs, studying it as if it were an alien artifact. Everything about the New Note impressed him: the portrait, the color-shifting ink, and particularly the watermark, which he immediately recognized as the most ingenious addition. Light beamed through the bookstore windows, and he held the bill up to a pane, marveling at how Franklin's ghostly image vanished with the slightest angular shift. He twisted the front, watching the nacreous play of color across the denomination mark. Even the feel of the bill, the hundreds of extra ridges on the portrait, was different. "They put a lot of work into this," he thought.

Art was silent on the way home from the bookstore. Seeing the new bill had roused not only his imagination, but also old feelings of possibility and challenge. The bill felt like a dare to him, a taunting and intricate lock whose challenge was as enticing as the reward behind it. But it was Natalie who first spoke the idea.

"How hard do you think it would be to counterfeit it?" she asked him. She insists that she spoke the question more out of curiosity than a desire to try. Although Art hadn't counterfeited in nearly five years, he'd mentioned the crime a few times since they'd met and she'd always wondered how he'd done it.

Art told her he didn't know. But right then it wasn't the new modifications he was thinking about. It was the pen. "It seems to me if people are putting so much faith in that damn pen, then they might not even be looking at the rest of the bill," he said. "Beat the pen and you've got a way in, you're halfway there."

"I bet you could do it," Natalie said gamely. Seeing her interest, Art started to wonder himself.

Once again a conversation had begun. When they got home, for the first time since his release, Art became animated and hopeful. Over beers, he told Natalie stories about da Vinci and the Dungeon days; about how he had learned from the best and, for a brief while, lived the good life. He told her about how he'd been treated like a king by Chicago's biggest criminal organizations, and the incredible feeling of seeing sheets of freshly minted counterfeit slide off a press. The hundred-dollar bill came out of Natalie's purse again and Art began theorizing about inks and chemical reactions, paper density and polymers.

By the end of the night, Natalie had agreed to front him three thousand dollars and let him set up a temporary print shop in her apartment. But this time it would function more as a laboratory. Its main purpose would be for experimentation, because their goal was not to merely print counterfeit, but to pursue what would become a Holy Grail quest: creating a perfect replica of the 1996 New Note.

CHOOSING WHICH DENOMINATION to counterfeit was a no-brainer for Williams. Even though the new fifty- and twenty-dollar notes were also circulating by 1999, the hundred-dollar bill offered the greatest potential profit, and it was the security prototype for every other denomination. If he could crack it, then the entire currency line would be vulnerable. He knew that there could be little room for error. The new hundreds were more scrutinized than any bill ever created before—a quality that made the potential reward all the more enticing.

Knowing that breaking the New Note could take months, Art planned to initially print and sell pre–Series 1996 twenties and tens, bills that were rarely subjected to the Dri Mark pen. The proceeds from these lower denominations, he figured, would allow him to upgrade his equipment and keep afloat while he experimented. He was so confident that no one would inspect the small denominations that he didn't even bother going to a printer for high-quality newsprint; instead, he bought several stacks of high-quality printer paper and ran off fifty thousand dollars in old twenties, then approached a friend he'd made at Lopez in the hopes of turning a fast deal. His friend was a stocky, amicable Irish kid named Toby McClellan, but

Art called him "Garfield" because of his pudgy face and red hair. Like Art, McClellan was fairly fresh out of prison and low on cash, so Art fronted him twenty thousand dollars in counterfeit on the condition that he'd get paid as soon as McClellan moved it. True to his word, McClellan unloaded the money within a week, paid Art, then presented him with another proposition.

"I know a heroin dealer who's interested in counterfeit," McClellan explained, "but he's cash poor right now and doesn't want to pay for it upfront. He wants you to front him so he can mix it into a heroin buy, then pay you after he's turned it around. Or he can just give you some of the dope."

Art was dubious. He had never fronted a stranger counterfeit before, much less a heroin dealer. But he was desperate for funds, so he agreed to meet McClellan's friend. The junk dealer, a guy named Ritchie, seemed serious enough when Art met him. He explained that he already had the heroin buy lined up with some Mexicans in Dallas—reliable sellers who he'd done business with before. Despite his misgivings, Art agreed to front Ritchie twenty thousand dollars with one provision:

"I'm going with you on the buy," Art told him. "I don't know you, and I've done this kind of thing before." Ritchie agreed, but what neither he nor McClellan told Art was that the counterfeit he had fronted McClellan a few weeks earlier had gone to the same Mexicans they were about to meet. In his haste to raise funds for his work on the New Note, Art had never asked McClellan that all-important question: Where are the bills headed? And when they showed up to the buy, Art immediately got a bad feeling.

"We pulled into this apartment complex, and these Mexicans were on their shit," he remembers. "They had walkie-talkies, earpieces, and all that stuff. We walk into the apartment, and there's two Mexicans in the apartment. One's sitting in the living room and one's in the kitchen. I follow Ritchie in, and the guy in the kitchen immediately gives me the eye. He looked crazy to me, a serious gangbanger."

"Who's this *vato*?" the dealer asked Ritchie, pointing to Art. After Ritchie explained that Art was on the level, the dealer nodded and they sat down at the kitchen table and got down to business. Ritchie told the dealer that he wanted an eighth of a key, about seven thousand dollars' worth, then dumped the money from a bag onto the table. Half of it was counterfeit.

At first the dealer seemed unfazed. He got on the walkie-talkie and ordered his associates, who were at another location, to bring in the drugs. At least that's what Art assumed, since the conversation was in Spanish. As they waited for the delivery, the dealer counted the money, his fingers moving ever more slowly through the stacks.

"You know, the last time you came here you gave me some bad money," the dealer said. "I go to the store, and they mark it with the pen, and it don't come back. What was that all about?"

Art's heart began to pound. He could tell by the dealer's eyes that he was fully aware that Ritchie was attempting to salt the money again.

"You're kidding me," Ritchie said, playing dumb.

"No, I'm not, *vato*," the dealer said calmly. "I bought a pen myself and found a whole bunch of them."

There was little doubt in Art's mind where this was heading. "This dealer was crazy, and he had his shit together," he says. "I knew that whoever was on the other end of that walkie-talkie wasn't bringing in no drugs. They were gonna come in and trap us in there. They were about to put bullets in us."

Art was sitting with his back to the door. He leaned his chair away from the table, listening for footsteps. The Mexican in the living room, he noticed, had his eye on the door as well, and once the bagman arrived their only exit would be blocked.

As soon as the door opened and the new arrival entered, Art leapt out of his chair, slammed the bagman to the side, then bolted out of the apartment. Remembering his Chicago street rules, he had parked Natalie's car on the main road just outside the apartment complex, far enough away so he wouldn't be trapped on the lot. He sped off and left Ritchie to his fate, later learning that the dealer survived the wrath of the Mexicans by blaming the counterfeit solely on Art.

The incident's lesson was loud and clear: "Right at that point I knew I had to step it up a notch," says Art. "I couldn't go with the old money that didn't mark properly. It had to change."

Art had already done plenty of research on the pen. He knew that because it reacted to the acidic starch contained in the newsprint, there were only two ways to beat it: either prevent the reaction from taking place by means of a chemical blocker, or find a new, acid-free paper to print on. He decided to pursue both options; while he searched for a substance that would block the pen, Natalie engaged in a phone campaign, calling as many national paper manufacturers as she could find and having samples sent to a P.O. box.

For all of the popularity and faith people put in the pen, Art was surprised by how fast they got results. After visiting several art- and printing-supply stores, he found numerous solutions that moderated the pen's effect—various gelatins, acid-free glosses, and even hair spray prevented the ink from turning dark brown. At one point, just out of curiosity, he even treated some newsprint with glutamine gel— a fitness supplement he used for bodybuilding—and found that it turned the Dri Mark ink amber. While neither it nor the other treatments produced the bright, affirming yellow of real currency, the important thing was that none of them marked black. Counterfeiting is an art of satisfying expectations, and the treatments were just yellow enough to be believable. The only drawback of the chemicals was that they tended to alter the surface of the newsprint, turning it slightly chalky or glossy, and it was only a matter of weeks before they decayed and lost their effectiveness. Despite his success at moderating the pen, Art hoped that Natalie's paper hunt would produce even better results.

Never one to aim low, Art had her start by calling Crane & Co., the Massachusetts-based paper company that's been supplying the Treasury Department since 1879. Other than its seventy-five to twenty-five percent linen and cotton formula, the precise technique Crane uses to create U.S. banknote paper—the most durable in the world— is a closely guarded national secret. When she asked a sales rep if they had anything available to the public that "approximated the wonderful feel and look of their currency paper" the response was a curt and resounding "No." But there are hundreds of other paper companies in North America. Using false identities, she called in dozens of samples, then tested them with the Dri Mark pen. Weeks of disappointment followed as sample after sample marked black. She grew increasingly exasperated as Art, convinced that a ready-made paper was out there, constantly badgered her to try more companies. "He acted like it was my fault we weren't finding the paper," she says, "I wasn't calling the right companies or looking in the right places." And then one day, after listening to Art complain once again that she wasn't producing results, she finally snapped.

"What else do you want me try?" she said as she stood in the kitchen with the pen in her hand. "Maybe these paper towels will work." She marked the towels viciously. "Nope, black. How about toilet paper? Or wait, here's a cereal box." She began running around the room, angrily marking everything she saw. "Aha, here's a phone book. The same phone book I've been using to call fucking paper companies. Haven't tried *this*," she said acidly, and stroked the pen all the way across one of the white pages. That's when both of their jaws dropped.

The ink marked bright yellow.

They gaped at each other in disbelief, then started marking again and again to make sure it wasn't some fluke of chemistry. When it came back yellow every time, they realized that the answer to the Dri Mark pen had, after all, been literally in the phone book: directory paper. They did a little victory dance, then Natalie found the name of the printer in the front of the book. She then called the printing house and asked them where they purchased their paper. The name they gave her was Abitibi Consolidated, and Natalie quickly learned on the Internet that Abitibi was the largest producer of newsprint in the world. Based in Montreal, it was an $8-billion-a-year operation, with mills, recycling centers, and offices in more than eighty countries. The company was such a monster that when she called the main office in Canada and asked for some samples of various thicknesses, they all but laughed at her. "Uh, we don't deal in *sheets*," a sales-department representative smugly told her. "We deal in the kinds of quantities if you were, say, a city." But Natalie was able to get the names of a few printing-house clients in Texas. One of them was only twenty miles away in Arlington. She hurriedly called the printer and requested samples. That's when they hit the first of many brick walls.

Paper thickness is measured by what's called "basis weight"— the amount that five hundred sheets weigh, according to standardized types and sizes. United States currency paper has a basis weight of about thirty-five pounds, but the thickest the directory paper came in was twenty-four pounds—far too thin. They called other companies that produced directory paper, but the sizes were all comparably thin.

They were crestfallen, but since Art had already figured out several workable barriers to the Dri Mark ink, they were still very much in business. Setting the Abitibi paper samples aside, they eagerly moved on to the bill itself.

THE OPTICALLY VARIABLE INK—OVI for short—was one of the most technologically advanced security features of the New Note. It appears on the denomination mark on the lower right-hand side of every bill above five dollars. Hold the bill in front of your face, turning it slowly, and the ink will "color-shift" from black to a glittery brass to metallic green, depending on the angle. The ink, produced by a company based in Santa Rosa, California, called Flex Products, is patented technology.

Art assumed it was unobtainable. The best he hoped for was an approximation—a glittery, metallic ink that provided the twinkling illusion of shift, just enough to keep the ruse going. While there was no shortage of glittery inks, none of them were convincing enough, and he once again settled into an uncompromising hunt. By now Art's eyes were constantly sucking in the shades and colors of his surroundings, his mind parsing them for correlative possibilities. He hoped that if he just kept looking he'd see the ink—or at least a material that mimicked the color-shift effect—somewhere in the world around him.

One day while he was walking through a parking lot in Dallas, he spotted a limited edition 1996 Mustang Cobra. The car itself was enough to inspire Art, a 'Stang connoisseur, to take closer look, but as he approached the vehicle something else caught his eye.

The Mustang's color shifted, from purple-black to deep blue.

"I kept walking back and forth, watching the color change, and forgot all about the car," he says. "Hell, I knew right away if I could get ahold of that paint I could buy my own Cobra! That mother-fucker was shifting color, just like the denomination mark."

Within an hour he was ringing auto-body shops and getting the lowdown on Ford's paint. What he subsequently discovered blew his mind. He learned that the paint contained a patented pigment called ChromaFlair, and although the '96 Cobra was the first production ve-hicle to feature it, custom shops had been using it for several years. ChromaFlair came in five different color shifts and was even available in spray-paint form, but the most startling thing about the pigment was its manufacturer: Flex Products, Inc.—the same company that supplied secure color-shifting ink to the BEP and window shading for NASA. Flex had gone ahead and marketed its technology to the pri-vate sector, meaning that citizens could legally obtain the same tech-nology behind one of the New Note's most lauded security features.

And as a private citizen, Art went about obtaining it. Although the green-to-black pigment was exclusive to the BEP, he easily bought a green-to-silver paint that beautifully replicated the true shift. "It was even better because it had a little bit of flash," he says, "and flash was what people expected when they looked for the shift." Unfortu-nately, the ChromaFlair couldn't be run through an offset press or an ink-jet printer because it was paint, but Art devised a novel solu-tion. He scanned the denomination marks on both the hundred- and five-dollar bills, then touched them up with Photoshop and rear-ranged the numbers so they read "1005." He then went to the most ubiquitous printing source on the planet—Kinko's.

"I'm a small businessman and I need to make an address stamp for my stationery," he told the clerk, explaining that he liked the font on U.S. currency because "it represents success." Could Kinko's convert his 1005 scan into a rubber stamp?

"No problem," the clerk told him. Of all the proprietary components in U.S. currency, it turns out that the most obvious element—the very style of lettering—is the least controlled. Companies like Adobe, Apple, and Microsoft possess exclusive rights to their fonts, but the most valuable font of all, that of the U.S. dollar, is public property.

Two days later Art picked up his stamp at Kinko's. He sliced off the 5 with an X-Acto knife, dipped the remaining 100 section into the automotive paint, then applied it to a sheet of newsprint. Once the paint dried, he took the sheet outside to study it under natural light.

As he turned it again and again, he marveled at what he saw. The paint shifted seamlessly from green to silver, like electric skin on some exotic, iridescent beetle.

WITH THE PEN AND OVI PROBLEMS SOLVED, Art took on the New Note's most daunting challenge: the watermark. Ever since he'd first seen it that day at Barnes & Noble he'd known that replicating it would be his biggest battle, one that he was by no means convinced he could win. "The watermark had nothing to do with printing or inks," he explains, "it was something out of my skill set, not something I was comfortable with. So I put it off as I looked at other parts of the bill, but it nagged me the whole time because I knew I'd have to deal with it, and there was no clear way around it."

The irony was that the watermark was the least innovative part of the bill—Old World technology that was virtually unchanged since the thirteenth century. Created during the papermaking process by a wire mesh device called a "dandy roll," a watermark is simply an area of low density in the paper's substrate that allows transmitted light to pass through. Because the watermarking process takes place when the paper pulp is wet, the mark itself is literally built into the bill and impossible to duplicate by printing.

One method by which counterfeiters were attempting to defeat the watermark was by taking new ten-dollar bills, bleaching them, then reprinting them as hundreds. This had the advantage of preserving not only the original paper, but also the watermark and the security strip, and as long as people saw both they usually accepted them—even if they were the wrong ones for that denomination. Later on, after the new five-dollar bill was issued, "bleaching" became even more economical, but it still involved altering large amounts of real currency. For this reason its practitioners were usually large criminal groups, many of them from South America, where drug cash is abundant. Art simply didn't have the capital to buy up thousands of ten-dollar bills and bleach them. More to the point, a bleached bill would never pass muster on that one vendor who actually knew his money. Art wanted a bill that would defeat that guy, or as he put it, "a bill that would go all the way to the bank."

At first Art dabbled with the idea of making his own paper. He dissolved some newsprint until it became an oatmeal-like pulp, pressed it onto a screen, and ran a homemade dandy roll across it, then baked it in Natalie's oven. Although the end result was indeed homemade paper with a watermark, the amount of work it had taken made it self-evident that he'd never be able to produce it in the quantities or quality he needed. He also tried soaking existing paper samples in water and various other softening solutions before stamping them, but the result was always the same: flaky, deteriorated paper that would never pass. After a dozen dead-end attempts, he was at a complete loss and on the verge of giving up. He says that the answer finally came to him in a dream.

"My mind had become like a computer program that runs during sleep mode. Even when I wasn't thinking about counterfeiting, I was. It was constantly there."

"He woke me up," Natalie remembers. "He actually said, 'I got it,' like I was supposed to know what he was talking about. I was like, 'Good for you, you got it. Tell me about it tomorrow.'"

In his dream, Art had seen two pieces of paper, like slices of bread on a sandwich. Nestled between them was a thin square of paper bearing Franklin's portrait, so thin that it didn't alter the feel or look of the bill, but thick enough so that it was visible under transmitted light. The next morning he had Natalie run out and buy the thinnest tracing paper she could find, then penciled an image of Franklin on it. That was the sandwich's meat, and Natalie had already found the bread three months earlier: the Abitibi directory paper. It had been too thin to replicate currency paper, but Art had never considered that two sheets pasted together would almost perfectly duplicate the thickness of genuine currency. After cutting out the image of Franklin he'd penciled onto the tracing paper, he dug up the samples from Abitibi, then laid the portrait between them and held the sheets in front of a light.

"The moment we saw it we knew we'd done it," he says. "It was just *there*. It sent chills up my spine. It was beyond anything I'd ever done. Even that first crappy drawing on tracing paper looked real. It scared me. That was something way beyond what Pete had taught me. He never did anything like that. That was me, my own innovation."

The beauty of the "twin sheet" solution to the watermark was that it also solved the problem of the security strip: Minicounterfeits of both could be slipped between sheets bearing the front and back images of the bill, which Art could then glue together and solidify using a select group of over-the-counter sprays. Once he realized this, he went out and bought red UV ink for his ink-jet printer (amazingly, that is an over-the-counter product too), then printed his own security strips on the same tracing paper he used for the watermark.

The final security feature of the New Note—the microprinting— turned out to be the easiest to defeat. Just as Treasury had miscalculated how fast reprographic technology would progress back in '89, by 1999 the ink-jets and software were good enough to render a convincing replica in the right hands. Those hands turned out to be Natalie's; she spent days working over scans in Photoshop until they shone like the real thing to all but the most trained eye. Even then, Art insisted that they still use an offset press for the seals and to color the background of the bill. "I don't care how good the technology gets. There are things an offset press can do that a computer never will. If I thought a computer could do those things better, I would have used it. But for me it wasn't about easy, I was obsessed. The funny thing was that there was this point when it wasn't about profit anymore. It was about the art, seeing if I could do it."

When the prototype of their New Note was finished—a good four months after Art had gotten out of prison—he and Natalie bought a digital scale. They'd been so caught up with how the bill looked that they'd never considered weight during their research process, and were now happy enough with the results that they didn't really care. But Art, as always, was curious, so they laid it on the scale. Their bill weighed exactly one gram. Precisely the weight of all genuine U.S. currency.

8

"EVERYBODY WILL WANT"

Despite all the grumping here about unresponsive government; and despite the tut-tutting abroad about American hegemonism and cultural decay—the eager acceptance of the new U.S. C-note proves that people everywhere have faith in the stability that flows from freedom in the United States of America.

–WILLIAM SAFIRE, IN *The New York Times*,
COMMENTING ON THE HIGH FOREIGN DEMAND
FOR THE NEW NOTE AHEAD OF ITS RELEASE,
DECEMBER 4, 1995

Tony Puntillo—Art's old wheelman from the Dungeon days—remembers being at a party in the fall of 1999 when Art walked in the door, Texas-tan with eyes bright with secrets. Puntillo hadn't seen Williams in four years, not since he'd run off to Texas after his relationship with Karen fell apart. After the two caught up over a few beers, Art asked him to step outside for a moment.

"We went out the front door, then he just sorta smiled and

handed me a hundred-dollar bill, one of the new ones," Puntillo re-members. "I looked at it and my first reaction was, 'What's this for?' Last I knew he didn't owe me any money. He just kept smiling and said, 'Just look at it.' So I did. He made sure I looked at everything. The watermark, the strip, the ink. Then he tells me it's one of his. I didn't believe the jagoff at first because I honestly couldn't tell the difference. It blew my mind. He's gone four years and then he shows up with *this*."

Art told Tony that he'd be calling and made sure he remembered the pager code they'd used back in the Dungeon days. He left one of his bills with him as a gift. They were about to become the most effective business cards in the Chicago underworld.

Over the next few weeks, Art made the rounds, always showing up unannounced and with a casual attitude before springing the new bill on his old clients. When they saw it, their reactions were universally ecstatic and so similar that he would later give it a nickname—the Glow. "They would get this look on their face," he says, "a look of wonder, almost like they were on drugs. It was like they were imagining the possibilities of what it could do for them, and they wanted more." Sandy immediately asked for three hundred thousand dollars, while Dmitri was so enthusiastic that he tried to convince Art to print millions. "He told me he'd set me up anywhere in the world, with bodyguards from St. Petersburg to protect me. He was serious. It sounded pretty good and I even thought about it for a moment, but the problem was that then I'd be working for him. Once I left the country, I'd lose control. I'd be like a bird in a cage."

Only the Horse was circumspect. While Art had been away in prison, he had gained intermittent access to what may well have been the only note on the planet better than Art's—the hundred-dollar bill that the Secret Service calls the "Supernote." Like Art's bill, the Supernote contained every security feature of the New Note, the major difference being that it was produced on an intaglio press similar to the ones used by the U.S. government. All of the bill's features and production processes, in fact, were so identical to real currency that distinguishing the notes usually required lab analysis. It had first appeared in Hong Kong in 1989 and since then the Secret Service has been oddly ambivalent about its origins. At different times, experts have linked the Supernote to Iran, East Germany, China, and, most often, North Korea—the sole agreement being that the only entity capable of creating it is a national government with accesses to tens of million of dollars. Some have even theorized that the Supernote is created by the United States government itself and used abroad to fund "black" operations outside of the national defense budget.

Whatever the Supernote's origins, On Leong had gained access to it during Art's hiatus from counterfeiting, and upon seeing Art's bill the Horse acknowledged as much, throwing him a backhanded compliment. "This bill is really good, Art," he said, "but we've still got you beat with the Supernote."

He then placed an order for a hundred thousand dollars, at thirty cents on the dollar.

Art found himself in the awkward position of telling all of his clients that they had to wait. Although he'd guessed that his new bill would be a hit, he had no idea that demand would come so quickly and with such high numbers—way beyond both his production capacity and his nerve. "They all wanted so much, and right then," he says. "And of course they had no idea how hard it was to make. Hell, at that point, I was still figuring out how to produce it on a large scale."

Mikey was at his lifeguard post at the Sheridan Park pool when Art showed up with the note. As his most trusted adviser, crime partner, and friend, he had bitter feelings when Art had left Chicago.

"We had made good money together, and Arty had thrown away a profitable business only to wind up in prison because of a stupid move," he says. But once he saw the new bill, his feelings of abandonment dissipated like midwinter spindrift off Lake Michigan. "He'd done it. That's all there was to it. He'd beaten the new bill. I wasn't surprised in the sense that it was him, because I always knew the boy had brains, but this was something special. That bill was perfect. You really couldn't tell the difference. Oh, I knew right away that we were going to make a lot of money."

Mikey wasted no time setting up Art's first firm deal with the new money. The client was a bookmaker he knew, Jimmy Amodio, who also ran a social club near Taylor Street. All he had to do was present Jimmy with the new money and a proposition: With the NFL play-offs approaching, what better way to cover his losses than by using this new *fugazi* for payouts? The bookmaker jumped on the idea and ordered up fifty thousand dollars. As always, there was a catch.

"He wants it tomorrow," Mikey explained to Art. "How can we make this happen?" Art told him that it was impossible. Although he and Natalie had printed and cut about a hundred thousand dollars in fronts and backs before leaving Texas, he had no place to assemble, dry, and wrap it, and it was a task he could never complete on time by himself. Mikey's solution would reveal one of the greatest strengths of Art's design.

"If I understand it correctly, your bill is kinda like a kit, right?" he asked Art.

"More or less."

"And you have all of the components made?"

"Yeah."

"So you just need a safe spot where you can assemble the

bills, and some help. Does there need to be anything special about the place?"

"As long as it's indoors, not too small, and nobody will find it, theoretically I could assemble anywhere," Art explained.

That's how the filtration room beneath Sheridan Park's pool became the first printing hole for Art's new note. Since Mikey was a lifeguard there, they waited until after hours on a weekend, then snuck in with equipment and set up shop between the pipes and pumps. Bolstered by half an eight ball of cocaine, they had more than five hundred bills drying on clotheslines between the pipes in just under four hours, with time to kill. "It was probably one in the morning when we got finished," Mikey remembers, "so after we were done we called up some hookers and told them to bring beer. They had a great time and so did we. They were swimming in the pool naked and we were literally throwing money at them all night. They had no idea all of it was fake."

The following morning, Mikey delivered the product to Jimmy, who put it into circulation with magnificent results. None of Jimmy's clients had any idea, but that year they were walking around with fistfuls of Art's money. Jimmy was so pleased with the NFL operation that he invited Art and Mikey to sit in on a weekly Texas Hold'em game that he ran in the back room. Provided that he kept twenty percent of their winnings, Jimmy allowed them to throw as much counterfeit on the table as they wanted.

No one appreciated the homemade nature of Art's bills as much as Wensdae, who allowed Art and Natalie to stay at her place while they looked for an apartment. A few days after Art and Natalie arrived, she came home from work to find a half-assed spider's web of clotheslines across her living room and kitchen. Hanging from them like spring leaves were dozens of freshly made, air-drying bills that

Art and Natalie had been gluing and stamping all day. Up until that moment, she didn't even know that her brother was a counterfeiter. "I was pissed at him for about five minutes. I mean, what kind of fucking asshole would do that to his own sister? But you gotta understand that when you look at those things, you can't tell the difference. I don't care who you are. If you had seen those bills, and fucking Art with all his assurances, you wouldn't be any different. You just want to spend them."

Art refused to give her any, which infuriated her even more. But in what would become an irresistible tradition for his friends and family, Wendz snuck a handful when he wasn't looking. "I went to Navy Pier, and I was dropping them like water," she remembers. "I'm a shopaholic, and I was in candyland."

DESPITE ART'S FLEXIBLE ASSEMBLY METHOD, he now had a supply deficit. In legal business, it's generally a good problem that can be overcome by partnerships and loans. In the criminal world, it's one of the most dangerous positions a crook can be in. Nothing increases a criminal's profile like expansion, and Art had not forgotten da Vinci's advice about occupying too much space. At the same time, he had to strike while the bills were hot, so to speak. And yet he lacked that most American of business essentials, the capacity for mass production.

The very thing that made his bills great—the fact that they were handmade—was also a limitation. Unlike da Vinci had done, it wasn't just a question of plates, paper, ink, and a press. Breaking the new note had required all those elements plus many more. Polyester paper, color-shifting paint, ultraviolet reactive inks, watermarks on tracing paper, spray glues and glosses, high-end scanners and printers and computers, plus a dozen other small steps like carrier sheets and spacers that could only be applied manually—they were all infuriatingly labor intensive. In his efforts to become perfect, he had become boutique.

To meet even a small portion of the demand, Art needed better equipment, a printing hole, and a labor force. Once again, Chicago turned out to be a propitious location. Every year, printers from around the globe converge on the McCormick Place convention center for Graph Expo—the world's largest graphic-arts convention. For three days the center's nearly three million square feet of display space exhibit the latest hi-tech presses, inks, papers, scanners, and computer programs—every innovation the industry has to offer. For a counterfeiter, standing above the South exhibition hall and looking across the floor of Graph Expo is perhaps the closest thing to a view of heaven on earth.

Counterfeiters aren't invited to Graph Expo, of course. Conventioneers pay thousands of dollars for the right to display and attend, and access to the floor is strictly regulated. But it is a little-known fact outside of Chicago that McCormick Place itself is heavily manned by Bridgeporters. From the suited managers to the back-braced laborers who set up the displays, most are either from the South Side or know somebody from the South Side who got them their union jobs, which at forty-five dollars an hour to start are among the best blue-collar gigs in Chicago. And so it was that in October of '99, Giorgi gave Art the keys to heaven.

Giorgi was working as a floor manager at McCormick Place that year, a job that gave him unfettered access to the entire exhibition floor. After seeing one of Art's New Notes and hearing about his need for good equipment, Giorgi personally saw to it that Art was given a necklace pass, complete with a photo ID, to the convention. He walked onto the floor that year with as much access as the president of Xerox.

His name was James Salino, and he was a small printer from the South Side. He spent three days roaming the floor, chatting up representatives from Adobe and Lexmark and Hewlett-Packard, attending demonstrations, and asking questions. At the same time, he was also shopping, because Giorgi made it clear to him that if he saw something he liked, then arrangements could made to obtain it.

On the first day he attended the Expo he fell in love. As he roamed the South Hall, his eyes fell upon a compact, two-color offset press made by Ryobi that was unlike anything he had ever seen before. Instead of using metal plates, it used plasticized paper plates, which distributed ink with far more uniformity and detail than aluminum sheets. Being mostly paper, the plates also burned quickly, which made getting rid of evidence a cinch. On top of all that it was downright sexy, "silver and yellow, like a race car." Plain and simple, it was "a bad motherfucker."

The Ryobi retailed for twelve thousand dollars. On the last night of Graph Expo, after the convention closed, a small army of South Siders assaulted the exhibition floor with forklifts and dollies to crate up the millions of dollars of equipment. McCormick Place is one of the best-run convention centers on the planet, and prospective visitors to those great exhibition halls would disservice themselves to be dissuaded by this anecdote. But that night, not everything made it safely to the loading dock.

ART SET THE RYOBI UP at an empty warehouse that Giorgi found for him on the South Side. Within a day he was experimenting, using it to color bill backgrounds and seals. Compared with his earlier offsets, it was a Rolls-Royce, with a touch so light and reliable that he wondered how he'd ever done without it. "That press even *sounded* good," he remembers. "It had a nice electric hum to it. I loved the feeling of turning it on, because when that fucker was rolling it was moneymaking time. It was going down."

His first hundred-thousand-dollar batch of the New Note was destined for the Horse, his oldest and most reliable client. With Natalie helping, they went from raw material to fully assembled bills in about ten days, twice as long as Art would have liked. There were paper jams, glue problems, cutting problems. Perfecting his methodology into a fluid system would take him many more months, but when they were finished and staring at ten shrink-wrapped piles of ten thousand, he knew that he was back in the game in a big way. "I felt like the caveman who had discovered fire," he says. "The bills looked so good I almost didn't want to sell them. I wanted to spend them."

During Art's hiatus from counterfeiting, the FBI had raided the On Leong Building several times, and the once legendary gambling den in the basement had passed into history. This time around, he met the Horse in his car at Ping Tom Park, and afterward they went out to a downtown nightclub.

"You'll have to be careful with these new bills," the Horse warned him at one point. "Everybody will want." Art was already seeing it. While superficially good for his ego, his social calendar exploded as clients, crooks, and even family members jockeyed for position next to the goose who was laying the golden eggs. "Everyone wanted money faster than I could make it," he says. "They all had big plans, they all wanted me to become exclusive with them. I could see that it wasn't really about me or my interests, but the money. It bothered me."

Dmitri was still pushing Art hard to travel with him abroad, specifically to St. Petersburg. Sensing Art's earlier reluctance, the Russian now talked about a short trip—three months—in which they would basically hang out and explore the architecture, but Art knew that once he was there he'd be seduced by Dmitri's friends and relatives into printing, or at least selling some of his secrets. At the time, the city was one of the largest producers of U.S. counterfeit in Europe, and all Dmitri needed to return as a conqueror was an unlimited supply of Art's bills.

One of the worst changes Art saw was in Tim Frandelo, an old friend he'd grown up with at the Bridgeport Homes. It had been Tim's little brother, Darren, who was gunned down outside the Dunkin' Donuts next to the projects. Back in the Dungeon days, Tim had helped Art out with a few deals, but once Frandelo saw the new bill, he pressed hard to become Art's full-time partner. Since Art desperately needed someone besides Natalie to help him with the backlog of orders, he brought Frandelo in on a trial basis. But from the very first print run Tim was frustrated.

"I don't understand why you're doing fifty- and hundred-thousand-dollar deals when we can be printing millions," he complained. "I know people who would buy a million."

Art didn't doubt it. Tim had solid Outfit connections, and that worried him. He explained da Vinci's rule about occupying too much "space" and the certainty that the Secret Service would catch them if they printed too much, but Frandelo derided him as being too cautious. "When you have an ability like you got, you need to use it to its full extent," Frandelo pressed. "These little batches will never make us rich, but with this product we could be."

A few weeks after they started working together, Tim informed Art that he had been offered another job; an Outfit associate named Ron Jarrett was smuggling cocaine into the city from an Indian reservation upstate, and he needed foot soldiers to help him move it. Since it was much better money than the five thousand dollars per batch that Art was paying him, Tim was seriously considering taking it.

"If you can promise me we'll print larger amounts, I'll stick with you," Frandelo told him. Art not only wouldn't budge, but he was incensed.

"You go with Jarrett and we're done," Art replied. "I won't be able to talk you. And if you tell him anything about me I'll find you."

Everybody in Bridgeport knew Ron Jarrett. A key member of the Twenty-sixth Street Crew, Jarrett had recently been released from prison for a 1980 jewelry heist, and since returning to the streets he'd been throwing his weight around the neighborhood, extorting money from locals and aggressively trying to tax any crook who smelled faintly of money. He was known for being a brute and a bulldog, and it was widely believed he was positioning himself to take over the Crew. That Frandelo was now associating with Jarrett spelled bad news to Art. "I figured it could be only a matter of time before I got on Jarrett's radar," he says. "If that happened I'd get taxed. The guy had a high profile. It was the kind of circle I didn't want to be anywhere near. Those guys are always watched by the feds."

As Art feared, Frandelo took the cocaine job, and he broke off all contact with his old friend. Worried that Jarrett or law enforcement would catch wind of his operation, Art grew intensely paranoid. He began spending thousands of dollars at the SpyShop USA, a "discreet electronics" store in downtown Chicago that specialized in high-tech countersurveillance equipment. Art bought a police scanner, bug and wire detectors, even night-vision goggles so he could look for stakeout cars in the dark. At the same time, he rarely answered his phone or allowed people to know where he was. When he and Natalie finally found their own apartment near Comiskey Park, he rented it under a false name and invited no one over but family. "I was like a ghost," he says. "Nobody could ever find me. People hated it, but it kept me safe."

"He was nuts," says Tony Puntillo. "I remember one day Art shows up at my apartment. He was worried that he was being followed. He comes in and he has this little box with an antenna sticking out of it—a bug detector. He starts poking the antenna around the whole place, the walls, the furniture. I'm like, 'What the fuck are you doing?' The jagoff's walking around my house acting like he thinks he's James fucking Bond.' Then he goes to the window and shuts the blinds and keeps peeking through them. He's convinced that one of the parked cars is following him."

Even though nobody knew where he and Natalie lived, Art decided that Chicago wasn't anonymous enough for him. The couple began searching downstate for a safe house, a country home where they could lay low and print if necessary. Eventually they found a farmhouse in Marshall, an agricultural community of about four thousand not far from the Indiana border. Located at the end of a dirt road, it literally sat in the middle of a cornfield. "No one was going to find this place," Art says. "I paid cash for six months' rent up front, used a false name. We didn't go there all the time, but when we did we usually printed. We did all the digital stuff there. My plan was to operate out of there and do what Pete had always said: Keep my batches small, avoid too much attention, and live a comfortable life. Things didn't work out that way, of course."

9

THE ART OF PASSING

"Papa! What's money?"

The abrupt question had such immediate reference to the subject of Mr. Dombey's thoughts, that Mr. Dombey was quite disconcerted.

"What is money, Paul?" he answered. "Money?"

"Yes," said the child, laying his hands upon the elbows of his little chair, and turning the old face up toward Mr. Dombey's; "what is money?"

Mr. Dombey was in a difficulty. He would have liked to give him some explanation involving the terms circulating-medium, currency, depreciation of currency, paper, bullion, rates of exchange, value of precious metals in the market, and so forth; but looking down at the little chair, and seeing what a long way down it was, he answered: "Gold, and silver, and copper. Guineas, shillings, half-pence. You know what they are?"

"Oh yes, I know what they are," said Paul. "I don't mean that, Papa. I mean what's money after all."

–CHARLES DICKENS, *Dombey and Son*

On the morning of December 23, 1999, fifty-five-year-old Ron Jarrett stepped outside his bungalow on Lowe Street, a quiet, middle-class section of Bridgeport that had long been a bastion of the Mafia. Like many reputed mobsters who lived in the area, Jarrett felt safe in the neighborhood. That morning, which was clear and cold, he was on his way to the funeral of a family member.

A few blocks away, two men started up a yellow Ryder moving truck and began driving toward Jarrett's house. The truck slowed as it drew up alongside Jarrett, then a man jumped from the passenger seat. He walked directly up to Jarrett, who turned to face him just in time to see a pistol aimed directly at his head. The gunman squeezed off at least five rounds, shooting Jarrett in the face, chest, right shoulder, and both arms. Jarrett would die in the hospital a month later.

The hit had all the earmarks of a classic Outfit operation. Police would later find the Ryder truck torched in an alley up the street, but they would have no good witnesses. In earlier eras, a single shooting might have drawn little law enforcement attention, but this was the first mob killing in Chicago in four years—one of the quietest periods in Outfit history. During that time the FBI had basked in the credit for tamping the organization's profile, a development that had more to do with the Outfit's self-policing than any law enforcement effort. For the Bureau, it was both an affront and a golden opportunity, a chance to take on its favorite Chicago nemesis.

Art heard about the hit from Jarrett's own son, Ron junior, who he frequently played basketball with at McGuane Park. He immediately knew that it was bad news. Since Tim Frandelo was a Jarrett associate, it meant that the FBI would probably haul him in for questioning or at the very least put him under surveillance. Frandelo's associates, which included Art, would be looked at as well. Art had no intention of being around when that happened. "Within two days after the Jarrett hit, the FBI was all over Bridgeport," he remembers. "You could actually see it. There were undercover vehicles everywhere and people were getting hauled in. Jarrett had so many enemies. It was a shitstorm. There was no way I was staying in that city."

It was time to print and run.

FIFTY THOUSAND DOLLARS in bill components, a box of equipment, a silver Mustang convertible, each other, and the clothes on their backs—that's all Art and Natalie had when they left Chicago (at the time Natalie's son was staying with his grandmother in Texas). No bags, no toothbrushes or maps, no reservations. They didn't bother packing anything. Their plan now was to buy everything they needed as they went—and make money doing it.

Their first stop was a sporting goods store, where they dropped about eight hundred dollars in fakes for camping supplies that included a high-end tent large enough to fit a portable table, a double sleeping bag, mats, toiletries, backpacks, cooking supplies, beach towels, hiking boots, canteens, flashlights, a first-aid kit, disposable cameras, suntan lotion, plastic containers, mosquito repellant. Within four hours of leaving, they had enough equipment to survive comfortably off the map for weeks.

Their plan was to keep moving west and see as much country as possible while changing up the counterfeit for real money. For the first time in his life as a counterfeiter, Art intended to go on a balls-out, hedonistic spending spree with his own product. He was going to ignore da Vinci's advice about not spending his own money and "really see what it could do" out in the world. Pete's advice was no longer applicable, he reasoned, because Pete had never possessed a bill like his.

Neither Art nor Natalie knew precisely how they were going to convert fifty thousand dollars counterfeit into genuine, but math led the way. Buy an item worth twenty dollars or less with a fake hundred-dollar bill and you get at least eighty dollars back in genuine currency. The faster you can drop the Benjamins, the more money you make. To spend money quickly, you need an environment abounding in shops, designed to make visiting all of them as convenient as possible. The solution was right there along the road.

According to the most recent statistics from the International Council of Shopping Centers, there are 48,695 malls in the United States. They range from quaint, open-air strips to megatherial indoor chambers replete with roller coasters, aquariums, and petting zoos. Collectively, they bring in about $2.12 trillion a year, accounting for 75 percent of all "nonautomotive" retail sales in America. During any given month, two-thirds of all Americans will visit a center, where they'll spend an average of $86.30 per visit. Malls even outnumber towns in America. The true cathedrals of capitalism, many of them rank among the largest indoor structures in the world. They employ more than twelve million people, and are so woven into the social fabric of suburbia that they are destinations in themselves and monuments of collective memory. As kids we wander their climate-controlled chambers looking for action and each other. As teenagers they become proto–mating grounds where girls test their first lipsticks while boys lurk hoping to test them too. We return to them as adults, working our first jobs in them and sneering at the kids we once were. We meet and sometimes even get married in them. We may detest their superficiality, but we never leave them.

Art and Natalie decided to rob them. America's malls were about to become gigantic, cash-spitting ATMs that would fuel a lifestyle that most of us only dream about.

• • •

PASSING MONEY INVOLVES ALMOST AS MUCH ART as making it. When Art and Natalie intended to hit a mall, he'd spend an hour leisurely driving through the closest town, noting the location of the police station, highway on-ramps, and general layout. If someone at the mall reported a bad bill, he wanted to know how long units might take to respond.

After surveying the town he'd move on to the mall itself, first prowling the entire parking lot for police cars. If he saw any, he would either wait for them to leave or abandon the operation alto-gether because "there was always another mall up the highway." Mall security guards were unavoidable, so in their case he at least made sure to register their vehicles and faces, get a feel for how they liked to conduct their rounds.

Most large malls, especially the older ones, are anchored by mar-quee department stores like Sears, Macy's, or JCPenney's. Art would usually park as close to them as possible, enter through their outer doors, then access the rest of the mall via their interior entrances. "We would never spend in that store, ever," he notes, "that was our get-away plan. And usually it would be through the department store door, to the car, then an exit to the highway in one fucking sweet move."

Once inside the mall, Natalie shopped while Art waited outside the stores and did his best to look like just another bored, dutiful husband beleaguered by an acquisitive wife. He'd keep an eye out for security guards and watch Natalie closely as she "did her thing." Natalie was a pro. She wore wigs and often sunglasses to avoid being identified on security-camera tapes, her favorite of the former being a black bob, like Uma Thurman's in *Pulp Fiction*. She'd pick an item under twenty dollars, browse for a few minutes more, then head for the cashier. If there was more than one register, she'd pick the attendant least likely to scrutinize the bill: "An old woman with thick glasses, or a young kid who looks like he doesn't give a shit about anything—those are the best people to drop money on. The worst is a woman in her mid-thirties who looks conscientious about her job."

Demographics also had a lot to do with how closely people inspected their bills. In populated, affluent states like California and New York, where counterfeits abounded, almost everyone would mark the bills with the pen or look for the watermark; in the Midwest and South, Art and Natalie might go all day without seeing the pen. Not that it mattered that much where they were. As Art and Natalie quickly learned, the new bills always passed. "We *knew* that we were gonna make money," says Art. "There was no 'might' about it, or 'I hope it's good enough to pass here.' It always worked."

After visiting three or four stores, Natalie would hand the bags and the change to Art, who'd look increasingly like a beast of burden. When he could carry no more bags he'd head back to the car, dump the goods in the trunk, deposit the change in a satchel, and pick up more bills to give to Natalie.

"We could hit forty or fifty stores in two hours, come out with about thirty-five hundred or four thousand dollars," Art says, "then we were gone."

NEITHER ART NOR NATALIE remembers the first mall they hit, but five minutes afterward they realized they had a unique logistical problem: a trunkful of brand new, unwanted goods. Given Art's experience with poverty and Natalie's churchgoing background, throwing away perfectly good merchandise was unthinkable. So they grabbed a phone book, located the closest Salvation Army branch, and drove straight over. Placing the goods into the donation bin gave both of them an intense charity high. Art would later describe it "as powerful as the high I got when I was making the money," and both he and Natalie would come to see it as a reason in itself for counterfeiting. From that moment on, the couple integrated charity into all their mall operations; if there wasn't a Salvation Army store in the area, then they'd leave the "merch at a church" with a note requesting that it be donated to needy families.

Once they started donating, Art and Natalie felt a little weird leaving poor people useless items like scented candles and other tchotchkes, so they began tailoring parts of their passing operations to include things that families could actually use: Baby clothes and formula, toys, and school supplies became mainstays. "Pretty soon charity became an important part of what we were doing," says Art. "We weren't satisfied unless we gave stuff away. It became a rule, not just donating items but also that we had to give ten percent of whatever real money we made away. Sometimes it was as simple as dropping four hundred bucks in a bucket at church, which we did a lot. Another rule was that we never dropped money on mom-and-pop stores—only the big chains."

They would later extend their charity to individuals as well. Natalie heard one Christmas about a friend of a friend living in Houston who was going through hard times. Her name was Brenda, and she had three daughters and two infant grandchildren. Brenda was on disability, suffering from severe carpal tunnel syndrome, and distraught because her children needed clothes, shoes, and hygiene products—Christmas presents were a luxury she didn't even consider. Natalie had her friend make a list, then Art and Natalie showed up at Brenda's doorstep two weeks later with everything on it and more: toys and clothes for the grandkids, music and shoes, jackets, shampoo, conditioner, bath soap, laundry detergent, toothpaste, toothbrushes, towels, washcloths, cleaning supplies. Every item was gift-wrapped, and even the dog got food and treats. Brenda herself was not forgotten. Art and Natalie bought her a paraffin-wax machine—a medical device used to relieve carpal tunnel syndrome. Brenda was reduced to tears by the couple's generosity, which did not end there. When Natalie noticed that the family had no Christmas tree, she and Art ran out and bought one, along with a full-blown holiday feast.

Years later, a therapist would suggest to Art that perhaps all the charity was simply an attempt to cleanse the tremendous guilt he felt for his crimes. "I don't think that was it," Art would tell him. "For that to be true I'd have to feel guilty about counterfeiting in the first place, and I never did. Not for one day. I only felt guilty about some of the problems counterfeiting led to." Guilt is rarely a by-product of counterfeiting. The money looks real, and the moment it passes, it effectively becomes real. And for Art it was even better than the real thing. "I liked *my* money more than real money. It was mine. I made it with my own hands and every batch was a little different, with its own personality." No one ever got hurt, and the fakes they left behind were trace molecules in the billion-dollar collection ponds of the national chains. Especially for Art, passing felt rebelliously empowering, each dropped bill a nip at the dispassionate system that he increasingly came to believe was as much a cause of his impoverished childhood as his father's abandonment.

HITTING AT LEAST A MALL A WEEK, Art and Natalie ran out of counterfeit fast. At night in the motel rooms, they'd assemble the bills. Art had a five-gallon pail in which he kept his glues, sprays, and finishing tools, along with a portable hydraulic press that could clamp onto tables and counters. Their only requirement was a fan in the bathroom to vent the chemicals. They'd dry the bills on a portable clothesline, hanging the fresh notes festively above the beds like the streamers of a capitalist cult. On one occasion, Art even assembled five thousand dollars in a tent they'd pitched in a northern California campground. "I had the little zip windows open and I'm in there with my kit and my radio going. I'm out in the wilderness putting money together. Natalie was pissed because I fucked the whole tent up. My glue got everywhere."

It was easy enough to buy a new tent the next day with the finished bills. Except for camping hardware and CDs, possessions became entirely disposable to them. They never did laundry or wore the same clothes more than twice. Once their clothes got dirty, they went into the donation pile with all the other goods.

With all the driving, traffic tickets were an omnipresent danger, especially since Art was a hopeless speeder. A single ticket could attach Art to a locale where counterfeit had popped. But like any conscientious criminal he carried fake IDs, or more precisely real IDs belonging to other people. He obtained them by getting trial passes from gyms in Chicago's more prosperous neighborhoods and visiting them on a regular basis. Not only did he get free workouts, but if he saw a fellow fitness enthusiast who looked like him, he'd note the time of his arrival. Gym rats often follow a precise schedule, and the next time Art's doppelgänger showed up he might return from a workout to find his locker ajar and his wallet gone. Art never used the credit cards; he was only interested in the driver's license and photo IDs. On two occasions that summer, patrolmen pulled Art over for speeding, but there would never be a trace of Art's presence anywhere near a papered mall. For years to come, guys in neighborhoods like Lincoln Park, Lakeview, and Old Town would receive receipts for tickets from places they had never been. The strangest thing was that all of them had been paid, in cash.

If the crime of creating counterfeit had brought Art and Natalie closer together, then the act of spending it on the road bonded them as surely as the twin sheets of their bills. They went river rafting in Wyoming, took a rock-climbing course in Utah. Hiking was their favorite pastime. One day in the Olympic Range, they stood on a cliff above a glacier lake.

"I want to jump in," Art told Natalie.

"It's at least three hundred feet, don't even think about it. You'll be dead."

"I can do it."

They joshed and argued over the jump for fifteen minutes until she won, then they clambered down to a beach for a safer entry. But Art liked the earlier view, so afterward they hiked back up and made love up above the tree line, cooled by nearby snowmelts with a granite boulder for a bed.

In western Nebraska, they had to stop the car when a herd of wild horses crossed the road in front of them. They left the car and marveled at the dappled crowd, making contact with eyes that held fear and ferocity. Then, it was the Art of romance.

"That's us, baby," he told Natalie.

All over America they saw twentysomethings like themselves laboring in restaurants and strip malls, burning away their youth in pursuit of paper. Cataleptic cashiers worked to their advantage, but also reminded them of what they had escaped. While everybody else chased the dollar and daydreamed of what they'd rather be doing, they were doing it. They became firm believers in the adage that retirement is wasted on the old. "We talked about how we should rent a motor home and just keep rollin' on forever," says Natalie. "We joked that we were doing life backwards, but was that any worse than what everybody else was doing? Waiting to get old to appreciate their freedom? I think we came closer to achieving pure freedom on that trip than anyone I've ever met. It sounds strange, but it was almost spiritual."

"I think we were what humans were meant to be," Art says, "completely free, almost like it was in the Garden of Eden. God wants us to play. I do not believe that people were meant to live the way they do. Slavery still exists; now we're just slaves to the dollar."

Time to philosophize about their lifestyle was just another one of its benefits. Whether or not freedom can be obtained through counterfeit means has been pondered for eons. Diogenes of Sinope believed that true freedom could be achieved only by rejecting both material goods and societal constructs. The path he ultimately took—hermitage—was one that Art and Natalie had no interest in. The goods and time they bought with counterfeit were real, and their perceived freedom didn't feel any less so. Great moments and memories, however purchased, always feel stolen.

Freedom from the past was a more complicated matter. Art wasn't even conscious of it at first, but the route they were taking—more or less due west from Chicago—shadowed the exact course his father had driven twenty years earlier when he had kidnapped Art and his siblings. Like a migrating animal, he had been navigating along the magnetic lines of his childhood. He didn't become aware of it until they were in southern Oregon, where he saw to the south the allusive and shimmering peak of Mount Shasta.

"That's where we're going," he told Natalie. "I used to live there."

Memories of the last days he had spent with his father flowed from the landscape. He told her about how he had never wanted to leave Mount Shasta, about riding horses with his first girlfriend, his first kiss, and the horrible trip back to Chicago in the well of the Bronco. He wanted to go back to the last good place of his childhood and plant a flag there.

They rented a cabin in the pines outside the town of Mount Shasta. During the days they hiked the Cascades and swam in the nearby rivers, and at night they ate out and drank microbrews on the cabin's porch. After a week, Art declared that they should live there, so they began driving around and looking at property. He talked about putting a few big deals together in Chicago, then building a house. "I liked the idea," says Natalie. "It was a beautiful little town and what he was talking about sounded *normal*. That was something I always tried to encourage in him, not that I was ever very successful." But normal wasn't free. Because they were now all but living in Mount Shasta, they couldn't drop counterfeit there without popping up on the Secret Service's radar. They had to spend real money, and as the weeks in the town drew out into a month, Art grew restless. Plans and dreams meant commitment, surrendering the unpredictability that now defined the way he operated. For a counterfeiter who spends his own product, staying free means movement. One morning, just as quickly as he'd decided to stay, he told Natalie they were leaving.

"We'll come back later," he said, and she wasn't exactly surprised. She wanted to see southern California anyway, and that's where they headed next. They broke for the coast, cruised down Highway 1, and wound up in Huntington Beach. There, it was long days on the beach and L.A. nightclubs in the evenings. They were also in the mall capital of America, but after hitting a couple of the larger centers they ceased spending; Art noticed that southern Californians paid attention to cash. The pen was omnipresent and every other cashier seemed to look for the watermark. Though the bills passed, Art felt like it was only a matter of time before a vigilant attendant sensed something amiss.

And so after three months on the road, they began backtracking. As promised, after Los Angeles Art drove them back to Mount Shasta, where they stayed for another week as he picked at the bones of his old happiness, but the past held less meat for him than the future. He still wanted to pursue his dream of land and a quiet life, but he was convinced that to achieve it he needed to return to the crucible that had always nurtured his life as a counterfeiter. Rather than staying in Mount Shasta and spawning, he steered them back to Chicago, the city in which, for him, pitfalls and possibilities are always indistinguishable.

SAILING ALONG ON THEIR CURRENTS OF COUNTERFEIT, Art and Natalie had been entirely oblivious to events transpiring back in Chicago. Just as Art had feared, during his absence Ron Jarrett's murder had led to a massive FBI investigation in Bridgeport, code-named Operation Vendetta II. By wiretapping a known Outfit member and Jarrett associate, the Bureau learned of Jarrett's cocaine smuggling operation—and the name Tim Frandelo. It had also uncovered that Frandelo was supplying many of Art's former friends in the Satan's Disciples with the drug, and that the SDs were dealing large amounts of cocaine out of the projects. In late October, Frandelo and fourteen other suspects would be swept up in a sting for trafficking in cocaine. Art's name never came up as a Frandelo associate, and in that regard his plan to flee the city worked. But it came at a cost.

He had ceased communication with his family during his absence, just at the time that Wensdae had needed him most. Right before Art left the city, her five-year relationship with the Greek dentist had come to a bitter end. She had moved into a new apartment on Sawyer Avenue, and for the first time in her life she was completely alone. Stoked by the recent loss, the depression, pain, and panic that had haunted her for as long as she could remember reignited with unprecedented ferocity. On the evening of May 15, 2000, she was alone in the apartment, dousing the flames with a fifth of Bacardi, when she decided to end her pain permanently.

Her new apartment was on the fourth floor, with a window overlooking an alley. That evening she opened window, then lay on the ledge on her stomach, testing the waters of her own death. She had flirted with suicide-by-fall many times before and had always pulled back, but this time she went deeper. She grabbed the ledge tightly, then slid off until she was hanging by her fingers. Then she let go.

She remembers very little about the fall, but two police officers on their dinner break at a White Castle fifty yards away saw her just as she dropped. According to the report they later filed, Wensdae plummeted down the wall, grazing it on the way down, then crashed feet-first into the cement below. As the officers radioed for a paramedic, they were stunned to see Wensdae stand up in the alley as if the impact hadn't even fazed her, then walk around the corner toward the building's main entrance. They ran after her, but her location wasn't clear to them until a few minutes later, when they spotted her at the same window, climbing out a second time.

They couldn't believe their eyes. She had somehow hobbled back to her apartment. Once again Wensdae crawled out on the ledge and dangled by her fingers, but now she decided she wanted to live. She screamed for help. One of the officers ran into the building, but just before he reached her, she lost her grip. Miraculously, a series of power lines running parallel to the building broke her second fall; she hit the wires, then spun forward, again landing on her feet, but this time she lost consciousness. The last thing she remembered was hearing one of the police officers yell to the other, "She jumped again."

Wensdae awoke two weeks later in a bed at Mercy Hospital. Both her ankles were completely shattered and her spine was broken. She spent the next three months in the hospital, and when she came out of it her right leg from below the knee was completely useless, a dangling, dead appendage whose only sign of life came from an immense, stultifying pain that never ceased. Doctors advised her that she would be much better off having it surgically amputated, but Wendz wanted to keep her leg. To fight the pain, she opted for a drug regimen that often left her completely debilitated and committed to an indeterminate series of reconstructive surgeries—a fight that would last nine years—longer and more harrowing than any prison sentence her brother would ever serve.

"Where were you? I tried calling around but no one knew where you were," she asked Art after he came back.

He didn't have the heart to tell her that he had been on a spending spree across America, having the greatest time of his life.

ART FOUND THE ROAD TRIP with Natalie so liberating that he decided to make passing his bills a permanent feature of his operation. From then on, almost every time he executed a deal in Chicago, he'd print up an extra twenty or thirty thousand, then invite a select group of friends or family on a prolonged shopping spree. He called it "slamming," and if you were one of the chosen few picked to participate in the adventure, it was akin to winning a game-show prize without ever having to compete. Not only would Art pay all your expenses, but you were allowed to keep twenty percent of the change and whatever goods you could fit into your allotted trunk space.

The trips were like abbreviated versions of Art and Natalie's first summer with the New Note. Part serious criminal enterprise and part play, they lasted anywhere from a weekend to a week, depending on how much counterfeit Art had printed and his sense of security, which could shift dramatically if he felt the slightest whiff of discovery.

As the orchestrator of the operations, Art never spent money himself; it was enough work managing three or four people high on unlimited cash from succumbing to stupidity.

Avarice would set in long before he parceled out the money. Prior to hitting a mall, he would hand out maps to everyone in order to review the layout and assign stores. At first he tried letting them choose the stores themselves, but that invariably led to conflict.

Friends would argue about who got to shop where until Art stepped in to say, "Listen, you assholes. You're going to go where I tell you to go." Even when spenders swore to follow a program, they'd invariably be tempted to sneak a visit to each other's targets, an act that Art strictly forbade because stores that discover a counterfeit immediately go on the lookout for more. To avoid this, Art warned everyone that whoever ignored his orders would be summarily dumped off at the nearest Greyhound station for a lonely bus ride back to Chicago. On two occasions, he delivered on the threat.

Like any good businessman (or parent) he found that positive incentives worked best. "A good spender knew they had a good chance of being invited on another trip, so I always encouraged them to compete with each other," he says. "Whoever cleaned the most money might get to keep a few hundred extra, or maybe I'd reward everybody with an expensive dinner." With three spenders competing, Art could suck five thousand dollars from a large-sized mall in less than two hours.

Spending trips were as much about living it up as they were about making money. During a trip through Missouri, one of Art's friends found that his assigned section of a mall included a costume store. He bought two clerical collars and declared that he intended to spend the rest of the trip passing counterfeit money dressed as a priest. After a philosophical debate in the car as to whether or not this constituted a mortal sin, Art declared that it was the best idea he'd ever seen. "So another friend of mine on the trip buys two black shirts, and these two guys spend the next three days passing money as priests, competing with each other the whole time. We destroyed Missouri on the that trip; absolutely slammed it."

By the time they reached St. Louis, Art had about four hundred dollars in singles alone, so he took the whole crew out to a strip club. He waved the brick-thick wad in front of a host, then gestured to his friends. "I want the best-looking girls in this place to be entertaining these guys at our table until this pile runs out," he said, then handed the host a fifty. The host happily complied.

ART ESTIMATES he printed four to five million dollars of his New Note within the first two years of its creation, and his money only got better over time. Small changes he made in printers, inks, and processes constantly added verisimilitude and allowed him to speed up production, so much so that he came to view his earliest versions of the Note with almost as much disdain as he did the pre-'96 money.

Yet despite how good the bills looked, they had an Achilles' heel. Art first noticed it at a mall in New Orleans while on a spending trip with Natalie. He was waiting outside a store, watching her do her thing at the counter, when suddenly the cashier—a young woman—exited the store and entered the shop next door. Art didn't think much of it, since cashiers commonly trot over to the neighbors for change. He had seen it a dozen times, but this time things played out differently.

When the cashier entered the adjacent store and approached the register, the male clerk didn't reach for the till. Instead he held up the bill and began picking at it. Art watched, horrified, as the clerk completely peeled away both sides of the bill as if it were a piece of single-wrapped American cheese. "Their eyes just popped, and the woman's mouth literally dropped open. And as soon as I saw that I ran into the first store and got Natalie. I told her it was time to get the fuck out of there and we did, fast."

It was the humidity. Art had assembled the bills in one of the nation's most tropical climates, and the glue had never quite dried. When he went back and inspected the rest of the stash, he found loose corners on many of them. He tried blow-drying them and taping them up to air conditioners and in front of fans. Nothing worked— the southern air was just too moist. He had to stop spending in Louisiana, and from then on he made a rule to never assemble his bills in a humid climate.

One of Art's friends from Chicago, Eric Reid, would learn that even bills made in dry conditions could also be susceptible to climatic influence. Reid was one of Art's square friends, a regular guy with no criminal history who worked as a personal trainer. He knew that Art counterfeited, but had never once asked for bills or requested to go on a spending trip. Under the right circumstances, however, there were very few people Art knew who were never tempted to spend a note or two, either for the spontaneous thrill of it or because they felt certain they wouldn't be caught. So he wasn't surprised when Reid nervously approached him one day and asked if he could buy a few thousand dollars. He and some buddies had long been planning a trip to Jamaica. Given that it was a foreign country, he figured that no one would be wise. "Eric was such a nice guy, I told him I wouldn't sell them to him, but that I'd throw him enough to have fun with. This was when it was fall. It wasn't hot or humid. I was able to do my thing and they came out beautiful. So I gave him four thousand dollars. I figured that would be plenty for him to go down there and have fun with, right? He comes back ten days later, and he looks all fucked up. He has a beard, eyes all bloodshot, he's looking stressed."

Reid explained that everything had gone well at first. Reid had no problem passing the money and was having such a good time with it in Jamaica that he gave some to his pals. Out of what he thought was discretion, he didn't tell them it was fake. Toward the end of their trip, the group went wild at a strip club in Montego Bay, ordering an expensive dinner followed by off-the-books backroom liaisons with some of the girls. When it came time to pay the check, however, the cashier split a bill apart right in front of him. Then he called the Jamaica Constabulary Force.

The JCF arrested the entire bachelor crew. During a night of interrogation, Reid—aided by the otherwise high quality of Art's money—was able to convince the cops that they'd had no idea that the money was fake. The JCF released them the next morning, but the saga wasn't over. Waiting outside the police station was the strippers' pimp, along with two muscular guys. They shadowed Reid back to his hotel room, knocked on the door, then bum-rushed their way in when he opened it. They wanted real money. In tears and lying to save his hide for the second time in twenty-four hours, Reid begged them to believe that he had had no idea, then ended up giving them whatever real cash he had left. "It ruined my vacation," he told Art. "I'll never spend that shit again."

The friends had a good laugh over the Jamaican episode, and Art learned that using his bills in the tropics could be just as dangerous as assembling them there. In the end, that seemed like a small limitation given that he could take steps to prevent it. Unfortunately, the next time someone found a flaw in his bills the results would prove far more costly.

1 O

HOUSE OF BLUES

The counterfeiter, the educated in his calling, and prince among the rascals of his clique, still finds his trade full of danger and difficulty.

–*The Merchants' Magazine and Commercial Review,* 1858

There's a sequence toward the end of Martin Scorsese's 1990 mob masterpiece, *Goodfellas,* in which the coked-up protagonist, Henry Hill, spends a long, exasperating day dashing around town performing errands for the mob while simultaneously arranging a feast for his family. In a wonderful rendering of the banalities of criminal life, Hill fights to stay in control as meatballs and marinara mix with cocaine and gun running. Meanwhile a police helicopter shadows ominously above the whole time. Just when Hill reaches the point of heroic exhaustion the trap is sprung; his street erupts in floodlights, cops come charging up his driveway, and out come the handcuffs. His babysitter/drug courier has made the mistake of using his home phone to arrange a deal. No matter how hard a criminal tries, there's always a wild card he cannot control, and that is usually what brings him down.

On February 19, 2001, Art woke up in Marshall with a similarly hectic day in front of him. He and Natalie had been up most of the previous night finishing a $160,000 print run, most of which he had to deliver to Dmitri in Chicago that night. At the same time, Natalie's mother and little sister were flying in from Texas that afternoon to visit for a few days and pick up Alex, who'd been selected to appear in a Sears children's catalog that was being shot in Dallas. So Art had to remove all traces of counterfeit supplies and chemicals from the house, drive 100 miles to Indianapolis to meet the family at the airport, rent them a car, then race another 180 miles back to Chicago and rendezvous with the Russians.

Everything went off without a hitch until they met Natalie's mother and sister in Indy. When Art explained that he had to run off to Chicago, Natalie's little sister, Amy, begged him to come along. Art didn't object. At eighteen, Amy had never seen the city, and she was also vaguely aware of Art's "business." The fact that she was a cute, precocious brunette like her sister didn't hurt either. Before leaving Marshall, Art had even grabbed an extra sixty thousand dollars to hit the town with after his deal. Having Amy along for company on the long ride and then showing her the city was what he needed to take the edge off the day.

After he'd rented Natalie and her mother a car, Art and Amy split for Chicago, arriving about two and half hours later. He arranged for the deal with Dmitri to go down at the House of Blues Hotel, a modern, tourist-oriented hot spot adjacent to one of the city's premier music venues on Dearborn Street. With a plush lounge and hip bar, it was the kind of place that a small-town girl from Texas would want to see, and Art had connections there that could get them into a private club on one of the upper floors.

Art booked a room, dropped off his satchel and the extra sixty grand in the closet, then headed upstairs to the club with Amy for some drinks. They were early, and by the time Dmitri arrived they were already fuzzily drunk, dancing to a live band. "Amy was danc-ing on the floor and she looked *great*," he remembers. "Up until that time, me and Amy had gotten very close. We'd never done nothing, but I had taken her out to dinner. Maybe we had talked sexy to each other, nothing real major. You gotta understand that I love Natalie. It was a game. I keep telling myself, 'You don't want to do this. Watch yourself around the little sister. Sister not good, sister not good.'"

Art and Dmitri caught up at the bar, then headed up to the room to conduct the deal and snort a little cocaine while Amy chat-ted and danced with two other Russians. Once business was taken care of, Dmitri invited everyone to a party over at his place, which Art thought was a good plan.

"Can't we go to another club first? I want to see more of the city," Amy pleaded after the Russians left.

Obliging her, Art took her to a nearby club where he knew the staff. Neither of them realized it was gay night until they entered and beheld an eclectic mass of writhing, shirtless men on the dance floor. Art wanted to leave, but Amy insisted on a few dances, so they started boogeying down with the guys. By now they were both trashed, and Art's powers of libidinous resistance—a Maginot Line even when he was sober—began to crumble. He became convinced that Amy wanted to take things further than flirting. The possibility ripened when, during one of the dances, Amy accidentally ripped her pants and ran off to the bathroom, returning shortly afterward with the embarrassing news.

"How bad is it? Do you want to leave?" Art asked her as they sat down at a cocktail table.

"See for yourself," she said. To show him the rip, she grabbed his hand and placed it in her lap.

Art pulled his hand away, but it was too much for him to resist. "She put on one of those sad puppy-dog faces. And so I put my hand back down there. And I'm like, 'What am I doing? If we're gonna do this, let's get back to the House of Blues.'" Back at the hotel room, Amy hopped in the shower while Art rolled a joint. She insists that she was preparing to go to sleep and that Art was having delusions of sexual grandeur, but whatever might have happened between them was moot, because he had passed out by the time she got out of the shower. Just as Amy stepped out of the bathroom wearing a robe, there was a knock on the door. Art jolted awake, and before he could tell her that it was a very bad idea to respond, Amy opened it a crack.

That's when four Chicago police officers pushed their way into the room.

Earlier that evening, a hotel security guard had called CPD after overhearing Art and Dmitri at the bar talking about scoring an eight ball of cocaine. Since hearsay didn't constitute just cause to enter Art's room, CPD told the guard that they could enter the room only if a disturbance was reported. Conveniently, the guard had reported a loud noise complaint shortly after Art and Amy returned.

One of the cops pinned Amy to the wall while the others moved toward the back. And once they were in, the sight of Art's marijuana on the coffee table was the only invitation they needed to stay and have a look around.

"This smells like really good shit, I wish I could smoke some," one of the cops joked as he sniffed Art's weed. "What else have you got in here?" They roused Art from the bed, sat them both down at a table, and began searching the room. Rifling though Art's suitcase, Amy's clothes bag, and a chest of drawers, they were frustrated to find nothing. Art had no outstanding warrants, and the possibility of nothing more than a marijuana violation seemed tantalizingly close. But just as the cops looked like they were about to wind up their search, a young, redheaded officer named Marty O'Flaherty opened the closet.

"I didn't see anything in there at first," remembers O'Flaherty.

"I was about to close the door again, but something made me run my hand over the top shelf. That's when I found this fat pile of cash, sixty grand." O'Flaherty assumed the money was real. But he took a closer look, holding the bill right up to his face. It was then that he noticed that the paper contained no red and blue silk fibers.

Art had easily simulated the fibers many times in the past, usually by taking hair from his own body, then burning a plate just for them, but he found that nobody really looked for them anymore after the '96 note was released. He had spent so much time perfecting the new security features that, on that particular batch, he had neglected to include the oldest one in the book.

O'Flaherty turned to Art and smiled.

AS AMY REMEMBERS IT, Art stayed "real calm" when O'Flaherty discovered the counterfeit. "He immediately told the officers that I had nothing do with it. He said that everything was his fault and that they should let me go." But the CPD was just getting started. After allowing Amy to dress, they cuffed and escorted both of them down to the hotel's garage, where the cops searched the rental car. Finding nothing of interest, the officers then hauled them to the Eighteenth District precinct house. It was there, at about eight that morning, that Art finally came face-to-face with the Secret Service.

There were two agents, a man and a woman, both in their mid-thirties and well dressed. The Service had been studying Art's bills for months, unaware as to who was creating them or where they'd been made. By the time agents showed up at malls or banks to inspect the bills, Art was always long gone, leaving no trace of his identity. To the agents, his only identity was his bills, and as soon as they inspected the notes that O'Flaherty had recovered, they became convinced that Art was the one they'd been after.

The male agent was pissed. Because the Secret Service had reason to believe that Art had been spreading bills across state lines, he'd been called in from D.C. on a red-eye. He was bleary-eyed and irritable, as tired as his suspects.

"I just left President Bush," he groaned to Art at one point, "so please, don't fuck with me."

Anytime the Service gets its hands on a counterfeiter, the first priority is almost always obtaining more evidence. They go after equipment, because seizing it is the best and often the only way to prove that a suspect is the creator of the notes as opposed to just a passer. When there are two or more suspects, standard interrogation procedure is to separate them and question the weakest one first.

That meant Amy. Young, frightened, and vulnerable, she was most likely to crack and provide them with information they could leverage against Art. While Art waited in a holding cell, they had at her. After confirming her identity—which also established a baseline for her truthful responses—the pair immediately demanded to know where the money had been made and who else had made it with her.

Amy was, of course, completely innocent. She knew nothing and told the agents as much. That's when the threats began. Interestingly, it was the female agent who played bad cop. "It was only the woman who was mean to me," she says, "the guy from D.C. was nice. But I hated her. She told me that I'd never see my mother or sister again. She said they'd arrest my mother, although that was ridiculous because my mother had nothing to with anything."

The agents brought up names and places: St. Louis, New Orleans, Minneapolis. They knew she had been involved. They even brandished a folder. Most of it was probably filled with blank paper, but it looked intimidating as they declared they knew everything, so there was no use holding back. Crying now, Amy reiterated that she knew nothing. This went on for eight hours, as the agents moved back and forth between her and Art. Other than a bag of M&M's, neither of them would be given any food or sleep.

"They absolutely tortured that girl," says Art, "and she gave them nothing."

Amy did know a few things. She knew that Art and Natalie were the ones who had made the bills, and that they had been doing it for some time. She'd heard stories about hitting malls. But she also knew that Art and Natalie were family, and that there was no way she was going to turn against them.

ART WAS FAR MORE COOPERATIVE. He told the agents outright that he alone had created the bills and that they should let Amy go. "He confessed," remembers O'Flaherty, who was in the interrogation room at the time. "And he was very arrogant. He told them that they had no idea who they had. He even told them how he had beaten each part of the bill."

"I figured that was it, I had been caught with the money and it was over," says Art. "I knew the conviction rate for counterfeiters. You don't beat the feds. They don't allow it."

Unlike their treatment of Amy, the agents let Art talk and talk. He had been dodging them for so many years that the interrogation took on the relieving air of a meeting that both parties had long desired. Who else but the Secret Service could truly appreciate what he had done? Art's weakness—his desire to be admired—flowered in that windowless room. The agents and O'Flaherty listened raptly while he affably schooled them on just how shortsighted the Treasury Department had been when it designed the New Note. "I thought he was real nice guy, he could charm his way out of anything," says O'Flaherty. "I told him, 'With all the right marks you had on your bill, you could have done anything. You could have had your own company.'"

Despite his long-windedness, Art's confession was far from total. He did not tell them what equipment he used, where it was, or the names of any of the other people involved in the manufacturing, distribution, and passing of his bills. He filled the airspace with time-consuming vagaries, and whenever the agents tried to get him to be specific, he smiled and shrugged, indicating—compassionately, almost—that he couldn't and wasn't going to help them.

At the same time, he was steadily bargaining. He needed to call Natalie, he told them, so that she'd know what had happened to her sister. By law he was entitled to one phone call, but the agents could postpone it for hours if they wanted. More than anything, the agents wanted an address where they could look for equipment. And late that afternoon they decided to gamble and let him call Natalie most likely in the hopes that they could trace the line and get a location.

"He got ahold of his girlfriend, and said he was in trouble, but couldn't talk much," remembers O'Flaherty. "And the Secret Service dropped the ball in letting him make that call."

Art was on the phone for a minute at most, long enough for the Service to trace the call to a fairly localized area in Marshall, but they still had to determine the address and get a warrant. The call was far more advantageous to Art. He was able to let Natalie know, without saying it, that she needed to destroy every piece of incriminating equipment in the house.

WHY THE SERVICE DIDN'T IMMEDIATELY DISPATCH AGENTS to Marshall is known only to them. An hour later, they decided to release Amy, and were even able to obtain directions to the house; Art wrote them down for her so she could drive the rental car back.

Poor Amy's ordeal was far from over when she left the station. Even though Art had more than three hundred dollars in genuine currency on him at the time of her arrest, the Service gave her only seventeen—barely enough for gas. Driving through an unfamiliar state with no food or sleep, she missed her exit and wound up in Indiana. After running out of money for tolls, she broke down crying at a gas station, where a sympathetic clerk drew her a map, gave her fourteen dollars and a toll card, then escorted her back to the highway. She got lost again on the back roads of Marshall, where she finally woke up an elderly couple living in a trailer at the end of a dirt road. Seeing her distress, they told her to leave the car till morning and mercifully gave her a ride all the way to the house.

Natalie was devastated when Amy told to her the story about the arrest. She was furious at Art, not because she thought anything would've happened with her sister, but because he hadn't been more careful about security. They were now on the Secret Service's radar, which meant that she herself would be under investigation. She had no doubt that the Service would obtain a search warrant for the house in Marshall, which still contained a computer they had used to work on scans. To top it off, she'd learned a few months earlier that she was pregnant, and she was now five and half months and showing. "Yeah, I was worried for Art," she says, "but I also had a baby to worry about. I was afraid he'd wind up in jail and I'd have to raise the baby alone. I was a wreck."

Luckily, Art's phone call had given her a head start. Within minutes of hanging up, she was stuffing a computer tower into plastic garbage bags, which she then hauled to a dumpster in downtown Marshall. Despite her rush, the Service didn't show up until the following afternoon. The women were away in Indianapolis dropping off the rental car at the time, but when they came home they saw the warrant taped to the front door. Despite the fact that Natalie had locked all the windows and dead-bolted the doors, they had entered without a scratch and searched the entire premises. The only thing they took was a camera containing undeveloped family photos. They never gave it back.

ART WAS ARRAIGNED A DAY AFTER HIS ARREST and charged with one count of counterfeiting United States currency, a crime that carried a maximum sentence of twenty years. But even as he stood haggard before the judge and heard the charge, agents and lab technicians were poring through bill databases and pulling up potential matches for other bills that might be linked to him. They turned up more almost immediately.

Six weeks earlier, Art, Natalie, and a couple of friends had taken a spending trip into Oklahoma, knowing that the post-Christmas bargain crowds would make a great slamming environment. Along Interstate 44, they had absolutely papered the Central Mall, near the town of Lawton. When the Secret Service later sent a couple agents from the Oklahoma City field office to investigate, they found that a whopping 80 percent of the merchants—or about sixty stores—had received counterfeit bills. In the report, they noted that the bills "differed in serial number, but possessed many of the same characteristics [as the Chicago notes] to include: mismatch Federal Reserve Bank number and letter, unique two-part note defeating the CFT detection pen, watermark and security fiber representations, unusual paper."

Proving that Art had made the Lawton bills would be difficult without his equipment, but if they could establish that just one of those bills was his, then there was a good chance he could also face at least one count of "uttering" counterfeit—an Old World term for passing. Uttering carried a fifteen-year maximum, but that wasn't the end of the bad news for Art. If they could trace any of the bills to another criminal he'd sold them to, then he'd also be facing a "dealing" charge, which also carried a twenty-year max.

The federal government enjoys a ninety-five percent conviction rate when it comes to criminal cases. Its law-enforcement officers enjoy the best training, equipment, and funding in the world, and their investigations produce evidence for not just a single prosecutor, but typically a team of a highly talented attorneys who often find themselves facing a lone defense lawyer or, in the case of multiple defendants, a loose and conflicted confederacy. The Department of Justice is also infamously selective; it likes to choose opponents it knows it can beat. In cases involving the Secret Service, the conviction rate is 98.8 percent, the highest rate of any law enforcement agency in the land.

Needless to say, Art needed a very good lawyer, which came down to money. Yet despite the millions in fake cash he had made and sold over the years, he had very little real money to spare. His lifestyle, and the confidence that he could always print more, had left him pathetically unprepared for financial emergencies. He had never established a way to launder his counterfeit earnings into savings; he had convinced himself that he could create a note that would fool anticounterfeiting devices used in offshore banks, deposit millions of dollars, then withdraw real cash. Such a plan, if feasible, would take years of research, and he had run out of time. Other than about fifty thousand dollars in assets, he had nothing, which meant that he was looking at a court-appointed lawyer who would invariably press for a guilty plea.

Natalie's mother, Sharon, decided that she wasn't going to let that happen. The morning after the arrest, she was hitting the phone, hunting for criminal-defense attorneys in Chicago. Conveniently, the town was practically built on them, and after several calls she was referred to a federal criminal-defense attorney named John Beal. The next day, she drove up to Chicago, visited his office downtown, and enlisted his services.

A few days later, Beal visited Art at the Metropolitan Correction Center, Chicago's federal jail, an ominous, eleven-story-high triangle. Art liked Beal immediately for his no-bullshit style. Beal asked Art to give him a step-by-step account of the arrest. When Art reached the part where the officers came into the room and found the marijuana, the lawyer became visibly excited. In the police report, CPD stated that their cause for entering room had been because they had seen—apparently through the crack in the door that Amy was holding open—marijuana on a coffee table.

"That's impossible," Art told him. "There was a hallway, and the coffee table was around the corner. It would have been physically impossible to see the weed, you'd have to have X-ray vision."

The next day, Beal visited the House of Blues. A police officer and the hotel manager escorted him to the room, which was blocked off with police tape. After the manager signed an affidavit stating the room had not been disturbed, Beal entered and took photographs. Just as Art had said, the coffee table was entirely out of view from the door. The manager also confirmed that the coffee table was in the appropriate position according to hotel policy, further indicating that it had never been moved. Beal developed the film and made a visit to the prosecutor, affidavit in hand.

"You've got a straight-up illegal search and seizure here," he told his adversary, and showed him the photos. "Not only that, but I have CPD lying about it on paper."

Three weeks later, the preliminary hearing had barely got under way when the prosecutor approached the bench and told the judge that the state wished to dismiss all charges.

Moments later, the gavel fell. After less than a month, Art was free.

11

THE LETTER

The world meets nobody halfway. When you want
something, you gotta take it.

—LINCOLN HAWK, IN THE FILM *Over the Top*, 1987

Art's elation upon beating the House of Blues rap was unabashedly visible. He bear-hugged Beal in the courtroom, then literally jumped for joy once he hit the sidewalk in front of the courthouse. Thanks to a technicality, he had escaped spending the rest of his youth in federal prison.

His rapture lasted about five minutes. His life as an underground counterfeiter was over. The Secret Service knew his identity, his capabilities, and the names of at least some of his associates. In the courtroom, he had seen two suited, short-haired men in the gallery. They glared at him as he exited, leaving him little doubt as to their affiliation and message. "They were so pissed," Art remembers. "By law, they had to burn all the evidence, sixty grand. I knew it wasn't over. There was no way they were going to let me get away."

Chicago was now way too hot for him. He believes the Service began tailing him the moment he left the courthouse. He stayed in the city just two days, then drove back roads all the way to Texas, where Natalie was waiting for him at her mother's house in Lewisville. Within a day of his arrival, black SUVs began appearing in his rearview mirror, or parked up the street at odd hours, the frozen silhouettes of their drivers in the front seats, waiting.

He stopped venturing outside, turned down the shades, and spent what was left of March beached on the sofa reading and watching TV. His plan was to bore the Service into moving on, but he became caught in his own trap. With too much time to think, he lapsed into a severe depression. "I didn't know what I was going to do," he says. "I figured that was it, game over. We lost the house in Marshall, and it was only a matter of time before the Service caught me for something else. I thought about the past, all the shittiness, my dad leaving, my mom going crazy, my fucking sister almost dying."

One day he found himself engrossed in a TV showing of *Over the Top,* a Stallone film from 1987 about an estranged father and son traveling across the county in a semi truck. Stallone's character, Lincoln Hawk, is an arm-wrestling trucker who hasn't seen his ten-year-old kid since he was a baby. His son resents him for leaving at first, but the pair gradually bond on the road. True to its title, *Over the Top* is one of the most shamelessly sentimental, manipulative, and ridiculously optimistic father-and-son movies ever made. By the end of the movie, Art was bawling.

Natalie found him breaking down on the front porch, trying to hide his tears. "I hadn't seen my dad in so many years. I didn't even know what happened to him, why he left. Then that fucking movie came on and got me thinking about everything. And I said to myself, 'Screw it. I'm gonna find him.'"

Natalie went back into the house, got on the computer, and enrolled in an Internet people-finder service for twenty dollars. Fifteen minutes later, she rejoined Art on the front porch.

"Your dad's living in Alaska," she told him. "I have his address."

•   •   •

ART HAD SPENT ENTIRE DAYS on the Internet researching paper companies and bill components; using it to answer his oldest question had never occurred to him. He had to run to the computer to see the address for himself to believe it.

Williams, Arthur J.
P.O. Box 1258
Chickaloon, AK 99674-1258

Art felt certain it was his father because, in a margin, the site listed the subject's age as fifty-two, precisely the age his dad should be. They entered the city into a map site. There it was, Chickaloon, a mote in the wilderness about sixty miles northeast of Anchorage. Art stared at the map point, transfixed. Farther away than he had ever imagined, but not so far that he couldn't picture it. His dad was right there, right now, probably holed up by the fire as the dark days ruled over the biggest, wildest state. No phone number was given with the address, but they called information just to be sure. The number was unlisted. Art decided that was better anyway; a phone call out of the blue after all these years would be too sudden.

That same night, Art sat down and wrote a letter. He wanted to pen an account of everything that had happened since his father had left, along with the only question that really mattered: Why? Realizing such an epistle would take a butt roll of paper and probably freak his father out, he kept it simple. He told his dad that he was living in Texas and doing well. He was married and had a kid, with another on the way. He wanted them to know their grandfather, and he had never stopped thinking about him. He understood if his dad was hesitant after so many years, but he still loved him. He left the phone number for Sharon's office line, telling his dad to leave his own number with her if he was interested in catching up. Art would call him back.

The next morning, Sharon took the letter to her office and deposited it in the outgoing mail.

ART KEPT A TIGHT REIGN on his hope that his father would respond, but the very act of reaching out made him feel like the future was opening up. Three weeks had gone by since he'd left Chicago, and sure enough, the Secret Service tails soon thinned out. That didn't mean that he was no longer under investigation; it only meant that they'd been occupied elsewhere. He knew that as soon as they had time they'd start checking back, like fishermen revisiting the magic spot where they'd nearly hooked a big one.

He started thinking about establishing a new printing hole, someplace even farther off the map than Marshall, where they'd never find him. Although Natalie had been forced to destroy the computers and printers, the Ryobi press and process camera were still safe in Chicago, and he had plenty of paper stock in Dallas. If he could find a spot, then pull off a large, swift sale, he'd be able to disappear—this time for good. "I still wanted to find a place and finally do it like da Vinci had taught me. Keep it small and contained, not occupy too much space, and just live well. I had wanted to do that in Marshall. Now I felt like I had learned my lesson and this was it. I wanted to get out, get a place where I could breathe some." It was classic criminal logic: He wanted to do a big sale so he could get back to doing small ones.

Finding a new house in rural Illinois was out of the question; not only was it too hot as far as law enforcement was concerned, but the House of Blues bust had given Natalie her fill of the state. "I told

Art that I was never going back there," she says. "If he wanted to be with me, then we'd have to live somewhere closer to Texas." Using the Internet and want ads, they started shopping for real estate within a few hours of Dallas. Since the humidity was worse to the south, they concentrated their search north so as to avoid the sticky problem of having bills peel apart. Eventually they found a listing for about a hundred acres of land in northwest Arkansas east of Fayetteville. Early one morning when the street looked clear of surveillance, they slipped out of town to take a look.

Both of them immediately fell in love with the plot. It included a small, one-story house, along with a twelve-acre lake, several streams, and it was thick with forest. The seller was an elderly woman who'd grown up on the land, and she was asking for $500 per acre. When Art asked her if she was willing to drop her price to $350 per acre in exchange for fifty percent cash up front, no questions asked, her generational preference for hard currency perked right up. "That would be wonderful," she told him.

To get real cash to pay for the land, all Art needed was a client willing to buy his biggest batch of counterfeit ever, and he already had a buyer in mind. As one of his oldest clients and friends, Sandy Sandoval not only trusted him completely, but for the last year he'd been begging Art for larger batches of money, five hundred thousand dollars and up. Art had always declined on the grounds that it was too dangerous. For this one-time deal, however, he was willing to make an exception if Sandy told him precisely how the money would be used.

Sandy jumped on the opportunity. "Okay, the money isn't for me," he told Art over a pay phone, "I'm just a middleman. The guy who wants it is my supplier, Beto." Beto, Sandy went on to explain, was even deeper into the cocaine business than he—one of five Mexican Mafia–affiliated suppliers in the Chicago area. Every month, each of the suppliers deposited anywhere from seven hundred thousand to a million dollars into the walls of an RV, which was basically a traveling bank. From Chicago, the RV went on to California, then Tijuana, Mexico, where the money was laundered and exchanged for more cocaine. "Beto wants to pad his shipment," he explained to Art, meaning that the supplier would mix the counterfeit into his deposit and pocket the savings.

Art liked the idea. Not only would the money be leaving the country, but he soon confirmed that Beto had been the one that Sandy had been selling to all along. In other words, the counterfeit-for-coke scam had a proven track record. After a few negotiating sessions over a pay phone, Art arranged to print the most exorbitant sum he had ever attempted: $750,000 at thirty cents on the dollar. Not all of it would be for Sandy; $250,000 would be for himself— rainy-day money that he intended to shrink-wrap and bury in the woods at his new place in Arkansas. "This was going to be it," he says. "One sweet move. Just print a shitload of money, then build my own place like I'd always dreamed about. Land, horses, the whole thing. I was going to design it and build the house with my own hands. I even had some kick-ass tools that I'd gotten from Home Depot stores. That was one of the places I'd hit hard over the years."

SEVEN HUNDRED AND FIFTY THOUSAND meant at least 15,000 bill faces. It meant 7,500 security strips and watermarks, and more print cartridges than many businesses use in a year. Since every bill had to be hand-assembled, Art and Natalie were looking at a minimum of two weeks of nonstop production, not to mention buying new computer equipment, arranging for a temporary hole where they could work, and transporting paper and supplies. Fortunately, the one problem they didn't have was getting the money to pay for it: Sandy agreed to front them five thousand dollars to pay for the production costs.

The operation would have to be done in Chicago—a sacrifice that Natalie conceded to, given the one-time scenario of the deal. Her only condition, which Art was happy to comply with, was that as soon as the deal went down they would hit the road for a long trip before setting up in Arkansas. Both of them were hungry to rekindle the romance from their earlier trips, and they wanted to do it before the baby arrived.

Setting all these plans in motion helped Art to forget about the letter. But as he and Natalie drove back to Texas, the possibility that his father had responded—or worse, hadn't—snowballed into an anxiety that grew with each mile. He suppressed it by mentally preparing himself for disappointment. It was certainly possible that the man in Alaska was a different Art Williams; if it was his father, why would he be willing to reconnect with him now after having remained silent for so long? And the way his father had always moved around, the address could be old, a cold lead. When they finally pulled into Sharon's driveway, he had primed himself for the inevitable letdown.

"Guess who called my office." Sharon said to him the moment he walked in the door. "He left a number; he wants to talk to you."

ART DIDN'T EVEN BOTHER UNPACKING. He drove straight to a 7-Eleven, got five dollars' worth of quarters, and dialed the number on a pay phone outside. A female answered. Despite the barricade of time, Art thought he recognized the voice. But given how impossible it seemed that his dad could be with the same woman, and the advantage of anonymity, he simply requested to speak to Arthur Williams.

"Just a moment, I'll get him."

Footsteps went away, then new ones approached.

"Hello?"

That voice he was sure of.

"Dad."

"Hello, son!" said Senior. He sounded more cheerful than Art had ever imagined.

"Oh my God, I can't believe it's you."

"It's me. I'm so glad you wrote me," Senior said. "I've been waiting for your call. When I got your letter, it made me so happy."

"That's good," Art said, and then they began the awkward process of reconnecting. With sixteen years and a continent between them, it was easiest for both of them to pretend like they'd last seen each other a few weeks ago. They stretched to speak in the possessive tones of family while touching on subjects that exposed just how much of strangers they'd become to each other. "It was simple things first," remembers Art. "I told him that he was a grandfather, that I had a wife who was pregnant. It was . . . there was too much to talk about over a pay phone. Baby steps. Of course, I had a shitload of questions I wanted to ask him, but I wasn't gonna do it over the phone."

Art was able to get some basics. After he'd left, Senior had driven back West and then moved Anice and her children to Alaska. He'd worked as a mechanic, had a house there in the mountains, and was "semiretired." Every subject led to more questions, but it was easier to stay general and keep to small talk. As Art suspected, the woman who had answered the phone was Anice. Senior had stayed with her the whole time. This both surprised and bothered him. Part of him had hoped that abandonment was congenital with his dad, a trait that hadn't centered on just the family he had left in Chicago.

"How are your brother and sister?" Senior asked at one point.

"They're good," Art lied. "They miss you."

"I miss you too," Senior said. Then he told Art exactly what he wanted to hear. "Why don't you come on up here? Why don't you just come as soon as possible?"

"Right now?"

"Right now."

Art didn't even stop to think before responding.

"You know what? I am," he said. "I'm coming as soon as I can." He explained that there were a few things he had to take care of first, but that a visit within the next few months was a given. They made plans to talk to each other again in a few days. Art hung up and raced back to Natalie to tell her the news that they would soon be heading north.

"He didn't even ask me if I wanted to go to Alaska," she says. "He just told me that that was what we were doing. He was excited; he needed to see his dad. I thought it was a good thing for him."

ART HAD NEGLECTED TO MENTION to Senior that he happened to be on the run from the United States Secret Service for perfecting a counterfeit of the 1996 New Note. Not the kind of detail you give your long-lost father if you want to rekindle a relationship, or even just get an opportunity to confront him face to face. Art wanted to do both, so when he touched base with his dad over the next few days he kept the calls short, light, and slim on specifics. Had Senior known his own son better, he might have interpreted that forced brevity as a sign that Junior was making serious criminal moves.

The day after Art contacted his dad, he and Natalie drove back to Chicago and started ramping up for the big print run. Sandy gave Art the five thousand dollars, and he bought a scanner, an Apple laptop, and a printer. He already had many of the smaller items—the glues, carrier sheets, hardening sprays, and hand tools—stashed away with the Ryobi at the warehouse. The run, Art decided, would take place in two locations; rather than breaking down the Ryobi and moving it from Giorgi's warehouse, Art would use it in situ to color his paper and print security strips and seals. He'd also take care of the faces and the color shifts. He would then take everything to Natalie, who'd have her own little shop set up in Sandy's back bedroom. She'd ink-jet the serial numbers and the "100" over the treasury seal, then they'd assemble the bills with the help of Big Bill, who Art hired on as a much-needed extra hand.

As the deal grew closer, in typical fashion, Art latched on to an even more grandiose scheme—one that could potentially turn the five hundred thousand he was making for Beto into millions. When Sandy had told him that his bills were destined to be stuffed into the walls of an RV full of cocaine money, the old drug pirate in Art began salivating. "Oh, God, I wanted to hit that thing," he laughs. "Can you imagine? You're talking five dealers depositing six or seven hundred thousand each. That's at least three million dollars inside that thing. Pose as a cop, pull it over on the road at night . . . that would set me up for life!"

Art had no way of locating the RV without tipping Sandy off to his plan, a risk that would not only ruin their relationship but probably also get him killed, so he visited his friend Mark Palazo, an electronics expert up in Des Plaines. He wanted to know if there was a GPS device small enough to fit inside a bill. "He told me there was no way he could do it," says Art, "and said that I was the craziest person he'd ever met."

Early retirement plans dashed, Art raced back to Chicago to begin work on the largest batch of counterfeit currency he'd ever attempted. By now, he had a commanding knowledge of a once torturous process, and production ran smoothly. Every morning, he and Big Bill ferried cardboard boxes of prepped faces and strips to Natalie, then returned to the warehouse to make more. Beholding the completed bills still gave Art a powerful rush, but laced into that feeling was now a persistent fear. The arrest, the prospect of seeing his father again, and Natalie's pregnancy reminded him that he was risking more than he ever had before. He wanted no evidence remaining. Two days into the print run, he visited Natalie with a somber air.

"Baby, I'm breaking down the Ryobi and destroying it after this is over," he told her. "I'm done. So make these bills good."

Natalie had heard similar resolutions before. It meant that in six months or a year, when they were out of money, they'd have to wrangle all the equipment again and start from scratch—easy enough to do with digital equipment. But the Ryobi was a special machine. When it came to shading the paper and the delicate printing on the strips, it was like a grand piano; it hit notes that no synthesizer ever could.

"Don't do it," she told him. "We might need it."

"That's what I'm afraid of."

She didn't really believe he'd throw away the best press he'd ever owned, and he didn't mention it again until a few nights later when he dropped off the last box of finished sheets and strips. Although it was midnight, he told her he was heading back to the warehouse. It was time to dispose of the press. Tired of arguing, she told Art to do what he needed to do.

Killing the Ryobi wasn't nearly as hard as he'd imagined. He and Bill broke it down within an hour, loaded the components into Bill's van, then drove to the Canal Street Bridge. They hurled the pieces through the bridge's old steel struts and into the South Branch of the Chicago River, where the press's final imprint was into the sediment, next to the bones and ballot boxes and rusting answers to questions best never asked in Bridgeport.

IT TOOK ART LESS THAN A DAY TO RUE THE RYOBI'S DESTRUCTION. When he swung by Sandy's the next morning to check on Natalie's progress, he picked up a bill front and noticed that the "100" mark over the seal wasn't black. It was blue.

"What's this?" he asked her. Before she could reply, he began thumbing through her piles of completed fronts. All of them bore similar blue marks.

While working on the mark in Photoshop, rather than destroying her early versions of its image file, she had separately saved all of them, until there were dozens of similarly named files on her computer. When it had come time to print, instead of using the final, finished file, she had used one of these old files, and the color was wrong. Art had warned her about destroying older files many times, but she'd been so busy with other details of the run that she'd forgotten.

Panicking, they tallied the misprints. The damage came to $400,000—more than half the deal money.

Art screamed at Natalie, who fired back that however bad her mistake was, it was at least an accident; she hadn't been the one idiotic enough to intentionally destroy the one device that would have allowed them to fix the problem. Their yelling tired into tears, as they both realized that buying the land in Arkansas was now impossible. Later that day, they dumped the bad money into the bowl of a Weber grill in Sandy's backyard, doused lighter fluid over it, and torched it. "That was the biggest burn I ever did," says Art. "I mean, I was in physical pain watching that shit go up, because my dreams went with it."

They still had enough good sheets to print a little more than $350,000, but the vast majority had to go to Beto. Because Art had promised the dealer $500,000, in order to keep things civil he had reduced his rate. After giving Sandy his cut, reimbursing him for expenses, and paying off Bill, Art and Natalie walked away with about $30,000 real, along with another $60,000 in fake that they assembled from extra paper they'd reserved for emergencies. While it wasn't a bad profit for a deal gone sour, it was nowhere close to the amount they'd need to quit, as if such numbers had any meaning left at all anymore.

Exhausted in body and heart by the end of the print run, both of them were eager to get out of Chicago. When it was all over, they beelined for Texas, where they bought a used Toyota off Natalie's friend Susan and hit the road within a day. Their plan was to take Alex, who was now five, to see the Grand Canyon and the Southwest, then hook north through Utah and work their way toward Seattle. From there, they would make the jump to Alaska.

Just before they left, Art placed another call to his dad.

"I'm coming, Pops," he told Senior. "I'll be there in three weeks."

SONNY

It is the same for all men. None of us can escape this
shadow of the father, even if that shadow fills us with fear,
even if it has no name or face. To be worthy of that man, to
prove something to that man, to exorcise the memory of
that man from every corner of our life—however it affects
us, the shadow of that man cannot be denied.

—KENT NERBURN, U.S. THEOLOGIAN AND AUTHOR,
Letters to My Son, 1994

In one of the photographs Natalie saved from the summer of
2001, she, Art, and Alex stand smiling at the railing on the
edge of the Grand Canyon—the most universally American
and wholesome family photo it's possible to take. Only when you
know that it was taken with a disposable camera bought right there
at a Grand Canyon gift shop for a fake hundred-dollar bill does the
impression shift. Then the moment and even the wide canyon itself
seem stolen and swiped out of time. But no matter how much you
remind yourself that the whole experience is predicated and floating
on felony, ultimately the family togetherness of the image prevails.

They hit the Southwest hard, slamming malls in Albuquerque,
Tucson, and Phoenix. In between cities the theme became "Billy the

Kid," as Art kept an eye out for any diversion where the outlaw had a history. By the time they got to Billy's grave at Fort Sumner he'd decided that the Kid was a spiritual cousin. "He was a guy from the inner city. His father died when he was eight. His stepfather was no good, dragged him and his mother around the country. He ended up getting swept into crime as a teenager trying to survive."

That little Alex was being swept along on a crime wave, accompanying his mom and Art into malls, was a thought that nagged at both of them. "I didn't like that he was there while we were doing this stuff," says Natalie, "but I believed, or told myself, that this was our last run, and he was having fun, seeing the world." By now counterfeiting was their way of life, second nature, and they were long past that first step into any life of crime—the denial of the consequences it might have on themselves or others. The conventional definition of crime is an act that violates the laws of a society, but it would not be less accurate to say that it is an outcome of acting almost completely in the present tense.

Art hadn't even thought about how he'd get to Alaska by the time they reached Seattle. Once he was there, it occurred to him that buying a plane ticket meant presenting his ID, which would then be entered into a database. His name was almost certainly flagged, which meant that the Secret Service would immediately know not only his location, but also where he was headed. He doubted his father would appreciate the extra company of a surveillance crew. For a moment, he thought about backing out.

Drawing on her experience as a ticket agent at DFW, Natalie devised a nifty tactic to avoid Art having to show ID. With Alex at her side, she bought three tickets to Anchorage, explaining that they were for herself and her two kids—one of whom hadn't yet arrived at the airport. She and Alex then checked in, receiving color-coded stickers on their boarding passes indicating that they'd already shown their IDs. She handed Art one of the checked passes, then checked Alex in again at a separate window with the third ticket. Nine-eleven was still four long months away, and in that wondrous world before, all three strolled through security and onto the plane.

ART WAS A BALL OF nerves on the flight to Anchorage. Even though he'd talked with his father several times over the phone, the prospect of actually seeing him had been abstract—a possible future in a life where most plans had more to do with wishful thinking and telling people what they wanted to hear than actual commitment. By the time they landed, his stomach was churning. It didn't help that, prior to passing through security, Natalie had duct-taped their remaining fifty thousand dollars in counterfeit across his belly.

Art had been a scrawny twelve-year-old when his father had last seen him; now he was twenty-eight and nearly six feet tall, with broad shoulders and an upper body powerful from working out. "A few minutes before we landed, I realized that my dad probably wouldn't even recognize me, and I wasn't even sure I'd recognize him," says Art. "I didn't want to walk past him, or even just up to him and see nothing in his eyes. It really hit me that this wasn't just going to be awkward, but awkward from the very first moment."

Senior had told Art he'd be waiting for him just past the security checkpoint at the main terminal, that universal nexus where everybody except your own people are vaguely disappointed to see you. Determined not to be a lost pup, Art concentrated on the older males as they entered the crescent of expectant faces. After a few anxious seconds he locked on to a man who looked like he was in his early fifties. The square jaw, the narrow cheeks—he was suddenly certain that he was looking at his father.

"Pops," he said.

"Arty!"

The Hollywood rule of estranged-father-and-son reunions is that the son must keep his dad at arm's length, while the father tries to win his kid back over with a combination of repentance and love, but Art hugged his father right there. Like it had been on the phone, it was easiest to go through the motions of normality. Anice was there, too, and Art embraced her as well. She seemed to have aged far faster than his father. Her face, Natalie would note, "looked like it had been wadded up at the bottom of a laundry basket," and her stringy hair, dyed orange, fell down to her chest in an attempt at youth. She was bony and frail, a weathered ghost of the woman Art remembered from childhood. Crowning her overall decline was the fact that she was in a wheelchair; a few weeks earlier she and Senior had fallen into an argument, apparently over a woman he had been seeing on the sly. They had been driving when the fight erupted, and in her anger Anice had jumped from the moving vehicle, breaking her right leg in several places.

After Art introduced Natalie and Alex, the party piled into Senior's truck, a big red dually, and drove to a diner for dinner. As the initial shock of the reunion wore off, both men began to relax. They ordered food, then Art said he was stepping outside for a cigarette.

"I'll come with," Senior said, and the two went back to the truck. Sitting in the front seat together, they small-talked a bit, then paused and looked at each other.

"I can't believe it."

"I know."

Junior started to relax. The one thing he had heard about Alaska, other than that it was extraordinarily beautiful and overflowing with dark and light, was that it was legal to grow pot there for personal use. He asked his father if this was true.

"It is," Senior said.

"I guess you don't know this about me, but I wouldn't mind trying some Alaskan bud, just for the hell of it," Junior ventured.

His father laughed and popped open the glove compartment.
He withdrew a Ziploc bag filled with the greenest, thickest marijuana buds Art had ever seen, followed by a pipe.

THE DRIVE FROM ANCHORAGE to Senior's house near Chickaloon was
about two hours, most of it along one of Alaska's most scenic routes—
the Glenn Highway. They'd arrived during the short night so there
wasn't much of a view, but outside the truck's windows was a landscape that would later take Art's breath away. A few miles north of
Anchorage, forests gave way to lush green flatlands framed by the
Chugach Mountains. As they headed north along the Cook Inlet,
crossing it near the town of Palmer, the mountains narrowed in from
both sides and they wound into the Matanuska Valley, carved by a
glacier and silvered by the wide Matanuska River. They hugged the
river for twenty miles, until finally Senior took a left off the highway
and climbed toward the Talkeetna Mountains along a dirt road.
There was nothing at the end of it but his house and two hundred
acres of forest that were his.

Art was speechless when he saw the house. Although it was un-
finished, it was a tavernesque, two-story A-frame, with a driveway
that swung around behind and a coach house on one side. Inside
were four bedrooms, all done in natural wood, as well as a library
and an interior balcony. "I had kinda imagined my dad living in a
shack or a cabin, real frontier stuff, but that house was huge and it
was comfortable. I knew right away that he had a good life, or at
least a good house."

After showing Art and Natalie the house, Senior led them out
back to a trailer set off in the woods. It was small and primitive, with

no plumbing, and Senior explained that he and Anice had lived there while he'd built the main house. He told Art and Natalie that they'd have privacy there.

"You can stay here as long as you like," he added to his son's amazement. Art was encouraged by the statement, but Natalie was not enthused by the arrangement.

"There was no way I was gonna sleep out in the woods in Alaska," she says. "I mean, I'm from Texas, but they had grizzly bears and wolves up there, who knows what kind of shit. I'm pregnant, and it just felt like we were being shoved off to the side." When she politely expressed her concern about the bear situation, Senior trotted off. A few minutes later, he returned with a 120-pound bull mastiff, a four-legged ball of muscle and slobber that was easily the largest canine she had ever seen. The dog hopped into the trailer, swaggered around and greeted everyone, then politely embedded himself on the kitchen floor like a battleship anchor.

"Whatever you're afraid of, this guy isn't," Senior assured her. "I take him with me when I hike and he backs down from nothing."

Natalie did feel better. She asked Senior what the beast's name was. Given the dog's size and breed, she figured it had to be something butch, like "Cannonball" or maybe "Brutus."

"That's Sonny," Senior said.

ONCE NATALIE AND ALEX WERE SETTLED in the trailer, father and son headed over to the coach house, which served as Senior's office and private getaway. It was all done in pine, with a black leather sofa, a twenty-inch TV, and its own kitchen, bathroom, and telephone. Art got the feeling his dad spent a lot of time there.

They sat down on the sofa. It was time for the Talk and they both knew it. To brace themselves, Senior loaded up a big bowl of

Alaskan bud and they smoked it down to dust. Wanting to keep the floodgates to the past under his control, Art took the initiative by asking his father what he had been doing for the last sixteen years. Senior gamely fielded the question. After he had dropped Art off with his mother in Chicago that day long ago, they had headed to Alaska to visit Anice's brother, who was stationed at Elmendorf Air Force Base, near Anchorage. While visiting him, they had fallen in love with the state, and for the first time in his life Senior had decided to put down roots.

"There are places here where you might be the first person to set foot there in hundreds of years," he told Art, then diverted into a story about how he and Anice's son, Larry, had once discovered an abandoned Russian settlement deep in the mountains. Buried beneath the collapsed huts they found old coins and small caches of gold nuggets. Senior still had a few of them, and he rose from the sofa, retrieved a wood box, and he showed Art some of the artifacts. Art held an old Masonic coin in his palm, imagining what it would have been like to have been there for the discovery.

Senior explained that within two months of arriving in Alaska for a "visit," they were all living in Anchorage. But rejecting his footloose past, this time Senior was determined to stay. He found piecework painting houses and fixing engines for fishing boats, and eventually saved up enough to outfit his own mobile auto-repair shop. For a decade he and Larry had built up the business, trucking hundreds of miles into the interior to assist isolated motorists. Only a year earlier, he'd sold the business and retired. Senior was now devoted to his two favorite hobbies: exploring the bush and raising dogs. Out past the trailer, he had kennels containing more than a hundred dogs, mostly large breeds or sled dogs, including a pale-eyed, hundred-percent timber wolf named King. In 1995, Larry had even taken some of Senior's dogs and run them in the Iditarod. In a race where simply completing the course is a victory, Larry had finished forty-eighth.

Art was quietly astounded as the stories flew from his father's lips. "My dad had gone completely Alaskan," he says. "The dogs, the fishing boats, even the goddamn bud. It was like he'd been born there. And he was still excited by the place. He told me there were a lot of places he wanted to show me."

And Art had missed all of it. Listening to the stories, he saw no reason why he and Wensdae and Jason couldn't have been there, at least for some of it. Part of him wanted to feel rage and strangle his father, but he was too fascinated. "He'd talk and tell stories and I'd just be amazed at what an interesting person he was. I realized that my father was cool, he was fun to hang out with. What was weird was that, at the same time, he was a fucking asshole who left us to rot in the projects."

Even when it was Art's turn to catch his father up on *his* life, he did not show him an angry face. He made sure Senior knew that while he had been frolicking in the wilds of Alaska, he and his siblings had been living in one of America's most dangerous neighborhoods, going hungry, and struggling with a clinically insane mother, but he did not assign blame. He told him about Jason being more or less permanently incarcerated, about getting shot, and about how they'd all been wards of the state after Aunt Donna nearly killed their mother, but there was never a suggestion that Senior's presence, or even financial help, might have mitigated some of it. He stopped short of telling his dad about his crimes, or of Wensdae's accident. Art wasn't yet sure how to break it to Wensdae that he had found their father, or how either of them would react.

Senior took it in silence. What could he say? He began to sob, and told Art that he had never meant for any of that to happen. Neglecting them had been the biggest mistake of his life. Not a day had gone by when he hadn't thought of him and Wensdae and Jason. He still loved all of them. He knew that what he had done was wrong and he hoped that they'd forgive him; he wished he could change things. Since he couldn't, all he could do was ask for Art's forgiveness and start fresh from there.

"I'll accept your apology if you tell me why you left us," Art said.

In his fantasies, he had always hoped the explanation was something heroic or at least criminally understandable, "like maybe people were trying to kill him, or he would have ended up going back to prison if he came near us." But flowers are few in the weed patch of deadbeat dads. Keeping it vague, Senior told Art that after he had fallen out of love with Malinda, she had "harassed" him, threatening him with lawsuits and arrest unless he came back to her. He knew that he would never be able to start a new life if she was around, and figured it would be better off for all of them if he stayed away. He added that he had looked for Art and his siblings "three or four times" but had never been able to find them.

"I knew it was all a complete lie," says Art. "My mom couldn't have harassed him much because she didn't even know where the fuck he was. And if he had looked for us it wouldn't have been that hard to find us. He could have phoned people. I didn't call him out on his lies, but let him say what he wanted to say. More than anything, I was just happy to be there."

ALASKA'S RESTIVE SUN had fallen and flown again during the first hours they'd spent talking. Unearthing the past was exhausting, but neither of them wanted to sleep. When Art's father finally asked him the question he'd been dreading, it came almost as a pleasant afterthought.

"So, Son, what do you do for work?"

Over the previous month, Art had vacillated as to whether or not he should tell his father the truth. He didn't decide until that moment.

"Well, I make money," Art told him.

Senior just looked at him, waiting for him to elaborate.

"Counterfeit. Hundred-dollar bills. I sell most of it," he said.

Senior just sat there, waiting for a punch line that would never arrive. Art stared right back at him, trying to gauge his reaction. "I wondered what he was thinking," says Art. "Was he upset? Was he blaming himself? Deep inside, part of me wanted him to say, 'No, son, you've got to stop. That's not how I wanted it to be for you.' I started to feel ashamed because I thought that's what he was thinking. But I was wrong."

"How long have you been doing it?" Senior finally asked.

"About ten years."

His old man began firing off the usual questions: Had Art ever been caught? How much had he made? Was it difficult? How did he learn? Then he finally came to the question that everybody wants to ask the most, but is afraid to ask too soon.

"Do you have any on you?"

"Some."

"Can I see it?"

Art ran out to the trailer, then returned a few minutes later with a bill and silently handed it to his father. Senior inspected both sides, rubbed his fingers across it, and held it up to the light. Art was now fully conflicted. "Even as I wanted him to get angry and tell me to quit, just as much of me wanted him to like it. I wanted him to see what I'd done for myself, that I'd created something beautiful. I know it sounds completely messed up, but I wanted him to be proud."

Senior shook his head in disbelief. Art watched as the Glow blossomed over him like it did with anyone else.

"I can't believe this isn't real," he finally said.

"Not many people can. Look close, and you'll see it has every-thing. The security strip, the watermark. It's all there. This is what I do, Pops."

Art went on to tell him about Pete, about how he and Natalie had struggled to figure out the new currency, the trips to the malls. Senior just listened, shaking his head and smiling. "He never asked me to stop. And when I tell people the story, they usually think less of him because he didn't. They see all those years of missed opportuni-ties and realize that he had a big chance to redeem himself by telling me to quit—as if it could begin to make up for the fact that he'd been gone for all those years. Sometimes I think less of him, too, because that would have been nice, but I don't dwell on it. The truth is that he really wasn't any different than anyone else who ever held one of my bills in their hands. He got the Glow. It wasn't any less surprising seeing it in my own dad, just maybe a little more real."

The next question Senior asked was also one that Art had heard a hundred times, but somehow now it came as a surprise. He pre-sented it in a joking way, his eyes bright with childish hope.

"Can you show me how you make it?"

Art laughed the question off without giving him an answer. Se-nior didn't press him, but he did ask if he could keep the bill as a memento. Art told him that was fine, as long as he didn't try to spend it or show it to anyone. Senior told him not to worry. He didn't need the money.

SENIOR HAD SECRETS TO SHARE that morning as well. After they ate breakfast, he took Art for ride in his truck. They drove for an hour, skirting the Matanuska River before turning onto a dirt road that rumbled deeper into the mountains. At a spot a few hundred yards up that appeared completely random to Art, his dad pulled over and killed the engine. They left the car and hiked off into the bush, following a well-worn trail through rampant spring brush. A few hundred feet in, Senior stopped and began clearing away piles of old brush and sticks.

Moments later, Art was staring at a trapdoor.

His dad lifted it, revealing a ladder. They both descended, and suddenly they were standing in an underground room full of the most beautiful pot plants Art had ever seen.

"They were in full bloom, budding with big canes coming off the tops. It smelled sweet, like flowers. I never thought weed could smell so good." The walls of the chamber were lined with silver reflective material, while long, fluorescent grow lights hung from the dugout roof. Art counted thirty-six plants.

"This is what *I* do," Senior said with a smile, then explained that, fifteen years earlier, he'd hooked up with an "old-timer" who taught him everything he knew about indoor marijuana cultivation—hydroponics, cloning, you name it. He'd been growing ever since, selling most of his harvest to a friend of his who lived down the highway in the town of Wasilla, which would later gain notoriety for its then-mayor, Sarah Palin. To power his grow room, he had surreptitiously spliced into the Matanuska Electric Association power line that ran along the highway.

The weed wasn't his only product, Senior explained. By feigning various ailments, Anice had obtained prescription pads from numerous area doctors. She and Senior were forging scripts for large amounts of the powerful painkiller OxyContin, then selling the pills on the side for a tidy profit. Art was almost relieved to learn that his father was still a crook. He'd found it hard to believe that his dad had stayed clean all these years, and at least his old man was finally beginning to go tit for tat with him when it came to honesty. It also gave them something in common.

They were more alike than either of them knew. Senior held back from telling Art that in 1992 he'd been convicted for assaulting and robbing a man of his cash and marijuana, the latter of which is legal in Alaska in quantities of less than an ounce. The crime had been part of a drug deal gone wrong involving two other men who had done the actual assaulting and robbing, but Senior had been the only one the victim knew and had taken the heat. He'd served five years in prison and was still on probation.

For his part, Art neglected to mention a word about the House of Blues arrest, or that there was fifty thousand dollars in counterfeit sitting in Senior's trailer.

OVER THE NEXT THREE WEEKS Art reunited with his stepsiblings, Larry and Chrissy, both of whom had stayed in Alaska. Chrissy was married and living in Anchorage. Unlike the bossy little girl in Art's memory, she was buoyant and friendly, and took to Art the moment she saw him again. To Art's surprise, she cried when she saw him, and confessed that she had always felt terrible about Senior leaving his children behind, especially him. "You got a raw deal," she told him. "If I could go back in time to when we were kids, I would have grabbed you up in my arms, run away with you, and raised you myself. You were so special."

Larry was also excited to see Art, and so unrecognizable from the jock that Art remembered that it freaked him out. He'd become even more Alaskan than Senior, with hair down to his shoulders and a Grizzly Adams beard. He had a girlfriend who looked as wild as he did, and her hair reached her knees. They would sometimes spend months by themselves in the mountains, hunting and fishing and exploring. Both were inordinately quiet and soft spoken, as if the solitude of the bush had permanently impressed them.

For the first time in years, Art began to feel like he was part of his father's family again. He never tired of learning new things about his dad, or being surprised by him. Senior had a mechanic's garage behind the house, and when Art saw the five cars inside he was speechless. The centerpiece was a white 1967 Mustang Fastback, a car prized by collectors. There was also a Camaro, a Chevelle, a 1979 Trans Am, and an old four-door yellow Caddy. Even though Art was a Mustang man, it was the Trans Am he fell in love with. Depending on the angle you looked at it, it was either purple or black. His father had also discovered the wonders of color-shifting paint.

"It's yours," his dad told him when Art voiced his admiration. "This is your car now."

They took it for spin along the Matanuska. As Art blasted off to a hundred miles an hour, Senior became a nervous, hectoring old man who begged him to slow down and chastised him for being unsafe. Art couldn't decide if the car would ever be worth more than that moment. Things were going so well with his dad, in fact, that he knew something wasn't right.

He discovered what it was three weeks after he arrived, when one morning Senior told Art he needed some help running an errand. They jumped in the truck and headed down the highway to Palmer. Their destination was the local feed store, where Art watched his dad throw down four hundred-dollar bills for eight hundred pounds of dry dog food. He and his dad loaded sixteen fifty-pound bags of food into the truck. It was a trip Senior made once a week.

Halfway back to the house, Art remembered the parking meters.

"How can you do this?" he asked his father.

"Huh?"

"You sit here and spend money on these fucking dogs, and we've had to fight to eat at times."

"What?"

"Pull over."

"What?"

"Pull over, and step out of the car for a minute," he yelled.

Senior did as he was told, and the moment they were free of the vehicle Art grabbed his father by the throat. He pinned him against the truck and asked him why he shouldn't beat the shit out of him when he had spent twenty years feeding dogs while his children went hungry. "How could you do this?" he screamed, over and over.

Senior was terrified. He begged his son to let him go so he could talk. Art eased up, but his fists remained clenched.

"I looked for you," Senior reiterated. "I should have looked harder." He told his son that he knew he was a failure, that nothing could excuse the abandonment. Art had every right in the world to be angry, and if whaling on him would make him feel better, then he was willing to take it. That calmed Art down a little bit. But he told his dad that the story about looking for his children was pure bullshit; if he had really looked he would have found them. His father had no idea what all of his children had endured. They had gone hungry, and his hundred dogs had not. He asked his dad over and over again if he had any concept of what it's like for a child to not know if he's going to eat. He told him he had no idea why he was there in Alaska; his dad was clearly a piece of shit. Why was he even bothering to try to have a relationship with him? If he hadn't tracked Senior down, his dad would have continued with his life, perfectly happy to never see his son again. In fact, he was going to leave as soon as they got back to the house.

"I'm a shitty father myself," Art said, "but I could never do to my kids what you did to us."

"I'm glad," Senior said. He was also glad that Art was there. "I want you to stay here, to live with me. We can build you a house on a corner of the property. We don't ever have to be apart again."

Art's anger shifted to wonder.

"Are you serious?"

"Absolutely."

It was the one thing his father could have said to make him stay.

IT WAS ONLY A FEW DAYS LATER that the pair took another ride, this time to Anchorage. Senior wanted Art to meet one of his friends. Other than a few townies in Wasilla, Art hadn't met anyone his father socialized with, and he was pleased that his dad was now bragging to his pals about his boy being in town. They pulled up to a large A-frame on the edge of the city. Parked out front were several Harleys.

"Bikers, huh?" Art commented. He tried to hide his disappointment. He loved motorcycles, but the memory of his aunt Donna riding off on the back of a Harley after putting his mom into a coma gave him an inherent distrust of anyone who embraced the lifestyle.

"Hell's Angels," his father said. "They're good guys, you'll like them."

And they were nice enough guys. The friend Senior had come to meet, Terry Cartwall, was a blond, pony-tailed Angel who reminded Art of a Viking. He was a fisherman who road-tripped between seasons. It was his house, and three other Angels from northern California were staying with him on a visit.

"I've heard a lot about you," Cartwall said warmly as they shook hands. "In fact, your pop can't stop talking about you." Art blushed, wondering how much Cartwall really knew. He doubted his dad had bragged much to his friends about how they hadn't seen each other in twenty years. Until a few months ago, probably none of them had even known he existed.

The five men small-talked about Chicago and Alaska and drank beer in Cartwall's TV room. After half an hour, Senior and Cartwall excused themselves and went into a back room. Art assumed that they were buying weed from his dad. Fifteen minutes later they popped back out, and Senior indicated it was time to head home.

"I got a question for you," Senior said once they were back on the highway.

"Go ahead, Pops."

"You can make more of that counterfeit if you want, right?"

Art didn't answer at first. He had been amazed it had taken him this long to ask, and had started to think that his dad might let it lie.

"You can always make more," Art said noncommittally. "Why do you ask?"

"Please don't get mad, but I showed Terry the bill you gave me. Before you say anything you have to take my word that I trust this guy with my life—"

"So what?" Art interrupted. "I asked you not to show it to anyone and you fucking did. I can't believe it."

"Just listen to me for a minute," Senior said forcefully. "I don't think you know what you got. Terry was completely astonished. He had to pull out a real bill and compare it to be convinced that yours was fake. Once he was sure, he said he'd buy as much as we can bring him. He has major connections in California. He'll ship the money down there and we won't be anywhere near it. We can do a few deals, then we're out. We'll use it to build your house."

It was nothing Art hadn't heard before. He was pissed at his dad for breaking his promise, but mostly at himself. These were the kind of things that happened once people saw the money, and he should have seen it coming. The tour of the underground grow lab his dad had given him was about more than honesty; it was about showing his son that he, too, knew how to operate. Luckily, Art had the perfect reason for telling his dad no: the House of Blues bust. On the way back to Chickaloon, he finally told Senior the whole story, emphasizing that, for all he knew, the Service was on the lookout for both him and his bills. Although his primary reason for coming to Alaska had been to see his dad, he now admitted to his father that it had practically been a necessity.

"I didn't tell you earlier because I didn't want you to think the only reason I'd come up here was to escape the Service," he explained.

"They don't know you're here, do they?"

"It's pretty unlikely."

"That's good. You wouldn't have to do anything other than make the bills. I'd handle the deals, and you won't have to be involved in any other aspect of it."

"Did you tell those guys that I was the one who made that bill?"

"No," Senior said, but Art didn't believe him. "Just think it over. There's no hurry. But I think we could make a lot of money with these guys. I know for a fact that they have access to lots of funds."

Despite his anger, Art found reasons to think it might not be a bad idea. Since their big print run for Beto had failed to produce a nest egg, he and Natalie had nothing but the fifty grand in counterfeit they'd brought with them, along with another seven thousand in genuine that they'd converted prior to their arrival. While that was good traveling money, it was hardly enough to settle down with, since they'd first have to convert it, which they couldn't do locally without alerting the authorities. They'd even discussed doing another big batch and proceeding with their plans in Arkansas once things calmed down in the lower forty-eight. But printing in Alaska made a lot of sense. Nobody knew he was there, it was off the map, and the land they'd be building their house on was far more beautiful and free. Best of all, he and his pops would get to make up for lost time.

"I'll think about it," he told his dad, but by the time they reached the house he'd already made up his mind.

CONVINCING NATALIE WAS NOT SO EASY. As a country girl who adored hiking and camping as much as Art, she found Alaska the most epic, awe-inspiring place she'd ever seen—even a great place to live if you could endure the winter—but she did not trust Senior. Although she'd kept it to herself, she had come to believe that the only reason they were still there was because Art had shown his dad a bill that first night.

"Granted, he hasn't seen you in twenty years, but don't you think it's a bit odd that he's so nice to us?" she said after Art related his father's plan. "He's been an asshole your whole life, and now all of a sudden he gives you a car, wants to build you a house. You really think that's sincere?"

"Yeah, I do," Art said. Although he'd told Natalie about the fight during the dog food run, she hadn't seen how shaken Senior had been, how Art had verbally ripped off his skin, and how beneath it he'd sensed genuine regret and fear of losing his son again. His father had told him that he loved him twice, but just as importantly, Art knew that his father liked him. Senior was having as much fun hanging out as he was. "You're wrong about him," he told Natalie, "I know you're wrong, because you haven't been there during these moments. This isn't about the money."

"You're right, I haven't been there," Natalie said. "I've been stuck in this fucking trailer, or getting away from Granny Clampett." She'd been trying to avoid both Senior and Anice as much as possible, often taking Alex on tours of the region in one of Senior's cars while Art and his dad bonded. "Fine," she told Art. "If you think your dad is so sincere, then tell him no. Refuse to print and see what he says about living here then."

That was as far she'd go. She saw how much Art wanted it, and there was no way she was going to insist that he couldn't live near his dad after being deprived of him for most his life. She didn't want to be *that* woman, the one who makes her husband choose between her and his family. She was also almost nine months pregnant and tired.

"If we're staying here, I'm not gonna have my baby out in the sticks," she said. "You either find me a place in Anchorage where I'm five minutes from the hospital, or my ass is going back to Texas. I'll have the baby and get a job, you can stay here yourself and have a nice life."

She meant it, but Art knew he'd won. He swore to Natalie that he'd start searching for a place in Anchorage the next morning. He hugged her with joy, poured out the sugar, then walked back to the main house to deliver the good news. Senior had the look of a man eager for an answer when Art walked in the door. For the briefest moment, Art thought about employing Natalie's test: What *would* Senior do if he told him no? But he wanted to see the look in his old man's eyes when he heard yes.

TRUE TO HIS WORD, Art got them into a place in Anchorage the very next day. It was too easy: At Senior's suggestion, Chrissy put them up at her place until after the baby was born and they had time to arrange something more permanent. The baby, a girl, arrived on May 30. In keeping with the tradition of having all his kids' names begin with the letter *A*, she was Andrea.

Once they were back from the hospital Art, having successfully copied his own genes, began searching in earnest for equipment to copy the money he'd need to pay for her.

In the Windy City, a counterfeiter can spend months visiting industrial printing houses and small graphic arts-shops and still not see all of them. In Anchorage, it took Art less than a week to visit every printer in the area. He could not find a single plate-burner, process camera, or offset for sale that met his requirements. He also struck out when it came to finding a local distributor of the all-important Abitibi paper.

While he could order some of the items he needed from Seattle, he knew that there was simply no way he could set up a proper shop without returning to the lower forty-eight, preferably Chicago, where he knew the lay of the land and still had a few items in storage. But he had never envisioned leaving the state when he agreed to his father's plan, much less returning to the city where he was hottest.

"It's going to be risky and it's going to be expensive, because these items are heavy and shipping them will cost a small fortune," he told his father. He was half hoping his dad would call it off.

"Then let's go, just you and me." Senior shrugged. "Why don't we hit the road? We'll fly down to Seattle, rent a car, and drive to Chicago and get whatever you need. We can have some fun spending money along the way."

A spending trip with his old man. The thought had never occurred to Art, but it had the ring of destiny. Suddenly the journey went from being a fretted chore to an adventure. Just the two of them on the road, freebooting across the country and slamming hard along the way. "I remember thinking, 'Me and Pops are gonna do it. Not Anice, not Natalie, not anybody—just us.'" He could already picture them laughing over the memories years later.

"Are you serious?" Art asked him.

"Sure I am. Don't you think it'd be fun?"

"I do," said Art. "You crack me up. You're starting to sound like me."

Natalie, having given birth only two weeks earlier, was less thrilled with the idea. The prospect of Art taking off on a spending trip made her worry that he'd get arrested and never return. Since she'd agreed to resume counterfeiting, however, she had little choice but to admit that the only way it could happen was if they obtained new equipment. Before they left, Art made sure to give her a project: While he was away with Senior, she'd be working on the computer, polishing up scans of the new fifty-dollar note. Although it was unusual for him to print fifties, he and his father would be dropping so many hundreds over the next few weeks that he didn't want to risk printing any more upon their return to Alaska. He wanted a new bill ready to go, something different, something that would allow him to embark on a new life with his dad without rousing the authorities.

1 3

FAMILY BONDING

It is simply impossible to convict counterfeiters, as a rule,
without the aid of their confederates. The lesser criminals
in this secretly conducted business can alone obtain the
confidence of the greater villains.

—GEORGE PICKERING BURNHAM

They flew to Seattle, where they rented a white Crown
Victoria, a model that satisfied Art's requirement of
looking as much like a cop as possible while committing
crimes. As they pulled out of Sea-Tac Airport, Senior turned and
gave him a devilish grin.

"You ready to do this?" he said.

"Hell, yeah."

Within an hour they were hammering gas stations along Interstate 90 East. Art had always avoided spending counterfeit at gas
stations because they bristle with security cameras, but three decades of nine-dollar change-raising scams had given Senior a tacti-
cian's knowledge of how to avoid being taped. They'd cruise down
the highway, wait until they spotted a forest of signage ahead, then
swoop in from the off-ramps. They'd circle a station once to get a
feel for its layout, then park away from the pumps, where the cam-

eras are usually aimed. Art junior would then enter and buy a pack of cigarettes and a soda. They'd usually be gone in less than a minute. "It was cigarettes and pop all day long," Art remembers, "and every time we'd get back ninety-two dollars in change. Sometimes there'd be four gas stations on one intersection, and we'd knock them all—bing, bing, bing, bing. At the end of that first day we counted out about $4,200 in a hotel room just across the state line in Coeur D'Alene, Idaho. We just started laughing because we'd never seen so many gas stations."

Based on their change returns, they calculated they'd hit roughly forty-five stations in just over three hundred miles—about one station for every seven miles of road. The closest call they encountered turned out to be right there at the hotel in Coeur D'Alene. Later that evening, Art ventured down to the lobby bar for a celebratory beer; he'd heard a healthy commotion from the bar when they'd checked in, but it wasn't until he walked in and sat down that he saw the source: The entire place was filled with cops.

"What's going on here?" he asked the bartender.

"Northwest State Police Conference. Washington, Idaho, Montana . . . they have a huge meet here every year."

Art got his beer to go.

He ran right back to the room, where he found his father smoking weed from a pipe next to an open window—a move so stupid and arrogant that, had it been anyone else, Art would have dumped him off at a Greyhound station and ended the trip right then.

"Put that out! We have to get the fuck out of here," he told his dad, and explained the situation. Senior casually finished inhaling from the pipe.

"They don't know what we've done," he finally said. "You look good, I look good, and we're driving a car that looks just like what they drive. Do you really think they'll think we're anything else but cops? We're safer here than anywhere."

Against all instinct, Art surrendered to his old man's assurances and calmed down. Senior's control impressed him. Art took a hit from the pipe himself, drank his beer, and they went to bed watching TV. "The truth was, I was having the best time in my life," Art says. "My old man was cool. I can't explain it. Yeah, he was a piece of shit, but he was cool. Maybe that's easy to say because that's really all I had, but I'd never give that trip up."

They slipped out of Coeur D'Alene the next morning while the hungover cops slept. Continuing down I-90, they hit the gas stations in and around Missoula and Billings hard, changing up almost as much money as the day before. They were having so much fun, in fact, that on the third night they almost died. Hoping to make up for all the time lost at gas stations, they drove late into the night as they entered North Dakota—and straight into a supercell storm system that was causing massive damage along the I-94 corridor. As lightning and rain raked the highway, the pair smoked a joint and cranked up the Led Zeppelin, oblivious to the fact that tornadoes were touching down all around them. "I thought it was a little weird because for a long time we were the only car on the road," remembers Art. "We didn't realize what had happened until we checked into a motel early the next morning. It took a long time for the desk clerk to show up, and when he did he said, 'What the hell are you people doing? Haven't you been listening to the news?' He'd been hiding in a shelter behind the motel."

After that little laugh at God's expense, they kept moving across the North Dakota plains. For hundreds of miles the land was empty and bright and mostly free of civilization. At that point they couldn't be criminals anymore; just father and son, stuck inside a speeding shell that could have doubled as a time capsule. Art couldn't help re-membering that the last time he had been on the road with his dad, the trip had ended with his father dumping him off on a Chicago curbside, then abandoning him for good.

BY THE END OF THE FOURTH DAY they had made it into Minnesota. Senior wanted to hit Minneapolis, so they spent the next day milking the gas stations there before bearing south for Chicago. Two hours from the city, Art called his sister from a gas station pay phone.

"I'll be arriving tonight, and I have a surprise for you," he told her.

In keeping with his practice of never allowing anyone to know his plans or his location, Art hadn't told Wensdae that he and his fa-ther were coming to the city. As far she'd known, they were still in Alaska. Her boyfriend at the time, a man who was, ironically enough, a successful Chicago printer, had a fifty-foot yacht that they lived on during the summers, and she was relaxing on deck when Art came aboard alone.

"Ready for your surprise?" he asked her, then shouted, "Okay!"

Senior, who had been waiting on the dock, ambled onto the deck and toward his daughter. "I was freaked out and happy," Wensdae remembers, "also relieved. Suddenly I had a parent that wasn't fucked up in the sense that I could talk to him and have a normal conversa-tion. My mom's sickness made talking to her pretty much impossible. Now I had this whole other parent who wasn't crazy. I had decided long ago to forgive him for what happened at Uncle Rich's. Life was too short to hold that against him, and I needed a father in my life."

While Wensdae and Senior visited all the next day, Art began a mad dash for supplies. Flush with cash, he rented a truck, then bought a used AB Dick offset from a shop on the Southwest Highway for three thousand dollars. He took it back to the storage space, where he still had his process camera and plate burner. Over the next two days he bought inks, blank plates, and various small items. He crated it all up, took it to a shipper, gave a false name and the address of one of Senior's friends in Alaska, and slapped down a wad of cash. It was the fastest he'd ever equipped a shop.

With the supplies taken care of, Senior decided that it would be fun for all three of them to hit the road together, so they jumped in the car and headed south. It went without saying that it would be a spending trip, but their first stop wasn't a mall. It was the Menard Correctional Center in Chester, Illinois. Only a year and half after his release from the boys' home, Jason had sold some cocaine to an undercover police officer. He was carrying a 9mm at the time, and the state threw him right back into maximum security, this time for five years. "They only got an hour together, but Jason was excited," remembers Wensdae. "We let them catch up alone. My dad was shaken up to see him in there. Every one of his kids had problems, but Jason had no real memory of our dad before he left us."

Seeing their son and brother in prison didn't deter them from the spree that ensued. The first mall they hit was in Kentucky. Tired from all the gas stations, Art and Senior took a rest, sticking to surveillance while Wensdae hit the stores. Prior to that, Art had given Wensdae a few hundreds to spend, and she had sneaked a few when he wasn't looking, but this was the first time Art had ever allowed her to accompany him on a full-blown slamming trip. And once he saw her in action, he regretted he hadn't brought her along earlier. Wensdae turned out to be a spending machine.

"I'm a girl, I love to shop, and I used to be a model," she says. "And when I say I love to shop you have to understand that there is nothing, nothing in the world I like to do more. I'm a born shopper. Art gave me all kinds of instructions about how to spend, but they just went in one ear and out the other. I *know* how to spend money. His money was so good that I just treated it like real money, and so did everyone else." Even on crutches, Wensdae could drop five thousand dollars a day. The crutches helped—no one was inclined to suspect a handicapped woman of handing over a fake hundred-dollar bill. Also, Wendz loved to chat up the cashiers and bond with them. She'd ask the ladies behind the counter if they liked the color of a bra, or which scented soap a man might find most appealing. She had the rare gift of being able to forget that she was committing a crime, at least during the act itself.

Wensdae tore it up through Kentucky, where Art insisted that they drive by Fort Knox and make a symbolic gesture of spending counterfeit as close to the depository as possible. It wasn't until they swung back up into Indiana that it occurred to Wensdae that her reunion with her father was massively dysfunctional. Fittingly, the revelation came on Father's Day, when the three of them went out for a celebratory breakfast at a diner in Kokomo. At the table, she handed him a three-dollar card that she'd purchased with a fake hundred-dollar bill. Both she and Art had signed it. After reading it, Senior reached out to give her a hug.

"Don't touch me," she suddenly snapped. "You disgust me. This is all wrong." She began crying.

Senior and Art were taken aback. They asked her what was wrong.

"Here it is, after all these years and we're out here on the road spending," Wensdae sobbed. "Is this what we are to you? Accessories? You're supposed to be our father. Fuck you."

It was her dog-food moment. She railed on Senior much the same way Art had, reciting the litany of Bridgeport sufferings. But this time Senior didn't take it. Hurt, he stepped outside of the diner. Art ran after him.

"We're done," Senior told him. "I'm going back. You can drop her off, stay here if you want. I don't care. This is too much."

"She's just overwhelmed, what do you expect?" Art said. He talked his father down, then went back into the diner to try to soothe his sister. He made no attempt to downplay Senior's shortcomings as a role model. Wensdae was right; their father was a shit, but neither of them was going to change that. They might as well make the most of the time they had with him, and no one was going to feel good if the trip ended prematurely. Wendz settled down, then crutched back to the car and made up with her dad.

They continued on, all the way up to the tip of the Michigan Peninsula, where they hopped a ferry to Mackinac Island, and rented a beach house on Lake Huron. They were all exhausted, and Wensdae's leg was hurting her, but on their first night there Art wanted to go out and hit some more stores on the island. Before he left the house, Senior took him aside.

"We've done enough," he told his son. "Let's just cool it while we're here. No more passing."

Art was relieved to see his father put some brakes on the spree; he attributed his hesitancy to the fight with Wendz. But once they left Mackinac Island, the respite ended and they were soon slamming malls again, this time as they headed West. Wensdae wanted to see Senior's place in Alaska, and the plan was for all of them to drive back to Seattle and take a plane back to Anchorage. But the closer they got to Seattle, the more Art began having doubts of his own, both about the money, and about where he was headed with his father.

THREE MONTHS EARLIER on Sharon's porch in Texas, Art had envisioned a far different reunion with his father. He'd pictured his pops living a more or less straight life, one that perhaps even inspired him to go clean too. Wishful thinking or not, it was a vision he had latched on to. But like always, he'd allowed the counterfeit into the fabric of their relationship. It was now dominating everything they did, becoming inseparable from not only the future, but also the past. Even now they were traveling the same sad highways that Art would forever associate with his dad's abandonment, except now Art was the one doing the driving. Twenty years earlier, his father had been the one in control, but as the creator of the counterfeit, Art was the one in charge. It was this realization that made him stop short of getting on the plane once they reached Seattle.

"I'm not going back with you," he told them at the airport. "I have some things I need to pack up in Texas, and you two should spend some time together alone." It was half true at best. Art indeed had a stash of Abitibi paper in Texas that he wanted to ship north, but he also felt the need to get away from his father. He needed space to think.

Senior was annoyed by his son's change in plans. He tried to talk Art into staying, but once he saw that Junior wouldn't be swayed he wished him luck and told his son that he'd see him in a week or so. Before they parted, Art gave Senior nine thousand dollars in counterfeit. He told his dad that he and Wensdae could have fun with it in Seattle, but warned him that if there was any left over he should not spend it in Alaska. They hugged each other good-bye, and Pops and Wensdae walked off to rent a car so they could spend a few days knocking around Seattle before heading home. "I got the feeling that that was the last time I was ever going to see him," says Art. "I was wrong, but it felt that way."

Now completely alone, Art embarked on the most forlorn spending trip of his life. He still had about fifteen thousand dollars in counterfeit, but the bills felt like a burden. Like an addict who's tired of doing drugs but still has an abundant supply, he wanted to blow it all and be rid of it. As he beelined for Texas, he hit every mall he saw, sleeping in his car along the way. He didn't even attempt to hide the remaining bundle of bills, but tied it with string and placed it on the passenger seat, almost as if he wanted to get caught. By the time he was nearing Oklahoma, there was still seven thousand in the pile, and finally he just pulled over, left the car, and walked down to the edge of the Cimarron River. He tossed the remaining bills into the water, feeling an immense relief as they drifted off to the east.

A few hundred miles later, he was back in Sharon's driveway, the very spot where the whole trip to Alaska had begun. He walked through her front door like a ghost.

"Where's Natalie?" was the first thing Sharon asked him. He found himself stammering to explain that she was still in Anchorage with their newborn baby. "Why aren't you with them? What are you doing here?" Sharon asked.

Breaking into tears, he confessed to her everything that had gone on with his father—the counterfeit plan, the road trip, his feeling that everyone was headed for disaster. The only thing Sharon could do was to throw out her hand to his and hope that he could hold on.

"We need to get Natalie back from there," Sharon told him. "Get her back here, then you two can break away. You can leave the counterfeiting behind. You have three wonderful children." She handed Art the telephone and told him to call Natalie and tell her to get on the next plane back to Texas. He dialed Chrissy's, but he had been largely incommunicado for the last two weeks. When he got Natalie on the line and told her she needed to fly back, she was pissed.

"I'm not coming back unless you come get me," she told him. "I've got two kids here and there's equipment to destroy. You think you can just leave me to clean up the whole fucking mess you started up here? You're wrong."   •

Art and Sharon pleaded with her to come back on her own, but Natalie didn't budge. She had compromised her needs for Art's all summer, and unless he came and helped, she was planted. Reluctantly, he agreed to return to Anchorage the following day.

ART'S SENSE THAT HE WAS LOSING CONTROL OF EVENTS was not misplaced. Anice was not enthused that her husband had spent three weeks visiting with his first family, spending time among both the offspring and the turf of her old rival, Malinda. When Senior and Wensdae arrived at the airport in Anchorage, the reception she gave her stepdaughter was almost inhumanly cold. "Anice didn't even say hello to me at the airport," Wensdae recalls. "She ignored me, like she was looking through me. I haven't seen this woman in twenty years and she's still pretending I'm not there. It was disgusting. She was mad at my dad, probably for bringing me up there. Then they dumped me off at Chrissy's. I knew it wasn't my dad, but her."

Senior knew of only one surefire way to disarm the situation with Anice, who after twenty years of having him to herself was now far less interesting to him than his children. He showed her some of Art's bills, telling her excitedly about how they'd crossed the country, twice, dropping notes the entire way without receiving so much as an eye bat from a single cashier. He also told her that they had obtained equipment, and that he would soon learn Art's secret of making the money himself. Thanks to Junior, they were about to become rich beyond their wildest dreams.

Art's bills, combined with Senior's story about the road trip, had an immediate and positive effect on Anice's disposition. To bolster it even more, Senior gave his wife eleven hundred dollars as a taste, along with some basic instruction on how to pass. A few days later, she passed her first fake C-note at a local store, using it to buy two cartons of cigarettes. Senior and Anice had now broken one of da Vinci's most important rules—they had spent money in their hometown.

It only took them a few more days to break another one. Having experienced the thrill of passing, Anice was thoroughly hooked. She grilled Senior for everything he knew about how Art made and passed the fakes. Since traveling with his son, Senior had become an armchair expert, and he regaled his wife with stories about Art using groups of passers to quickly convert large amounts of counterfeit. "That's what we should do," she told her husband. "Why expose ourselves when we can get other people to pass it for us?" she told Senior. She even had a couple of people in mind.

A few days later, Senior and Anice visited Vicki and Jim Shanigan, their friends from Wasilla, the latter of whom was also Senior's partner in the pot and OxyContin operation. They were slightly younger than Senior and Anice, and in addition to their "business" partnership the two couples often spent a lot of time socializing together. Anice thought of Vicki almost like a daughter, while Jim had looks remarkably similar to Senior himself, with a thin mustache and square-framed glasses. Since Wasilla was as comparatively populated as Chickaloon, and closer to Anchorage, Jim covered the distribution end of their drug business, dealing much of their product to local Native American tribes. With these connections, the Shanigans were the natural choices to include in a passing scheme. To boot, Jim Shanigan was a licensed bush pilot who owned a float plane, meaning that he could fly them to far-flung destinations in Alaska, Canada, and, theoretically, even eastern Russia, where they could pass or sell counterfeit at a safe distance from their home.

Like always, all it took to rope in Jim and Vicki was a gander at Art's product. They saw the possibilities right away and, interestingly, even before holding Art's bills they were already deep into greed's blinding grip. At the time, Vicki and Jim were themselves victims of a "419" scam, which derives its name from the criminal code of Nigeria, where the scam first originated. It usually begins with a "confidential" e-mail from a distinguished exile of an African government who needs help accessing tens of millions of dollars in frozen funds, often attributed to a defunct oil company, ousted political regime, or an inheritance. Through a series of highly convincing cross-references, the scam builds the confidence of the recipients, then engages them in a series of bureaucratic hurdles in which they must first deposit money in foreign bank accounts in order to realize the golden hoard of millions at the end. In Vicki and Jim's case, the money was in South Africa, where they would presumably meet with the banker or lawyer who would hand them the keys to happiness. For weeks they had been talking of little else except raising the money to go to South Africa.

"This can help you get to South Africa," Anice told them. She and Senior were apparently as caught up in the scheme as the Shanigans, because in return for helping them raise the travel money, they wanted a piece of the final cut. Since there would be plenty of money to go around, the Shanigans were more than happy with the arrangement, and as their meeting progressed it elevated into talk of buying yachts and mansions and luxury cars. The only real thing they had in front of them were Art's bills; fakes themselves, but real enough to make the wild fantasies seem as equally close. They stared at Art's bills, held them in their hands, and saw in them their own dreams.

"How much do you have?" Jim asked Senior, who had been hoping for just such an inroad. Senior explained that he still had five thousand dollars left over from the road trip. If the couple was interested, he and Anice were willing to give them all of it to try out. All they had to do was go shopping, buy items under twenty dollars, and bring back the receipts and change.

"There's a lot more where this came from," he told his friend.

"Spend this, and I can get you twice as much when you're done."
When Vicki and Jim asked how the bills were made, Senior and Anice revealed their source without hesitation.

"My boy made them," Senior said. "He's got a gift, and he's told
me how to do it."

The Shanigans were in. Soon afterward, Anice took Vicki spending just to show her how easy it all was. They visited the Northway
Mall in Anchorage, where they bought candles and incense and a
host of other cheap items. When they were finished, Anice gave
Vicki the rest of the five thousand in counterfeit, making her promise to keep the receipts from every bill she and Jim spent.

ART WAS COMPLETELY UNAWARE that his father and Anice had given
money to the Shanigans. He made arrangements to get back to
Alaska, this time enlisting Natalie's brother in the same ticket-switch
scheme that had allowed him to anonymously book flights twice
already that summer. He caught a flight north from Dallas–Fort
Worth, and in keeping with his policy of revealing his movements to
as few people as possible, he did not tell his father he was returning.
Instead, he waited until he was back at Chrissy's house in Anchorage
before calling him. When they finally talked, Senior made no mention of counterfeiting and Art was relieved.

Natalie was still on the warpath when he arrived. She'd lost
thirty pounds in water since giving birth to Andrea, and was infuriated that Art hadn't returned earlier with Wensdae and Senior.
Wensdae had already gone back to Chicago, but the sisters-in-law
had gotten into some petty squabbles—one more stress that Natalie
blamed squarely on Art. But once she calmed down, she took Art
into the back bedroom. She had a surprise for him.

While Art had been road-tripping, Natalie had been hunched

over a laptop, polishing up scans for the new fifty-dollar note. She'd gone ahead and assembled a few dozen prototypes, and Art was speechless when he saw them. "They were just perfect," he says. "The best bill we'd ever made. After she put on the finishing touches, it just sparkled. The lines, the color . . . I could have a spent a million of those."

He almost regretted that he wouldn't be staying in Alaska to make more of them with his father. The next day, he drove up to Chickaloon to inform Senior of his decision. But his dad was in a good mood when he arrived, and Art didn't have the heart to bring it up right away. Thinking a scenic drive might help relax them both, he suggested his dad hop in the Trans Am. As they drove along the Matanuska, Senior updated Art about their plans. All the equipment had arrived. Most of it was in storage, but now that Art was there they could set it up in the coach house. Senior had also reached out to Terry Cartwall, and the Angels were ready to receive money as soon as possible.

"They want a million dollars. How long do you think it will take to print that much?" he asked his son.

Art was dumbstruck. In his own head for much of the last week, he'd forgotten—or, more accurately, denied—that from Senior's perspective everything was going according to plan. And the optimism in his father's voice was infectious. Art could see the new fifties rolling out en masse—the foundation for his own homestead, a reason to stay. But given his production process, the amount of money his dad was talking about was almost unfathomable.

"A million dollars would take months," he replied.

"Well, we can break it up into several runs," Senior went on, unfazed. "And you're gonna love this, my friend Jim Shanigan has a float plane, and we can use it to pass or make money wherever we want. He knows the backcountry like you wouldn't believe. He says he can set us up on an island in a lake he knows where nobody would find us, real remote shit where nobody goes."

And that's how Art learned that his father had broken his promise.

"Shanigan knows about the counterfeit?"

"This guy can help us," Senior said, and continued to extol how valuable and trustworthy Jim was, how he and Anice had given Vicki and Jim money to pass, and how the couple was poised to receive a vast fortune from South Africa.

Art exploded. Once he learned that strangers were passing his money in Alaska, every fear that he'd been harboring about partnering with his dad came true. He pulled over to the side of the road and demanded that his father get out. He told Senior that he had made a mistake by not kicking his ass on the day of the dog-food run. Now he was going to rectify it.

Senior refused to leave the car. By now, he knew his son well enough to know that Art wouldn't strike him. He sat stoically in the passenger seat while Art screamed at him, throwing back admonishments for him to shut up and listen. Art finally let his father have his say, but since Senior had already broken his vow to not tell anyone, his new promises about Shanigan's reliability were meaningless. Art got back in the car, turned it around, and finally told him what he'd come to say.

"We're done," he told Senior. "You were a shit when you left us and you're a shit now. I'll probably always love you, but I can't do this with you. We're leaving."

Senior begged him to stay. When he failed to convince Art that he was overreacting, Senior told him that they didn't have to counterfeit at all. He still meant what he'd said about Art and Natalie building a house on his property. The Trans Am was still his, whether he stayed in Alaska or not.

"I don't want your car," Art told Senior. He said he'd leave the vehicle at Chrissy's house, then sped away without saying good-bye.

MINUTES AFTER ART ARRIVED BACK IN ANCHORAGE, he and Natalie began executing their plan to return to Texas. Since most of their equipment was at Senior's, the only evidence they needed to destroy was Natalie's laptop computer, along with about five thousand dollars in counterfeit. Both of these presented problems. The laptop contained Natalie's beautiful images of the Series 2001 fifty, as well as a new computer program they wanted to try out—a random-number generator that they could use to print variegated serial numbers. While the files could be transferred to CDs, a disk was just as incriminating as a computer, and by now—especially after the loss of the Ryobi—they were weary of constantly having to reequip themselves. They decided to risk keeping it.

The five thousand in counterfeit was also too juicy a nugget to just throw away. As usual, Art had burned through the fifty thousand dollars they'd built up over the summer. All the new equipment, traveling, plane tickets, and partying had left them preciously little to start on once they got back to Texas. Knowing that they'd need to lay low once they returned to the lower forty-eight, they decided to spend a day hitting the malls around Anchorage hard in a furious attempt to unload as much counterfeit as possible before skipping town.

At the same time Art and Natalie began spending, they had no idea that Jim and Vicki Shanigan were busy passing the five thousand that Senior had given them. Amateurs when it came to passing, Senior had provided them with no special instructions when it came to surveilling malls or selecting stores and cashiers. They were out on their own, dropping counterfeit with no method or understanding of how to pass.

On Wednesday, July 11, the Shanigans visited the Fifth Avenue Mall in downtown Anchorage, a high-end, four-story structure that constitutes the city's largest shopping center. The couple had already passed bills at the mall at least once before, and businesses were on the lookout for counterfeit. That day cashiers from at least two different stores noticed that the bills the Shanigans gave them were slightly hazy and flat to the touch. The couple was still ambling through the mall obliviously when officers from Anchorage PD approached them.

At first the Shanigans tried to the use the oldest excuse in the book: They played dumb, pretending that they didn't know they'd been in possession of bogus bills. While that denial often works in isolated cases, they'd already peppered the mall, and the officers knew full well that the couple was passing. Anchorage PD detained them on the spot, leading them to the headquarters of mall security.

Two U.S. Secret Service agents arrived within an hour: Resident Agent Michael Sweazey and Special Agent Robert Clark. The agents read the couple their Miranda rights, then sat down and examined some of the bills recovered from the mall. Both of them were immediately impressed. The counterfeits, Clark later noted in an affidavit, "were of good quality, and appeared to be most likely produced by a sophisticated computer, scanner, and printer operation. The bills had false security strips and were made of acid-free paper."

With their curiosity piqued, the agents separated the Shanigans and began interrogating them. At first both Vicki and Jim continued to deny knowing the bills were counterfeit, but Clark pressed Vicki hard. Exactly what he told her is unknown, but his tactics probably weren't much different from those employed on Natalie's little sister after the House of Blues bust. Her freedom, her family, and her future were now all but gone unless she cooperated quickly.

Vicki caved fast and thoroughly. She revealed that Senior and Anice had provided the bills, and that Art junior had made them. She even gave them Senior's address.

"Jim knows about all of this as well?" Clark asked her, forcing her to choose between telling the truth and protecting her husband.

"Yes," she told Clark, but the confession would have little impact. Minutes later, Jim himself broke. He corroborated Vicki's story and told the agents of Williams's plan to use the coach house as a printing hole. They also admitted to passing at least thirty bills in Anchorage and Wasilla. After their interrogations were over, they led Clark and Sweazey to their car, which the agents searched. Inside, they found several bags of merchandise from the mall, and a fanny pack containing bundles of genuine currency, with store receipts paper-clipped to each one. The agents photocopied everything.

Once they were finished, Clark and Sweazey, like true Alaskan fishermen, allowed Jim and Vicki to return home, releasing them back into the stream of their lives. The agents had caught their bait, now they were after bigger fish.

THE NEXT MORNING, the phone rang at Senior's place in Chickaloon. The number on the caller ID was unfamiliar to Anice, but when she picked up she immediately recognized the voice of her friend Vicki.

"I'm calling from my fax because my stupid phone battery—I need two batteries for my phone," Vicki explained, but Anice wasn't interested in such mundanities. She had news to report. A day earlier, she had attempted to pass money at a Kmart in Anchorage, and noticed copies of Art's bills taped above every cash register. She desperately wanted to warn Vicki not to pass counterfeit there, but she didn't want to be specific over the phone.

"Listen up. Kmart has bad PR, so you really don't want to go shopping there, okay?" she said, improvising a code.

"Okay," said Vicki, who was decisively less cautious. "Hey, we did really good in Anchorage yesterday."

"Good, I'm glad."

"We dropped just about all of it."

"Uh-huh. I'll talk to you in person," Anice said, fighting to stick with the program. But she found Vicki, a novice in the criminal world, annoyingly difficult to direct when it came to protocol. Vicki told Anice that she and Jim were "nearly finished with the money" that she and Senior had fronted them. "I've been pretty good for being at it for, what, just four days?" Vicki chirped.

"Good girl," Anice laughed, wanting to encourage her. When Vicki asked Anice for more money, the latter said she was expecting more from "the associates" in Anchorage—a thinly veiled reference to Art and Natalie.

"They need to start cranking that money out," Vicki said.

"I already know, Sis," Anice said, giving into emotion. "You're not telling me something I'm not aware of, because I want to go to [South Africa] too. I need a vacation."

After some small talk, Vicki wound up the conversation by making plans for Jim to stop by later that day to drop off the money and the receipts. Anice consented, telling her that they had "a few more" at the house, and that they were planning to "get more" from Art junior in Anchorage.

As planned, that afternoon Jim Shanigan showed up at Senior's house with a manila envelope. It contained the change he and Vicki had received from passing counterfeit, along with the receipts. Senior and Anice greeted him warmly and led him to a back bedroom. There, Anice counted the proceeds and tallied them in a notebook.

"Look how good they're doing!" she told Senior, showing him the notebook. Anice then tore out the sheet with her notes, stuffed it in the envelope with the cash, and placed it behind the bed's headboard.

Senior was equally enthusiastic. He told Jim that he was planning on picking up another twenty thousand dollars in counterfeit from Art that night, and that the Shanigans would get half of it the next day. Senior was presumably convinced that he could talk his son into printing more or, more likely, just talking big. But whatever his motives for the statement were, he knew that there was no twenty thousand dollars waiting for him in Anchorage, and he stayed home that night.

By now Senior was realizing that if he wanted to make a fortune in counterfeit, he was probably going to have to produce the bills himself, without the expertise of his son. Despite his complete lack of experience, he embraced the idea that he could make bills as well as Art, latching on to the layman's knowledge about procedures and equipment that Art had shared with him. The following day, when Jim and Vicki visited yet again, he and Anice reported that Art and Natalie were leaving, but it was no matter: Senior was now the new master printer, and he gave them a shopping list of supplies he needed. He threw out terms he'd heard from his son, asking them to buy "eighteen-bright newsprint" and a "sixty-four-bit color laser scanner" and acid-free gelatin—as if creating convincing counterfeit were simply a matter of following a recipe. Vicki, who had somehow become the workhorse of the group, promised to visit a paper mill, as well as get on the Internet and start ordering supplies.

"We need that stuff now," Anice told her, spurring her on.

Toward the end of the meeting, the two couples sat down in the living room and began waxing fantastic again about what they would do with the money. Once the bills were made, Senior's latest plan was to have Jim fly them all into Dawson City, Canada—a casino town about five hundred miles from Anchorage in the Yukon Territory. They would take ten thousand dollars in counterfeit each, using it to gamble and pass in the local gift shops.

"We could go through customs in the Prudhoe area," Senior explained. "They're looking for drugs. They don't give a shit about money."

"That'll be a nice vacation too," Vicki said.

"We'll be habitual gamblers." Senior laughed.

"Watch it, because I hit the pot," Anice chimed in. "I do hit the pot."

Underlying all the talk of crime was this sense of possibility and dreams. Only Vicki seemed nervous. "I don't know if I'm going to be able to do it, because I don't know anything about it," she said to Anice in reference to all the supplies Senior was asking her to acquire.

"You'll figure it out," Anice assured her. "And so will I. We will do it. I'm confident. I'm so fucking confident."

AGENTS CLARK AND SWEAZEY must have swooned in laughter, and maybe even pity, when they heard Anice's declaration of faith. They were apparently the only souls in Alaska more confident than she was that day, because they had taped every conversation the Shanigans had had with Senior and Anice since the arrest at the Fifth Avenue Mall. The investigation had required three days of intense handling and coaching, and Anice's statement was perfect proof that their infiltration of one of the biggest counterfeiting rings to ever appear in the state had proceeded flawlessly.

The number Vicki had used to call Anice on Thursday hadn't been her fax machine, but a line at the State Troopers' office in the town of Palmer. The phone had been wired up to a minicassette recorder, and both agents had been sitting within feet of her when she made the call. When Jim had delivered the envelope containing the change and receipts to the Williamses later that day, every item inside of it had been photocopied and registered as evidence, and he had been wired. Those two operations alone had provided Clark and Sweazey with enough evidence to obtain a search warrant for Senior's home, and the third meeting had come as an unexpected bounty, providing them not only with technical details concerning manufacturing, but the kind of cocky, conspiratorial dialogue that prosecutors love serving up at jury trials. Clark and Sweazey may not have been in the most glamorous post of the Secret Service, but they had rolled by the book, quickly producing dramatic results.

And now they made their first mistake: They decided to wait until Monday before serving the search warrant. Why they waited is known only to them, but it's quite possible that they believed they had plenty of time to establish Art's location and reel him in. Or they may have thought there'd be even more counterfeit at Senior's by Monday. And as it is with any bureaucracy, there are always logistical hurdles. To serve the warrant, they needed to coordinate with local agencies, which takes time. Whatever the cause of the delay, two days was a long time to let a couple like Art and Natalie run loose.

That was all the time they needed to unload the rest of their counterfeit. Over the weekend, they hit Anchorage hard, spending the last of their stash on Sunday at the Fifth Avenue Mall—the same shopping center where the Shanigans had been arrested five days

THE ART OF MAKING MONEY • 253

earlier. It also gave Art time to call a friend of his in Texas, Will Grant, who owned a ranch in Longview, and obtain permission to use it as a hideout until Art was confident that whatever heat had been generating in Alaska had died down. By Sunday evening, as they packed up their stuff at Chrissy's and prepared to head for the airport, they had a brick of cash, a solid safe house, and designs for a new bill, which in Art's world was a winning trifecta.

Just before they left for the airport, to Art's surprise, Senior's dually pulled up to Chrissy's house. He had come to say good-bye.

Art hadn't talked with his father since their last fight. He was still infuriated at his dad for including outsiders in their plans, and at himself for having introduced the money to Senior in the first place. For his part, Senior finally seemed resigned to the fact that Art was leaving. During the last minutes they spent together in Anchorage, he tried, however late, to patch things up with his son. He told Art that he was sorry that they'd had a falling-out and that things hadn't gone the way they had planned. Despite everything, he was grateful that Art had visited and given him a second chance. He told Art that he loved him, and fought to leave things on a hopeful note.

"I'd like to come visit soon," he said. "Call me when you get situated."

Art felt like that last statement about visiting was bullshit, but he was certain that his dad, as flawed as he was, did love him.

SHORTLY AFTER EIGHT A.M. ON MONDAY, JULY 16, 2001, Special Agent Clark sat in the lead car of a convoy of law enforcement vehicles barreling down the Glenn Highway toward Senior's house outside of Chickaloon. The knowledge that Senior possessed weapons, not to mention an army of dogs, meant that Clark was taking no chances. Accompanying him were at least twenty men, including a unit from the Bureau of Alcohol, Tobacco, and Firearms, and a narcotics unit from the Alaska State Troopers. At Mile 70, the convoy pulled off the highway and rumbled up Senior's driveway to his doorstep.

One of the ATF agents banged on the front door and shouted, "Police!" then another one bashed it open with a ramming cylinder. Then the snake-chain of agents moved in, screaming at the top of their lungs. The couple made no attempt to resist. Senior fell to the floor, and Anice, still on crutches from her car accident, was already sitting when they entered. Once the ATF team cuffed them and secured the house, Clark read them their rights, served them the warrant, and sat them down in separate rooms while he conducted his search.

In terms of raw hardware for evidence, Clark was not disappointed. In Senior's coach house he found an HP Deskjet printer, an HP Scanjet scanner, a Gateway computer tower, a Magnavox monitor, and an HP Color LaserJet printer. He also found a can of acid-free adhesive spray, an industrial paper cutter, and a box of newsprint. But interestingly, he found no counterfeit, nor did he find the genuine currency that Jim Shanigan had delivered three days earlier. When it came to currency, fake or real, all he found was the burnt corner of a genuine hundred-dollar bill, resting in an ash pile in Senior's woodstove.

The only logical conclusion was that, somehow, Jim or Vicki Shanigan had managed to notify them of their impending arrest. Given that the Shanigans' phone was tapped, Jim could have slipped Senior a written note during the "controlled delivery" the previous Friday. If that's true, then why Senior hadn't gone ahead and destroyed the equipment and paper as well is a mystery. The hardware was worth thousands of dollars, and he might have hoped that he could pass it off as simple office equipment, especially since Art and Natalie possessed the most incriminating evidence—the scans.

When it came to damaging evidence, the ATF and Alaska State Trooper's drug unit did just as well as the Secret Service. According to state law, Senior wasn't allowed to possess firearms because of his robbery conviction in '92. But the ATF seized a Glock 10mm pistol, a Ruger .458, a Winchester mag rifle, and a Coast to Coast 12 gauge shotgun, along with several boxes of assorted ammo. The troopers got their hands on 267 pills of OxyContin, six marijuana pipes, four containers of weed, a digital scale, and a prescription pad. They also found a bug detector that Art had left behind. Clearly, Senior hadn't used it.

The haul, coupled with the Shanigans' cooperation, was overwhelming and both Senior and Anice knew it. After arresting them both, Clark took them back to the jail in Anchorage, where he and Sweazey sat them down in the interrogation rooms. While Clark had been raiding Senior's, Sweazey had served another warrant on Chrissy's house in Anchorage, with far less success. He came up with absolutely zero evidence, and Chrissy had stood strong under interrogation. When Sweazey grilled her as to her stepbrother's whereabouts, she told him she wasn't sure, but "thought they might have gone to Phoenix."

Having failed with Chrissy, Clark and Sweazey were unequivocal with Senior and Anice.

"If you ever want to see your children again, you need to tell us, right now, where we can find Art junior," they told each of them.

Senior hawed. He admitted that Art had made the counterfeit that the Shanigans had passed—and that he and Anice had passed at least fifteen hundred dollars' worth of it themselves—but he did not initially disclose Art's location. Like Chrissy, he said he wasn't sure.

Anice was another story.

"He's in Dallas, and all of this is his fault," she told the agents. By the end of her interrogation, she had written and signed a two-page confession detailing her involvement, with certain curious caveats. She claimed that she didn't know the money that Senior had initially given her was counterfeit, and that it was only later, after the plan was well under way, that she embraced it.

Art has always been reluctant to believe what happened next. But it's there in the arrest report. The agents returned to Senior and asked him to confirm that Art had flown to Dallas.

"Yeah, they've gone to Dallas," he said.

For the second time in his life, he had given up his son.

ART AND NATALIE had not flown to Dallas. Though that had been their original itinerary, Art started "getting a bad feeling" during the layover in Seattle. On a hunch, he exchanged their tickets for a flight to Houston, deciding that it would be safer to head for Longview from there. He then called Will Grant and arranged for him to pick them up at the new location. The strategy was sound. Two Secret Service agents were in fact waiting for him at the gate at DFW when his original flight arrived.

In Houston, Art, Natalie, Alex, and Andrea piled into Will Grant's car and struck out for Longview. As they cruised up U.S. 59, Art could feel the dread that had been hanging over him for weeks now begin to slip away with the new course. Then, halfway to Longview, Natalie received a cell phone call from her mother.

Sharon explained that she had scheduled a photo shoot for Alex, and needed him in Dallas that afternoon.

Art thought it was a little strange that suddenly they were hearing about a photo shoot for Alex right after they'd decided to avoid

Dallas, but he trusted Sharon implicitly. She had been the one to convince him to follow his instincts and abandon Alaska, and had been there for him more than his own mother. But even with that faith, Dallas still felt like a bad move.

"Tell her there is no way we're heading back there," Art instructed Natalie. "We just went out of our way *not* to go there. She can reschedule the shoot."

Natalie was conflicted. She was tired of taking Art's orders, especially when they seemed driven by paranoia. In this case, her mom had made a commitment, and her boy had an opportunity to put away some money for college. They argued, inevitably drawing Will Grant in as the referee.

"If there was something going down in Dallas, you'd know it," was Grant's take. "Sharon would figure out a way to let you know." He was perfectly willing to divert there, although he didn't want to stay for long. After some argument, Art finally agreed to wait in a restaurant while the others swung by Sharon's. But Dallas was three hours away, and by the time they reached the city Art had relaxed enough to think that maybe it was safe enough to take a quick shower at Sharon's before heading toward Longview again. He wanted to clean up, and it would give his mother-in-law some time to visit with her new granddaughter. He was in the front hallway bathroom, enjoying the soft drum of water on his tired head, when four loud bangs came through the din like underwater explosions. They were followed by four words.

"United States Secret Service!"

Art didn't even bother turning off the water. "I figured they had me at that point, so I just tried to enjoy the rest of the shower. Good bet it was the last private shower I'd have in a long time! But those motherfuckers came right into the bathroom."

"Art Williams?" one of them asked, poking his head in the door.

"Yeah, that's me."

"Get out, get dressed. We need to talk to you."

Art toweled off, threw on some jeans, and stepped out of the bathroom to find himself facing two Secret Service agents and two deputies from the local sheriff's office. The lead agent identified himself as Adrian Andrews—a name that Art thought was a little too obviously fake. He was black, in his early thirties, with a polite yet determined air. He had wanted to be a Secret Service agent since the age of thirteen and would later go on to head the Oklahoma City field office. Since the Service refuses to comment, what occurred next is based entirely on Art's recollection.

"There are children in the house, so your mother-in-law has suggested we talk in the back bedroom," Andrews said. Art's heart dropped. Before jumping in the shower, he had set down the travel bag containing the laptop in precisely that room. When they entered it, Andrews handcuffed Art, read him his rights, then sat him down on the bed. Andrews took a chair in the corner. The bag, with the laptop actually sticking out of it, was literally inches from the agent's feet.

"So we went through your father's house," Andrews explained. "Your stepmother, Anice, pretty much told us everything. We know about the House of Blues, we know you went up to Alaska, we have counterfeit that you made and statements from four individuals corroborating that you made it. You're done, we know everything. But there are still things you can do to cooperate. We want the files, Art, your computer, the disks."

Art wasn't convinced he was in such a bad position. He and Natalie possessed no counterfeit currency. Secret Service agents have a long history of lying and exaggerating to extort confessions, and Art was thinking that the only thing that the agents knew was what one person—Anice—had told them. It seemed impossible to him that any other member of his family in Alaska, particularly his father, would be willing to testify against him.

"I don't know what you're talking about," he calmly told the agent. "Anice is lying. Take a close look at that woman and you'll realize it's all bullshit."

"Okay Art," Andrews said, "we're going to bring you and Natalie in, then. We'll sort this out behind bars."

"Do whatever you need to," Art said. All he wanted was to get the agents out of the room and away from the computer as quickly as possible. He was doing visual calisthenics to not keep staring at it himself, and the fact that nobody had seen it yet gave him hope. "It was right there at his fucking feet!" he says. "All he had to do was just look fucking down. Everything he needed to bury me, literally right next to his shiny shoes."

As they got up to leave, one of the sheriff's deputies suggested to Andrews that they search the house.

Art watched Andrews's face as he turned to the deputy; the agent's eyes turned inward, as if he were calculating the benefit of spending an hour obtaining a search warrant, then another digging through closets and drawers. The agent's response had an almost biblical mercy to it.

"Nah, there's probably nothing here," he said.

LATER THAT EVENING, both Art and Natalie visited the interrogation room at the local sheriff's office. Natalie entered first. She came out five minutes later in tears. "They told me I was never going to see my children again," she says. "They said that my mother would go to prison, my life as I knew it was over. They didn't mess around. It was, 'Either you cooperate or everybody goes to prison.'" When she came out of the room, she had just enough time to tell Art, who was waiting outside, that everything would be all right. From that, Art knew that Natalie had told the agents nothing. Andrews confirmed it minutes later when it was Art's turn on the hot seat.

"Your woman must really love you," he said, "because I pretty much used everything I could in the short period of time she was here. She didn't say anything. I suppose you're not going to be any different, are you?"

"No, because I don't know anything."

"Okay," the agent said obligingly.

Art was beginning to like Andrews. He knew that the agent had just been doing his job when he tried to turn Natalie, and now that he'd failed, he seemed relaxed and surprisingly respectful.

Andrews indeed released Natalie that evening, but the following morning Special Agent Clark e-mailed him two photographs from Anchorage. One was a photo Vicki Shanigan had taken of Natalie during a family outing; the other was a photo taken by an employee from a camera store in Anchorage's Fifth Avenue Mall who suspected the bill Natalie had handed him was counterfeit. Pretending to test a digital camera, he had snapped a shot of her before she left the store. Once Andrews compared the photos, he immediately worked up an arrest warrant for Natalie. Keeping with the original plan, she'd fled to the ranch in Longview after leaving the sheriff's office, but with two children to take care of she was in no position to stay on the lam for long. Within six weeks, she'd turn herself in.

By July 17, the Secret Service had effectively shut down Art Williams's counterfeiting operation—a criminal spree that had spanned fourteen years, minus the four he'd spent in Texas. How much money he had made, sold, and passed during that time is impossible to say. "I figure it was somewhere around ten million," he says, but Art was never one to keep records. If he made only half of that, then it was an extraordinary run, given that the vast majority of counterfeiters are arrested long before their first million ever hits the streets. He had taken one of the oldest criminal arts, evolved it, and—for a sweet time—defeated the most secure bill the United States government had ever created. And for an even briefer time he had made one thing that can never be counterfeited—his father—proud.

Now it was time to pay.

1 4

DEBTS

Punishment is a fruit that unsuspected ripens within
the flower of the pleasure which concealed it. Cause and
effect, means and ends, seed and fruit, cannot be severed;
for the effect already blooms in the cause, the end
preexists in the means, the fruit in the seed.

–RALPH WALDO EMERSON, "COMPENSATION,"
Essays, First Series, 1841

In the final, heartwarming sequence to *Over the Top*, Lincoln Hawk's estranged son shows up in Las Vegas to root for his father at the National Arm Wrestling Championship. Hawk has bet everything he owns on the outcome, and in true hang-lipped fashion, Stallone's character defeats his nemesis in the last round, securing a financial windfall and, most importantly, symbolically defeating the troubled past that separates him from his son. They drive away into the Vegas sunset, joshing about plans to form their own company.

For the Williams family, the contest would be *United States vs. Arthur J. Williams Sr., et al*. It would take place in an Anchorage courtroom, and this time no technicalities offered easy salvation. Agents Clark and Sweazey had been cautious and calculating. They had produced more than a hundred pages of phone and wire transcripts detailing the counterfeiting activities of what was now referred to by the *Anchorage Daily News* as the "Mat-Su" counterfeiting family, after the Matanuska-Sustina Valley where Senior lived. They had written confessions from Anice, Vicki, and Jim Shanigan. Senior's home had supplied them with physical evidence, including receipts of converted cash, and they had counterfeit currency from several stores in the Anchorage area. In Natalie's case, one of those stores had provided a photograph of her, taken moments after she passed a bogus note.

Every one of the six conspirators faced at least one count of utterance, while Art, Natalie, Senior, and Anice were also looking at one count of manufacturing each. But counterfeiting wasn't their only crime. Under federal law, all six were also charged with "conspiracy," which holds that anytime two or more people plan to commit an offense against the U.S. government, that, too, constitutes a crime punishable by up to five years. Of all the defendants, Senior had it the worst. The weapons the ATF had confiscated in his home severely violated his parole conditions, meaning that regardless of the federal charges he was most likely facing prison time.

Vicki and Jim Shanigan were in the best position of all. They had turned against their best friends and performed masterfully for the Secret Service, and in addition they had agreed to testify against the Williamses come trial. As a reward, the Service recommended that they do no prison time. But in the more ambiguous system of justice among thieves, they were rats, the lowest form of criminal. Their best defense against *that* was that Senior and Anice had been using them to do their dirty work, stringing them along with promises of riches that they were pathetically incapable of delivering.

James Singleton, the federal judge assigned to the case, recognized the fact that all of the Alaskans in the conspiracy were small-fry compared with Art. Senior, Anice, and Vicki and Jim Shanigan all made bail. With long histories of residence in the state, and their relatively advanced ages, none of them were considered flight risks. All of them had cooperated, and they basically told the same story: They'd been seduced by the authenticity of Art's bills, tempted by the prospect of money that appeared so real that it was easy to pretend that it actually was. They were scavengers. The real prize for the feds had always been Art, and they had wanted him long before he ever set foot in Alaska.

ART HARBORED NO ILLUSIONS about making bail himself; his history and ability to produce counterfeit on the run made him a tremendous flight risk. But only three weeks after he was arrested, Art would learn just how small an enemy of the federal government he was. He was in the federal transfer facility in Oklahoma City, in transit back to Anchorage to face arraignment, when the planes hit on September 11. He watched the footage on the rec room TV, part of that forgotten archipelago of two million incarcerated Americans who were as astonished, frightened, angry, and saddened by the attacks as the rest of America and most of the world. He was supposed to board an "air con" plane the next morning for Alaska, and like every other flight, his, too, was canceled. They told Art he might have to wait a couple weeks before getting on with his trial.

That same morning, by pure coincidence, Natalie turned herself in. She put on her nicest skirt and blouse, took extra time with her makeup, and drove to the federal building in Texarkana. She heard about the attacks over her car radio on the way, and didn't consider that it might be a bad day to turn herself in. Her world was already in collapse, and the fact that the rest of the country felt that way, too, didn't seem like a reason to prolong the inevitable. When she showed up for her reckoning with the Department of Justice, she found an office full of awestricken agents standing in front of TVs.

"We need to do this fast," a processing officer told her. "We've kind of got our hands full right now."

They booked and released her on bail in less than an hour.

By early October, Art was back in Alaska, awaiting formal charges in the Anchorage Jail. Of all the detention facilities he'd become familiar with, he found it the absolute worst. "It's already bad enough that most Alaskans are fucking crazy because they don't have any sunlight in the winter," he says, "so imagine what they were like in a cold, nasty jail with the worst possible food. I've been in a lot of jails and jails can get crazy, but in most places there's some sort of respectability in the inmates. They try to keep themselves clean, even though they can be mean. These people were nasty. They didn't clean themselves, it smelled, drugs were rampant in there. People were fucked up on all kinds of shit, mostly OxyContin. I hated it. I didn't talk to anyone and stayed completely to myself."

The first phone call Art made from the jail was to his father. He obtained permission for a one-hour contact visit, and later that week Senior drove down for what would be their only visit together. It took place in a small room, in the presence of cameras and guards. Senior came alone. He entered the room and smiled wanly at his son

"This was my fault, Arty," he said as he hugged his son. "I should have listened to you."

Art immediately felt relieved. But he wasn't convinced that was the truth.

"Pops, *I* was the one who fucked up," he said. "I brought it into your life. I shouldn't have. We wouldn't be here if I had just left it behind."

"Look, it ain't your fault," his old man insisted. "I knew better. I should have ended it."

"I'm sorry anyway."

Senior tried to change the subject by asking Art about how he was holding up, the jail conditions, whether he was eating enough. Art told him that everything was great. Silence crept in. Eventually they got around to the subject of the cases. Art finally heard from his father's mouth about how the Service had raided the house. Since they were being monitored, they avoided getting too specific about what had been found.

"So what does your lawyer say about your outlook?" Art asked.

Senior hesitated a moment—Art thought he was trying to summon up an encouraging response to the question—but he couldn't.

"I'm going down," he said. "I don't mind doing the time, I'm still young enough to have a life when I get out. But what really bothers me are the dogs. I don't know what will happen to them if we both go away. We won't be able take care of them. There's too many to find homes for all of them."

Art felt sick to his stomach. He had never had anything against the dogs themselves, just his father's devotion to them at the expense of his own kids. He began to cry.

"I never should have come up here," he said.

"That's bullshit," Senior countered. They went back and forth blaming themselves again, then more silence.

"What about Anice?" Art asked.

"Not happy, but she has a shot at staying out."

Based on the police reports his lawyer had shown him, Art had a pretty good idea why.

"She turned us in. Why did she do that?"

"She's a woman, she was frightened," Senior said.

"Yeah. She's a woman. My woman was frightened, too, she didn't tell them anything."

Senior shrugged.

"Anice turned me in because she never liked me," Art continued. "She never did, not even when I was a kid. She wanted us gone. I guess she's gonna have her way now."

"C'mon, that's not true," Senior said, but he didn't offer a countering argument.

They small-talked a little more about family members, and as the hour wore down Senior promised he'd visit again. As his dad prepared to leave, Art couldn't help apologizing again.

"Stop it," Senior said as they hugged each other farewell. "I don't want you worrying about me. Promise me that you'll take care of yourself, I'll take care of myself, and we'll get through this, okay?"

"Okay."

ART HAD NO INTENTION OF WAITING AROUND to see how the chips fell for his father. Following their visit, he decided to help not only his old man, but Anice and Natalie as well. Through his lawyer, he approached Joseph Bottini, the federal prosecutor assigned to all of their cases. Bottini was a rising star in the federal District of Alaska. In his late thirties, with a black brush mustache and square jaw, Bottini embodied the ruggedness of the state and could easily pass as a cop or a fisherman, while in the courtroom he exhibited the finesse and dynamism of a professional athlete. A native of Napa, California, he had a casual and conversational air wired up to a memory that was almost photographic and a presentation that was precise and deadly. Bottini would go on to participate in the takedown of the state's infamously corrupt legislature and its petroleum-industry bedfellows, ultimately finding himself a key member of the team that prosecuted Senator Ted Stevens. But he would never forget Art Williams: "I have one of Mr. Williams's bills sitting on my desk in an evidence bag," says Bottini. "It's been sitting there all these years as a memento. It is an unusually good counterfeit. I remember everything about the case. It was a sad case. Art junior hadn't seen his father in many years, and I wound up being the guy to prosecute this family."

Art was in a position of strength when he approached Bottini. Because the Secret Service had failed to recover the laptop with its image files, all the government had against him was hearsay—verbal and written statements from Jim and Vicki Shanigan and Anice. Without physical evidence, it was doubtful that even a prosecutor as skilled as Bottini could make the charges against him stick. In spite of that advantage, Art indicated to Bottini that he was willing to plead guilty to everything—provided that the prosecutor would go easy on his father, Anice, and Natalie. He relayed to the prosecutor that he was the mastermind and that he had been counterfeiting for years. None of the others would have gotten wrapped up in it, he explained, if he hadn't shown up.

Bottini appreciated Art's chivalry, but he was in a difficult position. Federal agents had worked long hours bringing down the rest of the defendants. They had successfully compromised a counterfeiting ring, run phone- and wiretaps, and executed a search warrant that had produced hard evidence against Senior and Anice. His case against them was rock solid. And when it came to the gun charges against Senior, his hands were completely tied since it was a parole violation. He demurred at Art's offer, but presented him with a counteroffer: If Art was willing to plead guilty to conspiracy, he'd recommend less than the five-year maximum. As part of the deal, he also wanted Art to admit to making the bills passed in Oklahoma, where agents had claimed they'd finally pulled a partial print matching one of Art's fingers from inside one of the bills. Because it was a weak case, Art wouldn't face charges; the Service just wanted to close the file.

That alone made Bottini's offer a great deal for Art, but the prosecutor also said that if Natalie and Anice pleaded guilty to at least one of their respective charges, he'd go easy on the women and recommend no prison time. But he could do nothing for Senior. Art's old man had violated parole and guns had been found on the property—state charges that were out of Bottini's control. Like Senior had said himself, he was going down. With Natalie's future on the table as well, Art had little choice but to take the deal. Although he was still angry at Anice, he also recognized that if he could help her, too, then so be it.

Beginning in mid-March 2002, the plea deals lined up fast and furious. Art's went down first, on the ides. True to his word, Bottini dropped all but the conspiracy charge and Art was sentenced the same day. Judge Singleton gave him thirty-six months' imprisonment, along with three years' probation and a fine of $13,200.

Four days later, Natalie pleaded guilty to one count of utterance, receiving five years' probation and restitution of $7,350—a sweetheart deal for a woman who had not only played a crucial role in Art's mastery of the New Note, but also made and passed enough bad C-notes at America's malls to pad the secretary of the treasury's bed.

Senior and Anice had scheduled their pleas for the same day, March 25. He went first. The arrangement he'd worked out with Bottini was to plead guilty to a single "dealing" charge, the most damning counterfeiting charge short of manufacturing. Combined with his parole violations, tacked on by the state's attorney, his sentence was a whopping seventy months, plus $7,350 restitution. In federal prisons, inmates must serve a minimum of eighty-five percent of their time, meaning that he was looking at a little more than five years—twice as much as his son.

Anice watched from the gallery as her husband received his sentence. From the moment Senior had abandoned his children, she'd had him all to herself. She had done nothing to encourage him to reestablish contact with his own children or provide them with financial support. When Art had popped back into their lives he was precisely the product of time and neglect. That smart little kid had grown into a master criminal artist, and she eagerly took his money without ever having taken him into her heart. Hers was a self-fulfilling prophesy, and what happened next would illustrate the depths of her capacity for denial.

PLEA HEARINGS are affairs of formality. Since the accused, prosecutors, defense attorneys, and judge have all consulted beforehand, everyone knows what's coming. In most cases, the prosecutor presents evidence supporting his case, then the accused faces the judge and acknowledges his or her culpability, verbally and in writing.

Largely thanks to Art, Anice had won herself a beautiful deal: five years' probation plus the by now standard $7,350 restitution. She would not spend a day behind bars, and with special permission she'd also be able to visit her husband.

Like clockwork, when the clerk called up Anice's case, Bottini presented his evidence, then her lawyer, Eugene Cyrus, informed Judge Singleton of her intent to plead guilty. As required by law, the judge then asked her if she understood that she was pleading guilty to the charges, thus surrendering her right to a trial.

"I'm doing this because my lawyer advised me, but I'm innocent," she said.

"You're innocent?"

"Oh, yes."

"It was my understanding that you were going to plead guilty. Do you wish to change your plea to not guilty?"

"I didn't do anything, Your Honor. I'm innocent. This all happened because of my stepson, Art. You see—"

"Mrs. Williams, this proceeding requires that you plead either guilty or not guilty. Your stepson is irrelevant here. Do you wish to change your intended plea?"

"I'm an innocent woman, Your Honor. Nothing should be done to me."

"You must reply either guilty or not guilty, Mrs. Williams."

"I'm not guilty."

Eugene Cyrus, Anice's lawyer, was standing right next to her at the time. Like everyone else he had assumed her guilty plea was a done deal; he now found himself in the unfortunate position of having won for his client a very good arrangement—only to watch her double down on a terrible hand. And Bottini wasn't just unhappy, but incensed. By any legal assessment he had been merciful toward Anice. He had her on tape arranging counterfeit deals, a ledger listing the proceeds, and the Shanigans to testify to it. In spite of that, he'd offered her no time.

"Do you understand what you are saying?" Judge Singleton pressed Anice. "That you wish to enter a plea of not guilty and proceed to trial?"

"Yes."

"Very well," said Judge Singleton, but he was far from convinced of her competency to stand trial. He ordered that Anice undergo a psychiatric evaluation prior to proceeding. The assigned psychiatrist, Dr. Irvin Rothrock, found that Anice was not only aware of her actions, but that she was "feigning an impaired memory hoping to avoid the legal consequences of her actions." Judge Singleton ordered her case to proceed.

Both her lawyer and her daughter attempted to change her mind. "Arthur had tried to take the fall for everything," Chrissy remembers. "He had tried to keep my mom and dad out of it, and she had gotten a good deal. I begged her to sign it. 'Mom, you could lose,' I told her. 'I've seen the police reports.' She blamed everything on Art junior. But she didn't want to admit that she had anything to do with it. To say she was stubborn would be putting it lightly. Her freedom wasn't enough for her; she wanted to clear her name."

But Anice refused to turn back, and so on August 12, 2002, the case went to trial.

Bottini had expended his mercy. His prosecution of Anice, as her own lawyer described it, "was flawless." Utilizing what was then the latest technology, he projected transcripts of the phone- and wiretaps, the ledger and the bill receipts, and her own signed confession onto a screen from a laptop computer. It was the federal flip-side of some of the same imaging technology Art had used to counterfeit. He put both Jim and Vicki Shanigan on the stand, as well as the Secret Service agents, and they confirmed every allegation against her. He also played back the audio of Anice's own voice, arranging the meet with Vicki Shanigan.

Once Bottini closed his case, Anice's attorney had little choice but to put her on the stand. Other than her word, he had nothing to contradict the evidence. But on the morning she was scheduled to testify, the box stood empty as the court waited in vain for her to show up. That morning, she suddenly started complaining about a sharp pain in her side. Paramedics rushed her to the emergency room, where doctors gave her a battery of tests and discharged her. They were unable to find anything wrong with her.

Back in court in following morning, she finally took the stand and answered the government's charges.

"I knew absolutely nothing about any counterfeiting," she told the court. On cross-examination, when Bottini asked her to explain where the money and the receipts the Secret Service had confiscated from her bedroom came from, she said that "it was from Jim Shanigan's drug dealing. Vicki gave it to me because Jim was a drug addict and she was afraid he would squander it." When it came to explaining her signed confession, Anice was flabbergasted. Despite her acute memory of holding the money for Vicki because her husband was an addict, she had "no memory of making any statements to the Secret Service agents." At the same time, she quite clearly remembered signing the confession, claiming that she "had been told by the agents she had to sign it or go to jail." It was the sort of contradictory testimony that prosecutors dream of and rarely see. On at least two occasions, several jurors were so incredulous at the boldness of Anice's lies that they actually laughed out loud at her.

The jury returned with a verdict in two hours. Anice was sentenced to forty-one months in prison, followed by thirty-six months of probation plus the restitution. Next to her husband's sentence, it was the longest of the six defendants'.

THE FEDERAL CORRECTIONAL INSTITUTION IN WASECA, MINNESOTA, is a low-security facility about seventy-five miles south of Minneapolis. Housing about a thousand inmates, it has no bars or cells, and inmates sleep in dormitory-style bunks, held in by little more than a chain link fence and razor wire. Compared with the prisons Art had seen in Texas and even the Anchorage Jail, it was a cakewalk, filled with mostly nonviolent offenders, many of them white-collar criminals.

His first cell mate, Kenneth Getty, was the former mayor of the Illinois town of Lyons. He'd been convicted of bid-rigging town contracts. His second cellie, a big-time credit-card scammer from L.A.

who faced $1.8 million in restitution, had been neighbors with Marvin Gaye. Prison had always been a likelihood in the world where Art grew up and in the life that he had chosen. Most of the boys from the Bridgeport Homes had done hard time in much worse places. A cynical reality of Art's life is that, compared with many he grew up with, Waseca could almost be interpreted as a sign of success.

Word travels fast in prison. A few weeks after his arrival, Art was jogging around the outdoor track when a fellow Chicagoan named Louis Bombacino approached him. Bombacino was an Outfit man, convicted for loan-sharking fifteen years earlier.

"You're from Chicago, right?" he said. "Taylor Street and Bridgeport?"

"Yeah."

"We don't get a lot of young guys from the neighborhood here. There are a few of us, but we don't get much news. We'd like to talk to you."

"Okay," Art said, waiting for a question.

"The only thing is, we can't really talk to you until we look into your past and who you are and what you did, you know? So don't take offense, but until then we probably won't even speak."

"That's cool, whatever," Art said, and started running again, perplexed and at the same time painfully cognizant that, after all those years of successfully hiding his operations from the Outfit, they'd finally discovered him in federal prison.

Art was heading out to the rec yard when Bombacino approached him again two weeks later.

"Hey, Arty. We just wanted to let you know that you're a good kid," he said. "You never said anything about anybody. We'd like you to come to breakfast tomorrow, if you don't mind. We'd just like to catch up on the neighborhood."

Now Art was truly mystified. Who was the "we"? And for a bunch of guys who didn't get much news from the neighborhood, they had tapped into the lowdown on him pretty fast. Art wondered whom they'd contacted. Giorgi? The Chinese? He'd never know.

The next morning at breakfast he brought his tray up to a table occupied by three old men. There was an empty seat just for him. Before he sat down, Louie introduced him to the two other men: Bobby Ferrare and Jerry Scalise. Art was awed. He had heard both of their names before. Ferrare was a well-known boss from Kansas City who was doing time for a vending-machine scam, while Scalise was nothing less than a legend. A longtime thief for the Outfit, in 1980 he and a cohort named Arthur "The Genius" Rachel had robbed a London jewelry store of more than $1.5 million in gems, including the famed Marlborough Diamond—a forty-five-carat stone once owned by Winston Churchill's cousin. Although Scalise was later convicted of the heist, authorities never recovered the diamond, and rumors were that he had buried it on his property in DuPage County. Scalise also had a famous nickname—Witherhand—due to the fact that he was missing four fingers on his left hand. Having already done his time in the UK for the jewelry heist, he was now serving a nine-year sentence for participating in a drug-running ring.

"I sat down, and we just started talking about the neighborhood," remembers Art. "They're asking me things like 'What changed here?' et cetera. And then the awe kind of fell off me, and I just started listening to them tell stories about the old days, about how when they'd steal shit everyone in the whole neighborhood would be wearing Armani suits or something. I'd get a real kick out of it." Art became a regular at their table, and along with reading, that's how he clocked his time at Waseca—hanging out with four old crooks and listening to stories of the glory days. Every once in a while Scalise would grill him for the details of his counterfeiting formula, and Art would just smile and give his patented answer: "I'll tell you how I counterfeited the Note if you tell me where you hid the Marlborough Diamond."

And so the months dripped by, bracketed by books, breakfasts, and a little piece of Bridgeport in the pen.

SENIOR WOUND UP at the FCI in Sheridan, Oregon, a combination medium- and minimum-security camp about ninety miles south of Portland. Counting Leavenworth, this was his second stint in federal prison. Almost as soon as he arrived, he and Art began writing each other on a regular basis. Sadly, none of their letters survive, but Art remembers many of the words he and his dad exchanged, at least the parts that mattered most to him.

"We did pretty much forgive each other," he says. "Both of us recognized that the way we made contact again was destructive. He blamed himself for not being a good father, I blamed myself for exposing him to my lifestyle. We both made huge mistakes. But the important thing about those letters was that they were full of love. Yeah, it had come at a huge price, really too much, but we did start to have a relationship again. We talked about picking up where we left off once we were both out. He wanted to see me. He told me that he didn't want anything to come between us again."

Chrissy, who visited Senior once at Sheridan and spoke to him on the phone frequently, echoes that sentiment. "He held absolutely nothing against Art for what had happened. He loved Art. His only regrets were for the choices he made. He accepted responsibility for his own actions."

Wensdae saved every letter Senior wrote her from prison. They are among the most valuable pieces of paper and ink she owns, and in many of them he evinces a desire to become the father he never was:

5-27-03

... God, honey, I can't express how happy I am knowing you're back in my life. I've missed you so very much. You're right about never being apart again. These days are over. . . .

I realize today that what pulled your mother and I apart were the world's persecutions, and because we were so young we let others in the world divide us and go our separate roads. When you talk to her again, please give her my best wishes.

Honey, I wanted to ask you again how Jason is doing? Have you heard from him? Is he still in prison in Illinois, or is he out now? I'd really like to be back in his life. I know it would be really hard for him to accept me, but I feel in time God can heal all things. Jason and I need to open that door and take it from there.

I'd love for you to send me some pictures of all of you kids. I got your picture hanging right next to my bunk, so when I get up in the morning I see my beautiful daughter. I even say good morning to you every day. . . .

Wensdae mailed him pictures, and Senior indeed sent a letter to Jason. According to Wensdae, the pair's correspondence was minimal. By the time he and his father connected, Jason had spent most of his twenty-four years in institutions and become more a child of the state than a son of Senior's.

• • •

COMPARED WITH HIS EARLIER PRISON STINT IN TEXAS, Art's time at Waseca flew by. He had already been credited with about six months of time served before he arrived, and with good behavior he was eligible to spend the last six months of his sentence at a halfway house in Chicago. And so less than a year and a half after he entered Waseca, he was walking toward the main gate, on his way back into the world.

Jerry Scalise and the rest of Art's breakfast crew, along with a few other friends, lined up near the exit to see him off. As each man hugged him good-bye, one of the men (he won't say who) handed him a letter for someone on the outside. "He told me not to read it and asked that I hand-deliver it," laughs Art. "I remember being scared, thinking 'What the fuck am I doing? I've gotta be out of my mind to take a letter from the mob and give it to someone. On the day I'm leaving, I'm already fucking up!'"

Natalie's probation requirements prevented her from leaving Texas, so she couldn't be there for Art's release. But he didn't reenter the world alone. Waiting out front to give him a ride to the halfway house was his first love, Karen Magers, and Little Art, who was now thirteen years old. Art jumped for joy and hugged both of them wildly, reveling in his first minutes of freedom. It was a strange scene. Two years earlier, after years of putting off her dream while she raised her son, Karen had completed her academy training and become a full-fledged CPD patrolwoman. Because she was about to go on shift, she'd shown up in full uniform and driving a police cruiser.

"If you two want to sit together, you'll have to sit in back," she told Art with a smile.

"I can't believe it," he said, picking up the bait. "I'm not out of prison five minutes and I'm already in the back of a cop car. That figures."

The halfway house Art was assigned to was in downtown Chicago. He had his own room, and was free to leave during the day, provided that it was for work and that he was back by the seven P.M. curfew. The provisions of his release required him to meet with his parole officer and undergo drug testing once a week. Any violation of the rules could be grounds for returning to prison, or an extension of his probation. He was also forbidden to be employed at any job that placed him in the proximity of "credit, credit cards, or negotiable instruments"—a condition that he would soon learn could be interpreted by his parole officer however she saw fit.

Art landed his first job within two days, working at a real estate brokerage run by his old friend, Mikey Pepitone. Mikey had gone legit while Art had been in prison, and when he heard that Art needed work he convinced his boss to hire him, swearing by his smarts. It was clerical work, filing and letters mostly, but knowing how quickly Art picked things up Mikey thought there was also the possibility that he could be selling houses himself within a year.

"Are there bank-account numbers on these papers you file?" Art's PO asked him on their first meeting, three days after he started.

"I guess so, probably," Art told her.

She insisted that he quit immediately. Shocked, Art explained that if he was going to commit a crime, it wouldn't be at the place where his best friend had vouched for him and it wouldn't be something so moronically traceable. He also reminded her that he had printed millions in counterfeit over the years, and that it wouldn't be logical for him to steal somebody else's money when he could just as easily print his own. But she wouldn't budge. The next job he took, waiting tables at a restaurant, needless to say had far less of a future than real estate. Even though he knew it required him to work a cash register and take credit cards, he took it anyway, thinking that such a dead-end job had to fall beneath the radar of even the most obtuse PO. When he reported for his usual Thursday check-in, she not only forced him to quit that job, too, but threatened to send him back to Waseca. The week after that, he made sure to show up with an airtight position: A friend of his had offered him a gig installing cigarette display cases in gas stations. It paid well, and the closest he'd get to a "negotiable instrument" would be to the pennies in the change dish. She refused to let him take it on the grounds that it would occasionally require him to leave the state.

From that moment on Art was convinced that his PO didn't understand him, had no interest in helping him, and was possibly even taking pleasure in dashing his hopes. The one job she finally allowed him to take was working at a boatyard run by an old friend of his aunt Donna. It was boring, menial labor for minimum wage, and until he had fulfilled his probation requirements, he was stuck.

Despite the setbacks, Art tried to look forward to the day when he could leave the halfway house and start fresh. The closer that day drew near, the more he thought about using his expanded freedom to rectify some of the mistakes he had made with his father. Three days before he was released, he received a letter from Senior, who had been counting the days before his son was finally free. He was excited for Art, and wanted to know if it would be possible for him to come visit him at the FCI in Sheridan in the near future. Art quickly wrote his dad, explaining that he wanted nothing more than to do exactly that. It would require some paperwork and wrangling with his parole officer, but Art was determined to see his father as soon as possible. "We'd wasted too much time," says Art. "Along with seeing my kids, seeing my dad was one of my main plans when I got out. He was back in my life and I wanted to keep him there."

•   •   •

NO SPECIAL FAREWELLS AWAITED ART the morning he left the half-way house. The setting's transient nature discouraged close friendships, and he'd had little interest in socializing. He simply packed up his bags, signed a few papers, and walked out the front door. It was February 25, 2004, a date he'd anticipated so much over the last few months that he'd awoken that morning charged up like a kid on Christmas.

He had the day planned down to the hour. Wendz would pick him up out front and take him to see his old limo driver friend, Mr. U., who had arranged for Art to borrow a black Crown Vic free of charge for the next month. Once he had his own wheels, he'd drive over to Wensdae's, relax, and call some friends. Then he'd pick his son up from school and spend a couple hours knocking around the city. His celebratory plan for the evening was to drive up to Lincoln Park, where one of his old friends from Bridgeport, Ned Cunningham, was starting up a Mediterranean restaurant. The launch party was that night, and Art couldn't think of a better culmination to his first day of freedom than a restaurant full of merrymakers and good food.

Art had just picked up the car and was driving down Twenty-fourth Street, on his way to Wendz's, when his cell phone rang. Checking the number, he was happily surprised to see that it was Chrissy calling from Alaska. They had written each other frequently over the past two years, and he was impressed that she had recalled the exact day that his freedom was final.

"I'm free! You remembered!" he answered cheerily, expecting to hear congratulatory whoops on the other end. Instead, it sounded like she was crying.

"Arty, I've got some bad news," she stammered. "I don't know how to tell you this."

"Just go ahead and tell me," he replied. "I'm free, nothing can bring me down today." By now he was convinced that she was playing a joke on him.

Chrissy began speaking again, and as she fought to deliver the words with precision it dawned on him that she was not playing a joke. She explained that earlier that morning she had received a phone call from the warden at FCI Sheridan. That morning, Senior's cell mate had been unable to wake him for the first count. Medics had rushed to the cell, and it was later determined that he had suffered a massive coronary attack. He had passed away in his bunk.

Art hung up the phone and pulled over at the corner of Loomis. He expected to break down, but he didn't. Other than telling his sister the bad news, he would continue with his day as he had planned. But that evening, when he attended the opening of his friend's restaurant, he didn't talk much. He didn't rush over to meet the people he had not seen in years, but waited for them to approach him, and when they did he greeted them politely and contritely. He was on autopilot. He listened to the waves of the party and watched it as if it were a genuinely beautiful miracle of denial. And then when it came time for speeches, he watched his friend's father climb onto a table to deliver his blessing. The old man was classic Chicago Irish, red-faced and white-haired, a face that could have passed in Bridgeport a hundred and thirty years ago. He held up a glass of whiskey and told the crowd how proud he was of his boy and how lucky he was to see him open up his own place. His eyes were wet blue flames and he toasted his son and thanked him for making this one of the best days of his life.

Art applauded vigorously, his hands like wings beating against a free fall. As soon as the old man stepped off the table, he ran out the front door, laid his back to the wall, and started sobbing.

EPILOGUE

I went to Missouri, then to Minnesota, then up and down
the west. I lectured in many places on the art of detecting
counterfeit money, and did well. Then I shoved a good
many notes, as I traveled—and the officers got upon my
trail again. I knew it. I watched them, while they watched
me. . . . I had no peace for a long time—anywhere.
And I wanted to get out of the business. But I couldn't
see my way.

—PETE McCARTNEY, INFAMOUS COUNTERFEITER

When I decided to write this book, I had high hopes
that Art Williams would be the next Frank Abagnale
Jr.—the young criminal genius who had exchanged
his life of crime for a lucrative career as a document-security consultant. Despite Art's long history as a counterfeiter, by the time I
met him in the spring of 2005 there were many reasons to believe
this was not only possible, but likely.

First there was the extreme price he had paid for his crime: It
had cost him the life of his father, who he had dreamed about reconnecting with since the day he had left. That alone, I believed, had
been enough to scare him away from ever taking the same road

again. Then there was the additional fallout from Alaska. On March 21, 2004, Jim Shanigan failed to return home after spending a day in Anchorage. Three days later his wife reported him missing. His fate would remain uncertain until April 26, 2006, when a surveyor working in some woods in Wasilla came across his skeleton. State coroners were unable to determine the cause of death, but according to several law-enforcement sources who wish to remain anonymous, there were rumors floating around that the Hell's Angels hadn't been happy about the fact that Jim and Vicki had testified in a case related to one of their associates.

Anice, despite her stubbornness and bottomless capacity for denial, arguably didn't deserve the five years she got for her role in the operation. She was no princess and she paid a traitor's price, but she was so hapless in her own defense that it's impossible to not wonder if her mental capacity was compromised after all. Claiming phantom illnesses even after her trial, she served out most of her sentence at the Federal Medical Center in Fort Worth, Texas, and was released in February of 2006. Only seven months later she was found dead in her apartment in Wasilla, apparently of heart failure. According to Chrissy, right up to the end Anice refused to admit her guilt, even though by then the only judge she faced was in the mirror.

Though Art wasn't to blame for the choices of his confederates, all of these losses were devastating testimony to the destructive power of his bills and counterfeiting in general. He knew that more than anyone, and there were people who still needed him. Natalie, who joined Art in Chicago after her probation was up, gave birth to their second child, a baby boy, in late 2004, bringing his total brood to four. During the writing of this book, Wensdae lost her long battle to save her leg. Doctors amputated it just below the knee, but due to complications it's still uncertain whether or not she'll have to undergo further surgeries. Succinctly, Art had abundant reasons to speak out against the very crime he had perfected.

Not long after the *Rolling Stone* story came out, he was approached by Document Security Systems, Inc., a publicly traded company based in Rochester, New York, that specializes in state-of-the-art protection systems against document theft, counterfeiting, and fraud. When they read about Art's innovative techniques for replicating the New Note, they offered him a speaking gig at a conference of law enforcement officers that included members of both the FBI and the Secret Service—the kind of men Art had spent much of his life avoiding. Like me, they wanted to know his trade secrets.

Art accepted the offer. He spent days composing a twenty-minute speech and wrangling with his parole officer to obtain permission to leave Illinois, and in February 2006, he finally flew to Rochester for the big reckoning. A few hours before he was supposed to speak, he called me. He was absolutely terrified.

"I don't know if I can go through with this," he said. "There's gonna be a lot of cops there. Feds."

"You already talked to me," I told him. "These guys will appreciate what you have to say even more. You're all in the same business, they're just on the other side of it."

"Dude, it's my stomach. I really feel like I'm about to throw up."

He actually did throw up, dry heaves about twenty minutes before he was scheduled to take the podium. He had peeked into the conference room and seen dozens of men and women filing in. Some were in uniform, but many of them were dressed sharply and conservatively, carrying themselves with the same confident poise and authority he had long come to dread.

Every instinct told him turn away, but he didn't. Pale and sweating, he stepped from the side entrance and stood before six hundred law-enforcement professionals. He had his speech typed out in front of him, but as he stared at the words, he found himself unable to begin. Awkward, silent seconds pressed down on the room, and finally he stepped back, took a few deep breaths, and abandoned his prepared speech.

"I'm sorry," he said to the crowd of cops. "I gotta tell you people that I'm really nervous. You gotta understand. I know I'm supposed to do this speech, but you people need to put yourselves in my shoes for minute. My whole life—a huge amount of it—I've spent trying to avoid *you*. I'm looking out at you and do you know what I am seeing? I am literally seeing my worst nightmare."

A dam break of laughter filled the room. From that moment on he had them. Soon he was rolling along, leading the crowd through his tutelage with da Vinci, his early life as counterfeiter, and eventually his campaign against the New Note. He focused mainly on the technical and business aspects, avoiding the personal details. By the time the question-and-answer session was finished, his twenty-minute speech had run to an hour. He exited the podium to applause and smiles, then snuck out a back entrance to the hotel and cried.

Art called me the next day with the play-by-play. I wasn't surprised by the warm reception he had received, nor was I a week later when Document Security Systems offered him a high-paying job as a speaker and consultant. He began calling me every day, telling me about ideas he was sharing with DSS and things he was learning from them, plans to move to Rochester. With each piece of good news, I saw another line of this epilogue writing itself.

Then suddenly his calls became fewer and farther between, and often he'd take a week to respond to mine. Every time we did speak, the news worsened; he couldn't work for DSS because his parole officer had refused to let him leave the state; he and Natalie had had a falling out, and she had taken the kids back to Texas. The most positive development in his life was a rekindling of his relationship with his oldest son, Art III—or the "Kid," as Art called him. The Kid had in fact moved in with Art, and showed extremely promising talent as a budding rap artist. When the subject of how he was supporting everybody came up, he told me he was working as a foreman for a contractor friend.

Six months after his speech, on August 14, 2007, he was arrested for counterfeiting.

It's unclear when he became active again. Because the statute of limitations has yet to expire, Art refuses to discuss the circumstances of his latest operation in detail. It certainly wouldn't have been out of character for him to have been printing even when we met and he told me (not to mention six hundred cops) that he was retired. That's what everyone, including himself, wanted to believe, and telling his story was an attempt to force his life as a criminal onto the page and into the past. He knew more than anyone the value of paper and ink; if it was written that he was retired, perhaps it would become true. The problem was that he was telling himself the same old story: that he would do just one more print run to get him and his family safely across the waters.

Art did tell me how he was caught. He came home one day to find a pile of counterfeit bills drying on his kitchen table. They had been made not by him, but by his sixteen-year-old son, who had read an article in *Rolling Stone*. Art went ballistic, and during the ensuing fight his son grabbed a pile of bills off the table and ran out into the street—just as a Chicago PD cruiser was passing by. According to the Secret Service, his son declared to the officer that the bills were counterfeit and that his father had made them—an act that the boy will probably regret for the rest of his life.

Within half an hour, Secret Service agents were searching Art's apartment, where they turned up both bills and equipment. Most of the bills were twenties of inferior quality that had been made by the Kid, but there were also high-quality hundreds that the Service knew could only have been made by Art himself. Ultimately, Art pleaded guilty to manufacturing over eighty-nine thousand dollars and was sentenced to eighty-seven months. He is currently incarcerated at the Federal Correctional Institute in Manchester, Kentucky, where he spends most of his time reading, writing, and keeping to himself. He and Natalie have made up, and she eagerly awaits his release, which should happen sometime in August of 2013. Manchester is too far from Dallas for Natalie to make the drive to visit, and they're hoping he'll soon be transferred to Texas.

By the time he is released, the next-generation hundred-dollar bill will be in circulation. It will be more technologically advanced than anything Americans have ever seen, featuring holographic images generated by "microlenses" wedded into the paper's matrix. Counterfeiters will find it the most daunting obstacle to their profession in history. Many will try to master it and the overwhelming majority will fail. But as Art Williams says, "There is always a way."

ACKNOWLEDGMENTS

This is the story of Art Williams, his family, and many of his friends, as he told it and as I interpreted it. If Art hadn't summoned the courage to share his secrets with me, it couldn't have happened. It was an immensely emotional process for him, and I thank both him and Natalie for opening the door to some very difficult parts of their lives and having the courage to share it with strangers.

The man who introduced me to Art Williams and his story was Paul Pompian, who became my great friend and mentor. He did his best to transmit to me his priceless understanding of and passion for the wondrous connections, histories, characters, and miracles of his native Chicago. I'd never even been to Chicago before writing this book; if I got anything right about this magnificent city, it's because of him.

Scott Waxman, my book agent, once told me that representing [wri]ters had been his childhood dream. As a kid, that's gotta be even [har]der to explain than wanting to *be* a writer. All I ever wanted to [do] was write and find a believer like him. Scott found me, and he [co]ntinues to be an inspiration.

Jim Kaminsky, my friend and editor through the years at various [m]agazines, was the first to publish my writings about Art Williams in *Rolling Stone*. Jim is the most dedicated, discerning, passionate, and talented magazine editor I've had the privilege to work with. Both of my books have been a direct result of our partnership.

Moira Meltzer-Cohen was the first person to read this book. Her insights and encouragement helped me through the hardest part, which is finishing.

Always last, always most, I'd like to thank my family and good friends, who endured the usual litany of angst, complaints about obscure narrative and reporting stuff, unfairly long episodes of burrowing and insensitivity, and the resulting cluelessness I typically display when I emerge. Out of them, no one deserves my gratitude more than Judy Dutton. The only genuine currency in this world is true love, and she's my mint.